THE BOY OF
BATTLE FORD
AND THE MAN

A SHAWNEE CLASSIC

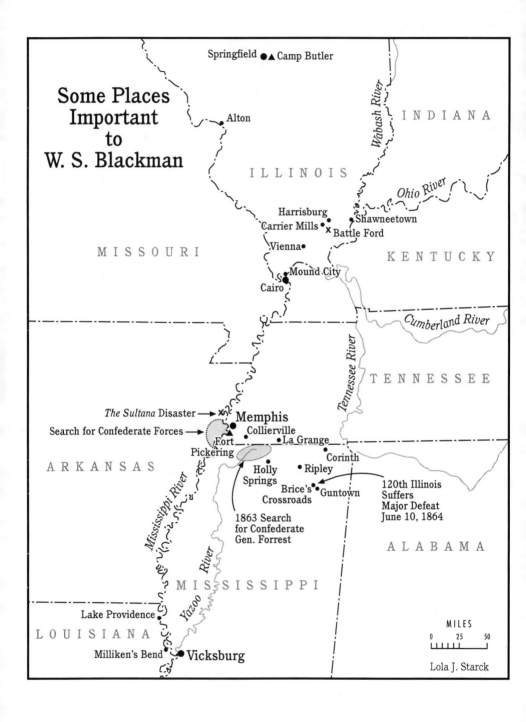

Some Places
Important
to
W. S. Blackman

Springfield ●▲ Camp Butler

INDIANA

Wabash River

Alton ●

ILLINOIS

Ohio River

MISSOURI

Harrisburg ●
Carrier Mills ●
✕ Battle Ford
● Shawneetown

Vienna ●

KENTUCKY

● Mound City
Cairo ●

Cumberland River

Tennessee River

TENNESSEE

The Sultana Disaster → ✕

Search for Confederate Forces →

Memphis ●
● Collierville
● La Grange

Fort
Pickering

Corinth ●

ARKANSAS

Holly ●
Springs
● Ripley

1863 Search
for Confederate
Gen. Forrest

Brice's ●
Crossroads Guntown

120th Illinois
Suffers
Major Defeat
June 10, 1864

ALABAMA

Mississippi River

Yazoo River

MISSISSIPPI

Lake Providence ●

LOUISIANA

Milliken's Bend ●

● Vicksburg

MILES
0   25   50

Lola J. Starck

THE BOY OF BATTLE FORD AND THE MAN

W. S. Blackman

With a New Introduction by

Herbert K. Russell

Southern Illinois University Press
Carbondale and Edwardsville

Library of Congress Cataloging-in-Publication Data
Blackman, W. S. (William S.), 1840–1913.
The boy of Battle Ford and the man / W. S. Blackman ;
with a new introduction by Herbert K. Russell.
p. cm. — (Shawnee classics)
Originally published: Marion, Ill. : Egyptian Press, 1906.
Includes bibliographical references and index.
ISBN-13: 978-0-8093-3128-4 (pbk. : alk. paper)
ISBN-10: 0-8093-3128-4 (pbk. : alk. paper)
ISBN-13: 978-0-8093-3129-1 (ebook)
ISBN-10: 0-8093-3129-2 (ebook)
1. Blackman, W. S. (William S.), 1840–1913. 2. United
States—History—Civil War, 1861–1865—Personal
narratives. 3. United States. Army. Illinois Infantry
Regiment, 120th (1862–1865)—Biography. 4. United
States. Army—Military life. 5. Illinois—Biography.
I. Title.
E601.B627 2012
973.7'8—dc23   2011051615

The paper used in this publication meets the minimum
requirements of American National Standard for
Information Sciences—Permanence of Paper for
Printed Library Materials, ANSI Z39.48-1992. ∞

Publisher's Note

This edition is a reprint of W. S. Blackman's history as it appeared in the first edition of 1906, but several editorial changes have been made. A map of places important to the author has been added, along with an introduction and an index of soldiers and regiments and names significant to the author and regional history. Three sermons and a religious essay that conclude the first edition have been deleted because of cost considerations and because many of the ideas appear elsewhere in the book. Pagination from the 1906 edition has been retained: the text of Blackman's story begins with his photo on page 10 and concludes on page 153: "And here I lay down my pen."

INTRODUCTION

The Boy of Battle Ford and the Man tells a true story as ancient as armies: a young person goes off to war, and an older one, changed by experience, returns. The best of these stories are usually told by enlisted personnel—the privates, corporals, and sergeants who bear the greatest hardships—and this is the case with author W. S. Blackman, who served in all three capacities during the American Civil War.

Born in 1840 near Harrisburg, Illinois, Blackman grew up near an old crossing of the Saline River known as "Battle Ford," a name that anticipates his crossing into maturity during his war years. Blackman's boyhood is primitive in the extreme: the Indian threat has ended, but his Saline County community has no luxuries such as matches or clocks and only a little money. A few primitive houses dot the few primitive roads, and the nearest markets are thirty miles away on the Ohio River. No-holds-barred fighting is common, and the backwoods doctors are as dangerous as the diseases they treat. Education is iffy. Superstitions involving black cats and witches account for phenomena that cannot be explained, and folklore reinforces religious teachings: the man in the moon was sent there for burning brush on Sunday.

Blackman (his first name is William) often seems pulled in two directions. He knows of the temptations associated with coming of age—and gives in to every one of them: dancing, drinking, tobacco use, card playing, gambling, and (apparently) the lure of prostitutes. He does not gloss over his shortcomings but is determined to "write facts," including the "trashy incidents" of his life. He shares the nineteenth-century prejudice that black people are inferior to whites but admires the only two African Americans he knows. He is usually comfortable around Christians if they are Protestants but is intolerant of other religions. He determines to marry a rich, educated, and beautiful woman, then settles for an honest face and church attendance.

Like his nation during the 1860s, he is sometimes at war with himself and no doubt similar to a good many other men.

Blackman is twenty-one when the Civil War breaks out in April 1861. He comes from a family of "war Democrats," a term applied to Democrats who supported the North. He enlists in the regiment of local congressman John A. Logan but is not formally mustered into the army and changes his plans when he learns that his brother Ben will enlist. They agree that one of them should remain at home with their mother, and Blackman delays his entrance into the army for a year until his brother returns home with a medical discharge.

In August 1862 Blackman and stepbrother Joe Harris gather with other Union Army recruits at a Gallatin County site near Shawneetown. Blackman travels by barge to Cairo, takes his first ride on the Illinois Central Railroad, and arrives at Camp Butler near Springfield in October. The Shawneetown recruits join other southern Illinoisans who had assembled in Johnson County at Vienna to form the ten companies of the 120th Illinois Infantry Regiment, approximately 1,000 men plus officers.

About half the men are from Johnson County, the remainder from the counties of Saline, Gallatin, Pope (Golconda), White (Carmi), and Williamson (Marion). Blackman becomes a corporal in Company F, composed mostly of men from Saline County. His pay will be $13 a month, and he will often live on bacon and "crackers" (hardtack) with coffee and sugar. Following stops at Alton and St. Louis, his unit proceeds to Memphis. He spends the remainder of his army time near the Mississippi River or elsewhere in states located on it either supporting Union forces or searching for rebels such as the South's legendary cavalry officer Nathan Bedford Forrest.

The most important battle in this region came when the Union Army and Navy attacked Vicksburg, Mississippi, a Confederate stronghold overlooking the Mississippi River. Blackman describes the Union bombardment, during which he served for a time on a communications team directing artillery strikes. The July 1863 victory at Vicksburg placed the river under control of the North and cut off the states of Arkansas, Texas, and most of Louisiana from the rest of the Confederacy. Blackman is seldom in the thick of fighting but survives several close calls, one of which comes when an enemy bullet buries itself in a rail in front of his forehead. His worst time comes near Guntown, Mississippi, in 1864.

As the Union Army's General Sherman was attacking Atlanta, he became concerned that Confederate General Forrest might cut Northern supply lines and ordered Union forces to seek out Forrest and defeat him. Union troops under the command of General Sturgis found Forrest near Guntown at Brice's Crossroads and Tishomingo Creek on June 10, 1864 (see map). Historian Bruce Catton would later describe the battle as "Forrest's supreme moment of glory." His force of perhaps 4,000 men routed a weary Union force of over 8,000 and sent the 120th Illinois and Blackman on a desperate, 115-mile retreat to Fort Pickering at Memphis. They arrived days later with little or nothing in the way of food, shoes, guns, or clothing. The retreat was so hasty that the Union Army left behind hundreds of men who were captured or killed, as well as wounded soldiers, food, guns, ammunition, ambulances, and mules.

Other southern Illinois units in this battle included the 81st Infantry Regiment, composed largely of men from the counties of Jackson (Murphysboro), Perry (Du Quoin), and Williamson, with lesser numbers from nearby counties. The 81st lost many men in the Battle of Guntown or its aftermath, and Blackman's story complements Edmund Newsome's *Experience in the War of the Great Rebellion by a Soldier of the Eighty-First Regiment Illinois Volunteer Infantry*.

The Boy of Battle Ford and the Man is unusual in that it provides details on matters often omitted from regimental histories: the nighttime dangers near army camps, including strong-arm robbery and murder, and the solemnity of military executions by hanging and firing squad. We hear too of the Southern guerilla known as "Dick Davis" and how his men captured and shot seven southern Illinois soldiers. (Their last names—Pankey, Parks, Mitchell, and others—live on in southern Illinois families and places.) In between, we learn of the everyday life of "Billy Yank," a once-popular nickname for the common soldier of the Union Army and the North's counterpart of the South's "Johnny Reb." The generic nickname is especially appropriate for an author whose given name is "William."

Blackman also alludes to other matters of continuing historical interest. One of the officers of the 120th Illinois Regiment is Bluford Wilson, whose later article in a publication of the Illinois State Historical Society helped refute the myth that large numbers of men from Williamson County enlisted in the Confederate Army at the start of the war. We hear too of Union Army desertions at the time of the 1863 Emancipation Proclamation: some Northern soldiers who had enlisted to maintain the Union balked at fighting when the purpose of the war was enlarged to free Southern slaves. In 1863 the author passes through Milliken's Bend, Louisiana, remembered now for the valor of the Union Army's African Americans who fought there and helped end doubts about the courage of black soldiers in combat.

At war's end, Blackman and his unit are traveling north on the Mississippi when they come across survivors of the *Sultana* disaster. A boiler explosion on the overloaded steamboat *Sultana* resulted in the deaths of over 1,500 people, many of them Union Army soldiers who had survived Confederate prison camps and were headed home. Blackman tells of his postwar conversation with a Benton, Illinois, survivor of the *Sultana*.

Blackman also tells of (but was not present at) the sinking of the *General Lyon* off the coast of North Carolina on March 17, 1865. On board were over 200 soldiers from the 56th Illinois Infantry Regiment, some of whom were from Blackman's home county of Saline, as well as the southern Illinois counties of Gallatin, White, Franklin (Benton),

Hamilton (McLeansboro), and adjacent areas. Veterans of numerous battles and skirmishes, they had accompanied General Sherman on his famous March to the Sea and were on their way home when the *General Lyon* caught fire. Two hundred members of the 56th Illinois perished in what was to be one of the costliest days of the war for southern Illinois.

In September 1865 Blackman arrives safely back at his mother's place near Harrisburg. He considers attending Shurtleff College in Alton and living elsewhere, but the Battle Ford area has a hold on him, and he soon marries a local girl named Allie Miller (whose first name he fails to mention in his book). In the ensuing decades he serves as a Saline County Baptist minister in addition to farming in the summers, teaching in the winters, and serving one term as county superintendent of schools. In 1905 he paused to write *The Boy of Battle Ford and the Man*. Published in 1906 with a cover of marbled paper and gold lettering on dark blue cloth (Union Army blue), it made for an attractive volume.

Blackman and his wife Allie had four children—Willie, Carrie, John Franklin, and Lizzie—but the nineteenth century's high mortality rate for youngsters claimed all of them. We endure Blackman's anguish as the oldest and last, seventeen-year-old Lizzie, succumbs to meningitis. "Our four dear children lie side by side in our church yard. There is room beside them for two more graves and there are two of us to occupy them." Blackman is still pulled in two directions as his story closes, the afterlife seeming as attractive as this one.

Before his book ends, however, Blackman ensures that readers learn of his transformation from soldier to minister by the manner in which he sequences his information. News about his marriage, children, and domestic life is scattered among pages detailing his spiritual growth and religious readings. The boy of Battle Ford wrote of the exciting times of the Civil War; the man from Battle Ford interrupted his narrative to make the points he felt a minister should make. He tells of his time on the "mourner's bench" (or "anxious seat"), a seat near

the pulpit reserved for those concerned about their spiritual well-being, and of his search for "justification," of being worthy of salvation. Church rituals of communion and baptism also receive attention.

Some readers may find that too much attention is given to these religious matters, but this mixture of personal and parochial details tells us much about the author and his times: *The Boy of Battle Ford and the Man* was written in an era when many Americans felt that good literature and art should illustrate moral goodness, as well as tell a story, and Blackman does not disappoint. His search for a faith to sustain him begins during his army years and culminates in his becoming a minister. He knew that details of his religious conversion would be welcomed by those of the Baptist faith, southern Illinois' largest denomination, and he certainly knew that veterans of the 120th Illinois Regiment would value his history. W. S. Blackman died in 1913 and is buried with his wife and children in Salem Cemetery near Carrier Mills, Illinois.

A century and a half after the Civil War, *The Boy of Battle Ford and the Man* remains the only extended, published account of the 120th Illinois Infantry Regiment. The revised Illinois *Adjutant General's Report* for the years 1861–66 offers a 2,000-word summary of the 120th Illinois but minimizes the mistakes of General Sturgis at Guntown in preference for lauding the behavior of junior officers. Frederick Dyer's *A Compendium of the War of the Rebellion* (1959) describes the movements and battles of the 120th in 400 words: among other statistics, the unit was mustered into service on October 28, 1862; mustered out on September 7, 1865; and lost 285 men, about a fourth of the regiment, to the enemy and disease. Other regimental histories allude to the 120th Illinois, but there is nothing as detailed as Blackman's book. William Tubbs' 2005 bibliography of regimental histories in the Abraham Lincoln Presidential Library, Springfield, cites just one printed or published work concerning the 120th Illinois Infantry Regiment—*The Boy of Battle Ford and the Man*.

THE BOY OF BATTLE FORD

By W. S. BLACKMAN

CHAPTER I.

I WAS born on the eighth day of February, 1840, in a log dwelling on a little farm seven miles south of Harrisburg, Illinois, and one mile south of the village of Independence. In November, 1842, my family moved from the home of my birth to the Battle Ford farm on the Saline river four miles west. The first event I remember was that move. I was just two years and nine months old, but I have never forgotten the corn husks the former occupant left on the floor from preparing to move his corn more easily. On the ninth day of November, 1843, my dear father died. I do not remember distinctly any event between those dates, except—dimly—that our place was a very public one for that early day in so sparsely settled country. My father was a very energetic business man, and he was sadly missed by the settlers there when he died. His affliction was called winter fever. It is now called pneumonia. My Aunt Allie, his youngest sister, held me up that I might see him again. He was in the throes of death. I remember to this hour his struggles for breath. I have hated death ever since. The rest is a blank to me till we arrived at the cemetery next day. I saw the grave and regarded it as a mere hole in the ground. I saw nothing more. I suppose they did not let me know that my dear father was being buried there. My father had signed someone's bond and he had just given up nearly all the property he had to pay it off. When we returned to our lonely home we found one mare, one cow, a few little

shoats and a few sheep! All we had, including household goods and provisions, could not have been sold for fifty dollars. Our family then consisted of my mother, myself and my little brother, Bennet Lee, two years and four days old at our father's death. I think I remember every event of importance that came to my knowledge from that date.

My maternal grandfather, William Empson, came from Cross Plains, Tennessee, in a short time to live with us, as he had been called to mourn the death of our grandmother several years before. Early the next spring his young son, G. J. Empson, then about seventeen, also came to live with us, as we were in great need of someone able and willing to labor on our little place.

At that time there were not many people in Southern Illinois, especially in that part of Saline county. If there were as many people there as there are sections of land, I do not know where they lived. The able-bodied men came to our place from their homes several miles away to drill, or muster, as it was called. I heard the men say they went ten miles sometimes to help roll logs in the clearings so they could be burned and to help raise buildings. They seemed to love to meet at any and all of those gatherings. The muster consisted of evolutions of the feet backward and forward of the simplest order. They had no arms except a few long-barreled flint-locked rifles, which were unfit to drill with. To call the roll, hear all the gossip of the country and to have a few wrestling matches concluded a fair day's muster duties. The men who came to muster and my kinfolks comprised the most of the people in the world I knew except the families of those near us—less than one hundred persons in all. When neighbors met anywhere they took time to tell all the news they had of whatsoever sort, sicknesses, deaths, misfortunes, removals, marriages and fights. The subject discussed with greatest zest, as I understood it, was fist-fighting. Sometimes there would be pitched battles arranged several weeks previous to the fight. Those were the outgrowth of hatred, and many persons gathered to see such fights. Usually fears were expressed by the more sturdy men that a tragedy might be the outcome. But often fights were impromptu and everybody would be on one side or the other. Several fights sometimes grew out of one. All would be friendly again as soon as they cooled off. Each wanted to be counted the best man, and they fought like bulldogs to prove they were the best. It was only their way. I had not seen a newspaper at seven years old nor even heard of one, and I believe all our neighbors reposed in the same blissful state of ignorance. Hence the necessity of carrying the news by way of the lips and tongue. I suppose ninety-nine acres out of each one hundred acres of land all over the country belonged to the United States government. The people were too poor to deed the land and settled on the United States land and cleared the little patches they called farms. Except these little farms the land was covered with timber of the finest quality. The varieties were, the gum, poplar, hickory, walnut, elm, sassafras, ash, plum, maple, mulberry, cherry, locust, cypress, persimmon, dogwood, birch, sycamore, post oak, red oak, white oak and several other kinds of oak, and a small quantity of cedar and hackberry. The timber, which was

then a real nuisance to the settlers, impeding their material progress and wearing out their bodies in its removal, would be worth twice as much as the farms made by its removal, were it here now. However, the farmers were compelled to have land on which they could plant gardens and produce grain. A field of four or five acres, with the large trees deadened by cutting the bark around them, and the bushes and saplings taken out and a fence four or five feet high made of rails ten feet long, and out of trees along the fence in the fence row or outside, felled so the top would not be to clear away, was considered a respectable farm for that day there. In the field were grown corn, potatoes, pumpkins, beans, peas, cabbage and cucumbers. A patch of cotton was invariably grown for the supply of clothing for the family the ensuing year. That was the source of the clothing supply, except the few little sheep of the country.

No wheat nor rye nor oats were grown there then. I was eleven years old when I saw the first of these growing. I think almost every family owned a nag, as the horse was called. The animal was indispensable. He pulled the sled containing wood or clothing to the wash place of the family or the barrel of water. He carried the sack of corn to the water-mill and back again with the meal as often as the family emptied the sack. He carried the members of the family hither and thither from one to five at a time as the exigencies of the case required and pulled the bar-shear or cary plow (a poor excuse) that plowed the ground. The boys of the present and the future will not have the privilege of being struck in the stomach or thereabouts with the handle of the plow when it met a root or stump and sent to the rear or to the ground all doubled up and crying as soon as he recovered sufficiently to breathe. The boys and men of that day needed no prize-fighting. All the most brave one needed to satisfy his ambition was a bar-shear plow. All he could attend to was the plow, lest he get a knock-out thump on the solar plexus. The fighters were not plowers. To the fellow who stood off and saw the battle it was very funny if he was not seen. Well, the horse boarded himself, except in very bad, sleety weather. However, that was pleasant to him, as grass was plentiful. Each family kept one or two cows at small cost, as they, like the horse, boarded themselves almost all the time. Each farmer kept a few hogs, as they were self-sustaining, and he fed them just enough to keep them from going wild. However, there were too many wild hogs in the woods to please the people, as they were dangerous to meet sometimes. Anyone could claim them. Capturing was the great question. The wolves were a great hindrance to their increase till they became numerous enough to defend themselves against their enemies. Some of the wild hogs had long, sharp tusks, and the herd put the small animals in the middle of the ring and, soldier-like, bravely defended them. The wolf who permitted the soldier hog to strike him once with his tusk was not apt to do any more mischief. The swine of that day were very different from those of this day. Then we met only those of long snouts, long, slim limbs and bowed backs. In color they were red or black or blue. Fifty per cent of them were decorated with a strip of white six inches wide around the body. A few were sandy and some were striped lengthwise with light brown and dark brown. The swine of those early days were supposed to be old enough to be used as pork and bacon after they were two years old. However, it was common to permit them to grow and mature to the age of three and even four years. The meat of those hogs was more palatable than that of the beautiful Berkshires of today. It was made largely from acorns and nuts and was not so fat. If one of the present Poland Chinas or other fine breeds had been on exhibition sixty years ago in this county, it would not have been received as a hog at all. It would have been thought a mongrel, a prodigy, a monstrosity, and a token of certain evil. Pork and bacon were so cheap then that it would not pay to raise it for sale. As I remember it now, bacon of the choice parts of the hog was worth less than three dollars per hundred pounds at Shawneetown or Elizabethtown, the nearest and the principal markets, thirty miles away. The people had a very poor way of delivering their produce to the markets. Flat-boats in the Saline river in the spring was far the best.

Strange as the swine of that day would be to us now, they served our hardy ancestors well in the opening of this great country so many years ago. In fact, the old-fashioned hazel-splitter and elm-peeler were well dated. They served their day and generation well and went away for better breeds.

The farmers who could do so kept a few sheep to furnish wool that the family might be clothed with woolen garments in the winter. The wolves were a continual menace to the flock, and great attention was required to raise them at all. The sheep of that pioneer day in this country would suffer in comparison with the sheep found in the hands of the farmers now as much as the hogs of that day when compared with those of today. They were light-bodied, with long, small legs, and their tails nearly reached the ground. They had little heads and usually little horns and short wool on their backs and sides; the nether part of the body was nude except the covering of hair that covered the legs. What wool the sheep yielded contained so many burrs from the field or beggar-lice from the woods that much labor and patience was required to manufacture it into cloth. No person would in this day receive such wool as a gift, yet our mothers and grandmothers manufactured very warm clothing out of it.

Wild game was very plentiful. It consisted in the main of deer, turkeys, squirrels and quail. The turkeys were taken in pens so built that they went into them through a trench beneath but were certain when once inside to overlook the only way out and were killed for the want of discernment. The squirrels were caught in deadfalls made by setting a piece of timber on a trigger, which fell on them when they went in for the corn put there to entice them. The quail were caught in traps made of sticks built in the shape of a conical pen, set on triggers as the deadfall. Quail were caught only for food. But squirrels were caught more for their mischief than for food. In the spring they scratched up the corn and when the crop was made they climbed the stalks and ate the ears. The beautiful but shy deer could not be taken by men's devices. They seemed to grow more numerous and less shy. It was not uncommon to see a dozen or more of them together, and they loved to get into the little fields. They could run very fast and even a small one could jump any fence to be found. Yet we were not strangers to feasts of fresh venison nor to the sweet dried hams of the choice ones saved by the hunters for special occasions. The handy cartridge of the present day was not invented then; neither the percussion cap. The hunter took his long-barreled rifle, put a charge of powder into it, pushed a bullet wrapped in cloth down the gun, onto the powder. Placing powder in a small pan outside the gun, opposite the breech, the hunter took aim at the object to be shot and, pulling the trigger, the flint in the hammer struck the steel

plate called the friz, arranged for the purpose when a spark of fire from the friction of the steel and the flint descended to the powder in the pan, the explosion of which reached the powder in the gun through the touch-hole in the barrel, and the bullet was sent home to the object aimed at.

The skins of deer, when dressed, were often used to make pants, as they were soft and white and would never wear out. But woe to the young man who went courting with deerskin pants on, if they got wet in the dew or the rain, for they would stretch twice their normal length; but if cut off to suit the emergency, they would be too short when dry again. The skins were very useful for other purposes, but they were generally sold to buy powder and lead with, as there was little money to be had for anything.

My little brother and I were too small to aid in the business of capturing animals and fowls, except to visit the traps and deadfalls late each morning and evening and bring in the catch. The best of the squirrels were used for food and the others were given to the dogs and cats. On one occasion I had a very painful experience. We found an old gray squirrel under the fall not yet dead. We knew nothing else to do but jump up and down on it till we thought life was extinct. Ben raised the timber and I took the animal out. But that squirrel put its teeth through the top of my middle finger before I knew it was alive. I cried and cried and cried, but the squirrel held on. I asked my brother to bite the animal. I begged him to do so; but he still refused. I do not know why. Neither do I know why I did not think to bite it myself; but I did not. I then asked him to break the squirrel's legs. He went to work in earnest and soon twisted the joints apart. But the teeth were still in my finger, firm and fixed. I continutd to cry and beg for help. After awhile I thought of choking it and said, "Choke him, 'Ben, choke him!" We turned that squirrel on his back and in a moment my thumb went to his throat and Ben's weight on my thumb. Results followed. I jumped up, glad to quit at that, and ready to run; but when I saw the animal hobbling along on its knees I changed my mind. I took it by the tail and struck it against the trees and stumps on all sides till the house was reached. The dogs had a mess of squirrel sausage for supper that night. I had a bad finger for weeks and I remember well to this day how those teeth felt in my finger.

The bear and the panther were almost gone when I began to remember. The wild cat and the catamount were there for many years, but were few and wild. The animal most hated by man and beast was the wolf. His tribe encompassed hill and valley, wood and field — anywhere, everywhere. He could howl as a single wolf or as half a dozen wolves at once, just as he pleased. He caught domestic fowls and small animals and sometimes chased the dogs to their homes for protection. I can remember well an experience of that kind which was very unpleasant to me. In some way the few sheep owned by my mother were not penned that night. An hour after dark the wolves found them at the farthest part of the little field, where they had chosen to camp, 150 yards away, and the cunning wolves hemmed them there and selected the largest lamb in the flock. The remainder ran for dear life towards the house. The dogs met them, but passed rapidly on till near the wolves. But on meeting an army of wolves, the dogs did well to get back. They did not stop till they went round the house and saw the wolves running back to the dead lambs. The dogs bravely ran to them again, to be turned homeward as suddenly as they went. The wolves, being hungry, were not willing to forego so rich a repast as the lamb furnished them, and the dogs were not in the habit of vacating their own premises at the will of intruders and robbers. Only the great outnumbering of the dogs caused them to retreat rather than to fight to the death. The wolves came within ten yards of the dwelling each time and ran back again till the lamb was devoured, and then they went away. The next morning we ventured to the place where the killing was done, but there was not a bone to be found nor scarcely a lock of wool. During the races between the wild dogs and the tame dogs, as our family had no gun, no one would venture to even open the door, much less go out and aid the home guards. And as for me, my head was covered from the beginning of the fray till quiet reigned again. In continuing my head under cover, ostrich-like, for safety, I suffered much for want of breathing air; but I feared to uncover my head with that awful contest raging so near our door. Such a running and jumping and clawing and scratching and grunting and whining and yelping and snapping as greeted our ears that night was well calculated to give a little six-year-old boy a fright to remember. I can feel some of that same terror now. If those dogs had stood their ground and fought that marauding gang of lupus they would have been killed and eaten bodily, as they were doubtless aware. The farmers were obliged to pen all small animals each night or run great danger of losing them.

The streams were well supplied with fish of various kinds. They were taken in traps when the water was at the proper stage. At other times they were caught with hooks; sometimes with the gig, and during long cold spells of weather while the fish were numb, men struck the ice above them, then cut through it and took them out. Anyone could have an abundance of fish with little effort during the greater part of the year. Persons often came to our house and stayed over night and my mother cooked for them and grandfather entertained them and aided them to get a supply of fish. Sometimes when the hour for starting came next morning they could not carry all they had ready. At that time I had never heard of anyone charging another for entertainment. There were thousands of pounds of fish taken away from that place. But our folks never refused shelter and food to those fishers who desired it. Grandfather greatly enjoyed the company of those who came. I think they caught one that weighed seventy-five pounds and many twenty-five-pounders. It is said that a hundred-pounder was taken out of the trunk of the water-mill at Whitesville a few miles below. The catfish were the largest. Grinnel, eel, buffalo, perch, bass, gar and snakes were caught in our trap. The two last-named classes were not wanted, but had to be slain as enemies of us and the fish.

There were many reptiles, including snakes of the adder, the moccasin, the copperhead and the rattlesnake varieties of poisonous ones, beside non-poisonous snakes. Yet, strange as it may seem, very seldom was anyone bitten by them. However, they bit cattle and horses more frequently and often rendered them useless or nearly so even if they did not effect their death, by the bite.

On one occasion, when I was five or six years old, I had just received a licking and desired to get lost in the corn if I could do so without incurring another one. So I told brother I would go frog hunting. In a few minutes I came to a huge rattlesnake coiled in a hill of corn. I ran to the house proclaiming the find. They paid but little attention to me, as I was not regarded very reliable and I was sometimes cruelly informed so. But I would not let them rest and at last my mother came to my aid, declaring that I had seen what I claimed. That settled the matter and the three dogs, with mother, grandfather and Uncle Jack, started for the snake, which they said was not a large one if any at all. The dogs went ahead and to the south of the place and found a rattlesnake larger than any of us had ever seen before. It struck viciously at the dogs, but as poisonous snakes are blind in August, the dogs escaped unhurt. When the monster had been dispatched and laid outside the fence and I was being eulogized, I told the folks that we had not gone to the snake I found yet. But they hooted at me for thinking that two big rattlesnakes would be near our house at once. As before, I would not stop repeating my story in such earnest tones, that my mother declared that I knew what I was saying and that I had seen another snake. So dogs and family started to track me backwards, for my heels went into the ground every time I jumped as I ran from the snake. We soon came to it, coiled just as as I left it. They killed that snake also and laid it outside by the other one. The news went over the country in a hurry that two of the largest snakes ever seen in that country were killed near our house. The people came far and near to see them till they had to be removed. Grandfather would tell each comer of the snake killing and how it all came about through my industry and intelligence, and I could feel myself fairly swell at each repetition of the story. Stock in me never was so low any more. It was said that the snake could charm birds and animals and even persons. To do so it had to get the eye of the object to be charmed. Then the victim charmed moved slowly toward the snake's mouth, chattering with all its might, with its feathers or its hair turned toward its head and moving rapidly from side to side as it advanced; the snake all the time keeping its eye on the eye of the object hypnotized, and by some mysterious influence gradually drew its prisoner into its mouth and then swallowed it.

Snakes, like men, sometimes undertake too much, however. As Ruffin Travis came to our home one morning; he discovered a large rattlesnake by the roadside with a squirrel in its throat partially swallowed—both of them dead. Dr. F. F. Johnson, living near Stonefort, Illinois, related to me the following strange incident regarding the snake. Some years ago while in Texas, he and a friend were strolling over the prairie, when they came upon a large chicken-snake whose hindmost half was wrapped closely around its middle part, presenting a mysterious appearance indeed, which was unraveled only when the snake had been killed and examined. In stealing the eggs from some hen's nest it mistook a stone egg for a hen's egg and swallowed it. Of course the lady who put the egg there to fool the hen with, thought some boy stole it, but the snake knew he had it and would be glad if he did not have it. He tried to crush it with the tail end of himself by wrapping and squeezing. As he failed he continued till that part of the body grew rigid there, assuming an ugly and frightening appearance. By that one discovery, the manner in which the snake crushes its food is learned. And by the merciful killing by the Doctor and his friend the snake was relieved of a slow but certain death.

CHAPTER II.

DURING the first seven years of my life, the date of the events of which I am writing, I saw only one wagon except the clumsy truck wagon whose wheels were sawed from black gum logs. Sleds were used generaly in moving what could not be carried easily on the men's shoulders. The roads of that date were not capable of admitting the passage of a wagon in most places. As to bridges, there were none in that country. If our neighbors knew there were such inventions as bridges in the world, I did not hear them speak of the fact.

One day in March, 1846, Stephen Duncan asked my grandfather to accompany him to the creek, 300 yards away. I was permitted to go along and we witnessed him swim the full river with his clothing tied on the top of his head. The ford extends from the east bank northwest to the west bank, nearly seventy-five yards, I think. His clothing did not escape the water entirely. We waited till he dressed and departed on his mission, before returning home. I do not know why the man did not make a raft or dugout, unless he liked to swim in cold water. I stood on the same bank fifty years later, long after the others had gone to the world unseen by us and recalled the incident and remarked the striking similarity of the Battle Ford of 1846 and the Battle Ford of 1896, as recognized by me. In a short time afterward there was a bridge at the ford and they soon became common.

The residences of the people were of simple construction. Yet they answered their purpose well. A pen was built of logs sixteen or eighteen feet each way and seven or eight feet high. The sides of the logs were sometimes scalped off. The house was covered with boards four feet long and very wide, placed on rib poles and held in place with weight poles, as there were no nails to be had. One door was cut in the side of the house and sometimes one was cut in each side of it. The shutter was made of thin, long, split boards shaved with a drawing knife and hung on wooden hinges. If there was any ceiling overhead it was of split boards or rough sawed plank. The floors were of thick split puncheons, six feet long, with spaces between them often an inch wide. The fire-place was a hole sawed out of the end of the pen, of large dimensions, and a wooden pen outside raised to the top of the house and a jamb of dirt or rock built inside of it as a casing between the fire and the wood. The hearth was either of rock or dirt, and extended nearly three feet inside the house from the fire-place. The hearth was the place to cook the meals for the family. The skillet to bake the three nearly triangular cornmeal cakes in, the oven to fry the meat or bake the potatoes in, and the tin coffee pot to make coffee for the right old people in, were set on beds of live coals on the hearth till cooking was done. No chimney was complete till a wooden piece extended crosswise from side to side seven feet above the hearth in the chimney and an iron rod swung from it, four feet long with a hook on its end. On the hook the good women, by means of pot hooks, swung their articles to boil and heated their water for any and all uses. The instrument was called a "pot-rack."

There were no stoves in the world at that time so far as we knew, either for heating or cooking purposes. The first stoves we ever heard of were some used on a steamboat on the Ohio river some years later, which were seen by some of our young men who went to the river to work when they needed money very much.

Wages were low at the river, but much better than at home. Some of them cut cordwood at a stipulated price. I heard them say that Dan Turner was the best woodcutter that ever went there. The men had an art by which they could make three cords measure four cords by bad cording. The manager of the works sometimes docked the unfair choppers. The boys received some experience as well as money.

They told us that a great iron frame with a fire in it on the boat did the cooking. But they said that the victuals were not good like the food cooked in the skillet and oven. We did not think of ever using one. But the knowledge of their use spread rapidly and in the summer of the year 1853 my stepfather brought a new stove to our home. I suppose it was the first one ever used in that country. People came from all direction to see it. I soon had as my task the supplying of the stove wood and the building of the fires in the stove.

Such things as common matches were unknown. In winter the fires kept in the chimney and in the summer some old log near by was kept burning in order that each morning fire to cook the meal with could be had easily. But sometimes our fire failed. Then we took a flint and struck the back of a closed pocket knife against it, when sparks of fire would fall on powder and cotton beneath and an explosion would set the cotton on fire. Blowing the burning cotton with the breath and holding fine dry splinters to it soon terminated in a good fire. Sometimes the friz of the flint-lock gun was used to get the spark. When neither gun, knife nor flint was at hand the women put copperas thread on the spindle of their spinning wheels and turned till fire was produced. I have seen that done, but I scarcely understand the art of the action nor the philosophy of it. I suppose every person sixty years of age has seen it done often if he lived here then. If there were any other ways to generate fire on the earth, we had not been informed of the fact. Yet we progressed well.

We had no wheat to make flour. Therefore we had no biscuit nor pancakes nor pies. However, we had long bread and ash-cake, and short bread, and crackling bread and corn light bread and hoe-cake bread, and best of all, Johnny-cake bread made from the meal ground in the water-mill out of the Indian corn raised on our little farms.

We had a sufficiency of wild meat and tame meat and fish. Though the cooking was a little unsophisticated, our appetites were exactly suited to the requirements. It was all received with good grace. And if there was an opportunity to board with some old timer now who could duplicate the old-time food and the old-time cooking he would be much crowded for a few days at least.

All the cooking, eating and sleeping were done in the same room. Besides that, the women did all their carding, spinning, knitting, sewing and weaving there also. The loom occupied seven feet square of space. It was mighty close times when the loom was there. But we were shifty; what we could not have we could do without, of course. Such a thing as parlor or sitting room or waiting room or drawing room or reception room, none of us had ever seen or heard of. We used the one room we had for all necessary purposes. If it was too cold we filled the chinks with wood and mud; if it was too warm we knocked them out again. Our rooms needed no paint nor screens. Neither would they wear out in a lifetime. Yet they would not suit us now. But "We are nearly all dead!"

I had a spell of fever in the summer of 1846, and as I was recovering old Aunt Ann Cole, a colored woman, brought me a biscuit, the first I had ever tasted or seen. It was made of very poor flour and water and lard. I remember how the inside looked and how it tasted. I enjoyed it very well. It had been worked with her hands. It was flat, hard and heavy; but it was sweet and delicious to me. Her husband was one of the best farmers in our knowledge. I think he had raised his first

patch of wheat that year. It had been taken from the field and flailed out and fanned with a cloth till separated from the chaff. Then it was ground at the water-mill and bolted with a hand-bolt. It did not make very white bread. The Coles were an excellent family. The man's name was Joseph. Yes, Joseph Cole, and Ann Cole was his wife. They were servants of God, and Baptists. They lived three miles west of us in what is now known as the colored settlement. They have been dead nearly fifty years, and doubtless are reaping their great reward. The intelligent and religious citizenship of the large colored settlement of the present day there were largely influenced for good by them and their three children, who were also servants of God and Baptists. "Blessed are the dead which die in the Lord from henceforth; yea, saith the Spirit, that they may rest from their labors; and their works do followe them." Rev. 14:13. They planted; God gave the increase; they have their reward.

The clothing the people wore there in those days was manufactured by the mothers and daughters, of the poor quality of wool grown on the sheep and of the cotton raised on the farms. The wool was clipped with shears from the sheep, while one, usually a youngster, or two youngsters, held it down. It was a very unpleasant work for me and I often managed to get a licking for my impatience during the shearing. After saving as much wool as we could from the burrs it was washed and carded into rolls and spun into thread on a spinning wheel. It was colored with walnut bark, either light brown or dark brown, as the maker desired. The cotton was gathered from the boll in which it grew, the seeds picked out by hand and, after being washed and dried, was carded like the wool and spun into thread. The picking of the cotton was a tedious task and usually devolved on the men and boys and the little girls. Rows of it would be piled before the log fire in the winter evenings and as it warmed it worked more easily. After a few songs were sung—of the father, mother, brother, sister variety; and a few witch tales told, we little folks began to grow sleepy. I think even now that our tasks were too hard. But we had to finish them before we went to bed.

Those songs were of much value to us, as we could not read and we could learn them easily and they were orthodox and inspiring. Their doctrines were generally believed. But the witch tales which were told in most households and believed by almost every one were horrible and injurious, especially to children. Many a time I stood before the wood fire-place and kept turning around to avoid blistering till I could do so no longer, for the heat, lest something would catch me if I receded from it toward the center of the room. And the foolish and the cruel business of tale telling was as common as periods of leisure. One of the alleged practices of a witch, which was usually some old woman of dreadful appearance or eccentric actions, was to come into the home and select some member thereof and turn it into a cow, or brute of some kind, and take it out of the house through the chimney and ride it all night on such runaways as the witch had to do in her business and return it again through the chimney to its home, when it became a human again immediately. It was usually the men who were said to be made riding stock and had to pick all the briars out of their hands and heal them for several days. The women and girls were said to be changed into black cats by the old witch; and to afflict those the witch did not like, she brought fits of insanity and even death, besides despoiling the property and the happiness of the people in many other ways. But the cat invariably became the person she was before the witch had used her as long as desired, at or about the break of the ensuing day. I think that most of the people believed in those fabrications, as I never even once heard anyone express doubt as to their reliability. However, some few persons may have regarded the whole business as a relic of heathenism, but feared to hint their suspicions lest the witch punish them or the people might rail on them. Most of such beliefs went forever from the minds of the people as schools came to the country. A few old fogies would not be convinced of the folly of the belief of witchcraft, however, and talked of it till death relieved them of their benightedness. The last of those I knew were a brother and sister who died about 1885, nearly seventy years old, after rearing a large family each. They were so steadfast in the belief of these gross and groundless lies that no argument could jar them. It is astonishing that anyone of ordinary mother-wit could ever be imposed on by anyone to believe what we of that age believed. But it was not quite so bad as the cruelties suffered by the people of Salem, Mass., when some persons were burned for being thought witches. The credibility of our simple folk of sixty-five years ago was of the same unsuspecting stamp as the much-humbugged Mormons who trust their all on the home-manufactured falsehoods passed off on them by Joe Smith and his later leaders of that un-American tribe of human dupes, and also that tribe of dupes who look to St. Mary to aid them and adore St. Patrick, and depend on the priests to intercede for them. But as the real education of the people advances the superstition of the Catholic, the Mormon, and all other superstitions disappear, as that of witchcraft has done.

The cotton thread was colored purple with maple bark or yellow with copperas, or made into white cloth. After sizing and spooling and warping, the warp, as it was called, had to be put through the harness and sley, thread by thread, before the weaving began. Putting the thread through the harness was the task that I dreaded most of all. I had to sit and hand one thread to my mother after another till it seemed I could not stand the confinement longer. I frequently claimed to be a little sick and sometimes I was so ugly that my mother gave me the much-deserved licking. What few of the boys of that long ago time, who are yet alive, remember to this day how a boxed ear or jaw feels when given by an irate mother from the other side of the sley and harness. When that job was done I was very happy, for I could play for weeks before another one would be on me. My mother was happy, too, for she, like most of the mothers, loved to do work that she could progress well in, not having anyone to bother her.

The women always seemed to be happy when making cloth. And I remember well how they talked about the cloth they were making and the chickens they were raising or were aiming to raise, their gardens, etc., when they were together. I do not remember that I ever heard them say any mean thing about their neighbors. In due time the long web of cloth would be finished. Then Tom, Jim and Harry and the remainder of the male members of the family had to have their coats cut and made if the cloth was woolen, and if it was cotton they were made into shirts and pants.

Well do I remember the first pants I owned. They were white. Of course they had to be washed at least twice a week, and as they grew less at each washing and I grew larger every day, I was too large for them in a few months. Then my brother took them through a similar course of usage as I had done and when they were

too little for him and had to be abandoned as of no further use to us they did not have a hole in them as I remember. My uncle bought Brown domestic to make for himself a Sunday shirt, as he had become about grown, and the scraps left furnished a collar and wristbands for one shirt for me and that shirt of mine was so much more storelike than the other little boys had that I think I could not avoid strutting like a gaudy peacock. Those homemade goods were rough, but had staying qualities worthy the honest toilers that produced them.

The women and girls made their own clothes, even their wedding suits. They were ringed and streaked and striped. They had three colors, white and copperas and purple. But the combinations, when sizes of stripes and colors were both considered, were endless. Their aprons and their bonnets were of the same material and color, but differently combined. The children of both sexes till eight or ten years old wore in fair or warm weather only a single garment, viz., a kind of Mother Hubbard shirt. The shoes the children were provided with were made of jeans, a moccasin or nothing but a thick rusty skin that nature furnished to feet long exposed to hard weather.

The men and women wore shoes made of the skins of cattle tanned long enough to remove the hair from them, and each shoe was formed on the same last, as if both feet were of the same shape. Said shoes did not wear out that I ever heard of. The shoemaker knew that they would not. For they were of such poorly tanned leather that they would run down on one side or the other or backward or in two or even in all three directions. The toe always turned up and the whole shoe turned red as the lampblack wore off, and ere long the ugly thing grew so hard and unhandy that it had to be abandoned. The owner went barefooted thenceforward till next winter again. It was a noted event in the family circle when about Christmas the parent brought from the shoemaker several pairs of shoes for the different members of the family. They were very black when new.

The hats or caps were not costly, as they were manufactured at home. Some made little caps out of homemade cloth for the little boys and some made them out of rabbit skins. These last may have been bought from the stores. The knit cap for old and young alike was the common head covering in winter time. The palmetto hat coming into fashion as I began to remember, was sometimes the hat used in summer. As wheat and oats and rye began to find a place on the farm, the straws were often plaited and sewed into the shape of a hat. The long stove-pipe cannon hat was the first I ever knew. But that style was a costly one and did not prevail except as a Sunday hat. They were very fine. And one may now be seen on the head of an old man sometimes. The coat buttons were brass; the pants buttons were made at home out of cows' horns. The shirt buttons were made by the women out of thread. The thread was wound into a little cone and fastened with an eye to it.

One physician lived in Equality, fifteen miles away. His name was Watkins. I think the given name was William. Beside that one I did not know of any other. If anyone was stricken with sickness it was not the practice to run for the doctor. In each community someone kept a lance and he was the person to be invited at once. He bled the sick person in the arm or the foot or both. I have carried from my boyhood the mark of the lance in my arm. Teas were given freely, of roots, leaves, barks and berries. Sweats were much depended on in some diseases. In connection with the teas, peach leaves were crammed around the body under the clothing and the person to be sweated was covered with bed clothing as long as it was thought useful, and left to sweat. That treatment usually produced sweat enough. I knew one splendid young man killed by the sweating process.

Tartar was the specific for biliousness. Some good people had to have an exceedingly sick tartar day each spring. Then such person had better health the remainder of the year. That statement seemed to be really true. But of all the remedies for general purposes known to the people of sixty years ago in that part of the country, calomel was the one mostly depended on. The only fear from its use was salivation. The people did not know how to stop the eating of the mouth and throat when it started. Many a one was literally eaten up. That is, their vitals destroyed by salivation caused by taking calomel. My own maternal grandmother was killed in that way. Her mouth and neck were destroyed till bleeding from the eating process ended her suffering. Yet calomel was the common medicine because the people knew nothing to use in its stead.

The most plaintive recollections I have of useless suffering by the sick in those days was their want of water. It was universally understood that the sick must not have water while the fever was present. The sweating process was to go on till the water was out of the sufferer, but no more was to be given him. The sick would plead for just a swallow, while the mother would suffer as much for the child as the child suffered for himself, yet in love for him she turned a deaf ear to his pleadings. The sick one partly sleeping or frenzied from fever dreamed of drinking from the clear spring, but never could be satisfied. I experienced that delusion time and again. I enjoyed the drinking in my frenzy or in my dream, but when I came to myself I was burning up, as it were, for water. Once in awhile when the family were sleeping or were out of the house, the sufferer crawled to the pail and filled himself full of water. The cry was at once raised that the sick would die, as he had drunk all the water he wanted while he had fever. On being asked why he would kill himself he would say, "I do not think it will hurt me. If it does I can't help it. I had better die that way than to die for want of water." Such rash action as the sufferer was supposed to have committed always brought health. Though it was expected that the violator of the foolish tradition would die soon, he never failed to recover even once in all my recollection. However it was a long time before the people could break loose from the tradition of the fathers and give the sick the good cold water they needed. I fear many poor sufferers died from want of water that their friends would gladly have given them had they believed it was best for them. The truth is emphasized in such mistakes that it is not enough for one to think he is right but that he must be right to avoid serious consequences.

A very good reason for not sending for the doctor was that it was a difficult matter to pay him for his services. But a better reason was that it would be a mere accident if he was found at home. And if he was not there, to undertake to hunt him up, in a territory thirty or forty miles in diameter, would be a very discouraging undertaking, and if found and taken to the sick, the patient would most likely be well or dead. Many people died, doubtless, for want of medical treatment. But it has been so from the beginning of sickness in the world, I suppose. It has always seemed to me a pity for life to be frittered away through ignorance. I believe everyone should make the very best use of his life possible. I have held this view from the time I was a little boy to the present, and I know I am right in this view.

CHAPTER III.

THERE was one school of three months duration taught in 1846, four miles from home, by a man named Blair. That school was the only one I ever heard of till I was eight and two-thirds years old.

Our family library consisted of an old Bible printed in italic letters, with only one letter for the f's and s s. They were f's. It was so difficult for our family to read that it was not used much. The other piece of book in the library was a part of John A. Murrell's life. It was called "The Murder Book." Everybody wanted to read it to see what an awful rascal John A. Murrell was. I do not know what became of it. There was one whole Bible in our community. It belonged to Polly Hill. I remember that my mother borrowed it and read it in the monotone style a few Sundays. I think the people read and talked more of the Old Testament occurrences than of any of those of the New Testament except the crucifixion of Christ, and of his resurrection. Everyone that was in any way civil towards the word of God was acquainted with the case of the flood and the destruction of Sodom and the offering of Isaac and the case of Jacob and Esau and that of Moses and Joseph, and David, and Daniel in the lions' den.

Sunday was observed more reverently than it is now. The man in the moon was believed to be a warning to Sabbath breakers. It was said that he was sent there for burning brush on Sunday.

Bryant Wilkins and Polly Wilkins, his wife; Elias Carter and Lovice, his wife, and Polly Hill, and the members of the Macedonia Baptist church, five miles east of our home, were all the Christians I heard of, besides the Coles before mentioned, and these were Baptists, except the possible exception of Mrs. Hill.

My mother took me to Macedonia church in her lap on our family nag one Sunday. During the services Grandmother Blackman began to shout and praise the Lord for his love and kindness, but she did not rise from her seat. She was from sixty-five to seventy years old at that time and she was too feeble to rise, I suppose. I was very much excited over the matter and clasped my mother and asked her what made grandmother do so. She simply told me she was happy because she was soon to go to heaven where my papa was. That satisfied me and I continued to sit quietly on her knees keenly observing the exercises of that, the first meeting I had ever seen.

My father had professed faith in Jesus Christ awhile before his death, and was a Baptist in principle, as were all the Blackmans and also the Empsons, my mother's people who were religious; but he had not become a member of the church where he expected to, because of his earnest wish that my mother would be prepared to unite at the same time with him, as she was anxiously inquiring the way of life. The Baptists, during all the nineteen centuries of their history, have earnestly contended that no one should be baptized and received into membership in a Baptist church till such person had been born again and was a child of God and fit for the heavenly home, and she was not yet a fit subject for baptism. He understood that the saved ones were under obligation to God and to themselves to be immersed in the name of the Holy Trinity, and he intended to obey God in the matter, but he so much desired to be buried with Christ in baptism at the same time as his wife and by the hands of the same godly old man whom the people delighted to honor, that he deferred the matter too long. Elder William Ferrell, the father of Elders Hezekiah and Wilfred Ferrell, was the minister. Those three stood as a stone wall, together with Thomas Vance, Hosea Vice, Silas Williams, the Lemens, Levi Browning, Elder W. F. Boyakin and others, in the 30's and 40's, against the soul-enervating, God-dishonoring and hope-destroying doctrines of one Daniel Parker, who, being a minister in the Baptist denomination, began to teach anti-nomianism and succeeded in dividing the Baptists, drawing perhaps one-half of them in Illinois and Indiana after him. Those faithful men of God are all dead now except Elder W. F. Boyakin. Levi Browning, the last to die, went to rest in his eighty-fifth year, on July 22, 1905, honored by all who knew him. He had lived to see prosperity crown the efforts of the stern soldiers of those early days of their cause in this country and to see the followers of Parker, after a few years of successful proselyting of others, divide and subdivide till their power to paralyze Christian effort is little more than a historical reminiscence. Such heresy, though honest people were argued into its acceptance, could not survive an age of independent investigation, and therefore was doomed to decay in the light of practical Christian activity.

Elder Boyakin resides in Blue Rapids, Kansas, sound in the faith, eloquent in deliverance, rich in experiences, honored for his works, happy in his hopefulness, and ripe for heaven, more than ninety-nine years old.

After the death of my father, our loneliness was great and the broken-heartedness of my mother was very pathetic. Someone in my hearing remarked to her that we all had to die some time. That word was a sad word to me. To that time I had honestly expected to escape death some way and live on a very long time. I did not want to die and believed I would be spared. After our visitor had gone I, with a heavy heart, asked mother if the person did mean that every one in the world would be bound to die some time. She answered: "Yes, child; every one of us must die some time, and be buried as papa was." I believed her and gloom immediately shrouded my expectations. My light went out and I was a miserable little boy. It was in the early afternoon. I remember it was a still, pleasant, cloudy day. A dagger went through my heart then that has never ceased to pain me. I hated death then and I hate death yet. I love to hate it. I am sane on that subject and have been so those sixty years of life. Life is the only part of human beings worth anything. Insane persons destroy their lives and morally insane persons insanely lose their souls. Only when Christians know their lives are hid with Christ in God and they will live again forever are they willing to die. Death is not what man was made for It does not fit him. It is an enemy to him and it is cowardly to court death to excuse us from the duties of life. If I could have done so, I would have effaced that decree from the fiat of God. I by nature was a happy little boy, and if it had not been for that shade on my heart I think I should have been happy always. Outside of death in the world it suited me well. I feared no task nor doubted my ability to do what could be done, and only craved to be let loose to do my part.

In the spring of 1844 some of our kin whom we did not often see, called, in passing, to lodge over night. They had us to sing for them. We sang:

"Away over in the promised land;
  I hope, one day, we'll all get there—
Away over in the promised land."

If I had sung any song previous to that I do not remember it. Perhaps we had both sung before. The visitors raised a collection for us and divided it between us. My brother's share was five cents and mine

was six and one-fourth cents That was the first money we ever had or had ever seen. We were white-headed and they said we sang very well.

About the first of May grandfather began to plow up the ground of our little farm to plant the crop. Elm bark or hickory bark lines had been the kinds used, but at Hancock's store, four miles away, home-made ropes or lines were being made of cotton, and my mother, seeing the trouble of the bark lines to grandfather, took our money and bought plowlines for him. I remember hearing him tell someone of her action. It did not displease us to be left without money, as we had never seen a store and did not know what it was for.

I remember most vividly the enlisting of several young men in the spring of 1846, who lived not far from our home, to go to fight the Mexicans. They were Jim Hill, Jim Hamilton, Bill Hancock, Bill Creed, Jonce Reed, Ad Boyd, Steve Duncan and Wess Ingram. One or two of them were young married men. We all felt sad to see them start so far away on so perilous a mission. We did not know the merits of the war, but supposed our contention was just, else our nation would not have gone to war. About August following Jim Hamilton was brought home very sick. He had come across the Gulf of Mexico and up the Mississippi and Ohio rivers to Shawneetown, and on some conveyance to his home. Everyone who knew him felt sympathy for him. But after a month's care and friendly nursing he died. That was nearly sixty years ago, but my heart is sad at the remembrance of his, our dear neighbor's, death to this day. But few live to remember him now.

About October of that year a noted pitched battle was fought one mile north of the village of Independence, in which four men were engaged—David Stiff and

Thomas Duncan against Lewis Owens and Berry Owens. It had been the talk of the people for some time. They shuddered at the probable results. The four men were powerful men and it was feared that the consequences would be bad. The old man Duncan plead with his son Thomas and his son-in-law Berry Owens to desist, that the consequences might be awful; but his tears effected nothing. A crowd gathered; the men fought—David Stiff against Lewis Owens and Thomas Duncan against Berry Owens. They were to use no weapons. Yet Thomas Duncan cut his antagonist very badly during the fight and walked by the other men, who were lying across a log fighting with all their strength, and put his knife in the side of Lewis Owens once only and passed on. The fights were then stopped and the two wounded men cared for. Berry Owens recovered after much suffering; but Lewis was too badly hurt to live and, after dwindling several days, died. Duncan escaped. Stiff was not held responsible. Public sympathy was with the Owenses, and the fatal termination of that pitched battle had much to do in rendering fighting unpopular in the country afterwards. Hearing of the death of Jim Hill, and then of Lewis Owens, so soon afterwards and so close to us, kept me sad all the time, for I hated death with all my powers still.

Late in February, 1847, grandfather contracted pneumonia (then called winter fever) and, after beginning to recover, relapsed and died. He was not a servant of God, but had great respect for religious people and their good intentions and advice. He had contracted the habit of drinking whisky and, though he knew it was wrong, he seemed to be unable to avoid getting drunk sometimes. He was a real good-hearted man and one of the funniest men of that country. All liked him even if he did drink whisky. He was pleasant even when drinking. It was thought he intended to enlist in the Lord's service later, but he delayed that most important act perhaps too long, doubtless thinking if he were a Christian he would not be allowed to have his fun. The deceiver of souls made him think if he became a Christian he would be bowed down in grief all his life. My mother said she heard him praying many times during his sickness, for the Lord to save him. She indulged a faint hope of his salvation, but to be lost means so much that to the day of her death she carried a burdened heart lest her own dear father was lost forever. She bore that unwelcome dread for fifty-three years, which would have been joy all that time if he had taken the Lord's advice in Matthew 7:33. After he became unconscious, and the ominous rattling in his throat told that death was nigh, mother was wetting his dry lips to help him all her willing hands could do, when William Hase rebuked her for her solicitude for him. He said he would soon be dead and would be then no more than a beast; that he would never live again, neither would anyone else. I was already heart-broken at the bereavement suffered at seeing my beloved grandfather ruthlessly removed from our family. I had been named for both of my grandfathers. I had heard him time and again exhort my mother to educate me if it ever became possible to do so. He said I would be a power for good some time and that she would be proud of me when I arrived at manhood. To hear a man of mature years exhibit such lack of sympathy as those unfeeling words of Mr. Hase indicated he lacked, and to learn that anyone could be so glad as he seemed to be, to believe that death ended all there was of us, sent a sickening shudder through my heart and utterly amazed me at the new ideas I had never heard before. We needed sympathy then, not words like those. Though I was only seven years old, he planted a seed of skepticism in my mind that did untold mischief to me in later years. I had already, though unwillingly, accepted the fiat that all must die some time. The next query was what shall I do with myself, till death shall claim me. Now to hear that there would be no future for me or others was intolerably displeasing to me. I thought if there was no life to live after the one now possessed had gone, then this one was not worth living. But if we were to live again when this life was finished, I was willing to be anything and do anything to live again. I did not suffer from the fear of hell as I did from the fear of never living again. I intended to do whatever I ought to do to live in heaven always. I had decided that matter and till I heard those hateful words, had believed the kind words spoken to comfort my own dear mother during her continued bereavements. I could not see why the man would utter those cruel words unless he believed them; neither could I see why he should believe them without some fair reason. I was very sad and dejected.

The neighbors went with us and buried grandfather beside his dear wife in the old Mitchell cemetery, and we were at our lonely home again the same evening. My mother had been sorry to hear him speak so in our presence, but it had no influence on her belief. She assured me that Mr. Hase was an irreligious man and very wicked and only wished there would be no resurrection of the dead. She said that Mr. Hase knew he would not go to heaven if he died, for he was too wicked. She said that Christian people knew what he did not know—they know that the Lord had blessed them and made them happy. She named several Christians who had been saved from their sins and who did

not want to sin any more, and who said they were taught by the Lord that they would rise from the grave some time and then go to heaven to meet the religious people that died in all the years since the world was made. That the Savior would come down to this world to get the people who loved him and they would live with him always. She said that she did not know about this like those who had religion, but she hoped to know some time when she became religious. She said there was not much in this world but trouble. But the real Christians were doing the best they knew how to do and were perfectly satisfied that it would be well with them after awhile. That many of them rejoiced in the near approach of death because heaven was so near. That I must not believe the words of a man who spoke as if he knew all about it when he knew nothing at all about it.

About one year after the occurrence just related, a very sad event took place in the life of Mr. Hase and ended in his death. He had reared several grown-up girls and as many grown-up boys. I think that they were about like other young people except they were reared without any respect for Godliness or religion. But they nearly all died early and left no descendants. The name has been gone from the earth a good while. Mr. Hase was an overbearing man. He was a brother-in-law to Thomas Hamilton, a small and peaceable man. While at a gathering of the men for some purpose, perhaps an election or a sale, either for very hatred, or merely to exhibit his superior strength and foolhardiness, he grasped Hamilton around the body and carried him to a well, deep and dangerous, several rods away from the assembly, in disregard of the protests of friends, declaring that he would drop him into it. The well is on the old Randolph farm, near the old stone fort, in the south part of the county. When Hamilton became convinced that he was in danger of losing his life, he managed to draw his knife from his pocket and stabbed his persecutor just once. Hase let him down instantly in such a way that he missed the well and he hurriedly left the country to return to it no more. Hase died in a few minutes after being stabbed. The sympathy of the people was altogether with Hamilton, as he was a small man and a man of peace. Hase was a large man and rather independent and rough. No doubt that if Hamilton had stayed and stood his trial he would have come clear, as it was in defense of his own life that he committed the awful deed. But he regarded the killing of a man, even in self-defense, so great a calamity that he wanted to get as far away from the place and the people who knew it as possible. I think it is possible that he wished many times that he had let Hase alone, even if he did fall into the well. An humble, conscientious man can scarcely be reconciled to the killing of a person under any circumstances. Let no boy contemplate murder at all, if he ever expects to be happy.

CHAPTER III.

MY MOTHER had three sisters living near Brushy Fork creek, eight miles south of Galatia, ten miles north of our home. They and their husbands asked us to sell our claim and buy one near them. My oldest sister had died before my father, and another sister, who was born two months after my father's death, died at three months of age, and my father and grandfather, making four deaths in a few years, caused my mother to make the change.

We sold our claim to William Watkins, for a consideration of $100, to be paid in property, one-half down and twenty-five dollars worth each autumn for the next two. Elias Carter was the witness to the agreement. Every condition of the agreement was carried out to a tittle. I remember that a second-rate cow and calf, or yearling, were to be valued at $8. No interest was to accrue. I never forgot the honor and fair dealing of Mr. Wilkins toward us. In less than one month after we buried grandfather we were moving away—household, live stock and family. It was a dark and cloudy day. I looked back at the old place as long as I could see.

It was the only home I could remember. I hated to leave it. It was dear to me. Twenty years and three months passed away before I visited the old place again. I sat on my horse alone and my eyes scanned every part of the little meadow to discover something I had known before. Every tree and stump and log and fence had gone. Much of the outer edge of the little field had been allowed to grow up in trees. The old muster ground was a hazel thicket, except a path through it. I was surprised to witness so great a change. There were no people living within three miles of the place whom we had left there a score of years previous. The Hills, the Hancocks, and Hamiltons; the Creeds, the Coles, and the Carters, the Wilkinses, the Travises, the Hases, had died or moved away. My mother, my brother and my uncle, who lived with us there, were still living. The first three were Christians and members of the New Salem Baptist church, two miles north of Carrier Mills; the last named three were returned veterans of the late Civil war. I recognized the merciful providence of God in sparing me and mine through the long period since I had seen the old home, and there offered myself anew to the Lord as his servant, during my pilgrimage that summer day in 1867.

When we came to our new home on Brushy Fork I was about seven years and two months old. Our house was fifty feet above the creek to the north, and the descent of sixty degrees covered with white oak trees and shrubs. The five-acre field on the south came to the yard. As I look back over the intervening fifty-nine years to our little home and the trees and the birds making sweet music for us, and MOTHER being there, it seems a veritable earthly paradise. We were so happy in our single-room home, so snug and warm that we did not want to go back to the Battle Ford again. Our kinfolks were not a mile away and many friendly people were less than two miles distant. The people were just as good as the people we had left and were closer together and perhaps had better conveniences. My mother was not so lonesome, and we had more playmates. Among the good neighbors we found there were the Boatrights, the Abneys, the Pankeys, the Carsons, the Medlins, the Smotherses, the Reynoldses, the Rices and the Vineyards. Some of those names included several families. All of them were our friends and their memories are sweet to me to this day. There was a large house built of hewn logs, 400 yards east of us, for church purposes. Aaron Sutton, a minister of what was known as the Anti-Mission Baptist church, calling themselves the Regular Baptists, decided that he did not agree with his brethren, and organized a church in the large church house, and they called themselves Campbellites, as I understood it. They were splendid people and had true religion. Sutton, for some reason, left soon after we came to the place, and settled in the middle of the state. The church scattered, and in 1854 nearly all of them went into a Baptist church called Bankston Fork, just organized, two miles southeast. They were Baptists all the time if they had understood themselves. I remember that we attended the church till the preacher left the country, and my mother said he preached the gospel. When the house was vacated two families moved into it, one at each end. I judge it was forty or fifty feet long, and had two very large fireplaces in it. When a preacher came to preach there was room between the families in the house for the people. They did not care for standing.

On one occasion a very exciting incident took place there. Though dangerous, it turned out all right. I'll relate it as an expletive: Mrs. Annis Henderson and her little son and daughter occupied one end of the house while waiting for possession of a place she had bought near by. A very unpopular white dog belonged to the family, which had to be permitted to lie under the bed during the services and during the visit of any person not connected with the family, lest he creep up and bite the visitor. John S. Harris was conducting the services and his exhortations were of the most gifted and eloquent character ever heard in that country. Francis Medlin was so much encouraged that he began to shout and jump and clap his hands. That was entirely too much for the dog. He rushed at the shouting man. The congregation sat stone-still lest things would grow worse. The people sat all around the house and on beds, and a large space in the center was vacant. Medlin kept his feet together. He jumped about twelve inches each time, perhaps, and the dog snapped at him once or twice at each jump. The preacher exhorted as fast as he could talk, and very loudly, as he always did. Medlin shouted at the top of his voice, and the dog barked furiously and snapped viciously till Medlin had gone all over the floor frequently and stopped. The dog darted under the bed as if to save his life. We all thought the poor man would certainly be bitten, but feared to move in his behalf.

I believe the dog snapped at the man's legs forty or fifty times and almost caught him every time. We were all much relieved when the shouting was over and the dog gone without biting the man. The preacher and the shouting man died about thirty-five years ago and doubtless went to the rest of the people of God. The poor dog died a score of years earlier; but he did not go to heaven to mar the peace of man.

Shouting was common then, and it has always been right, in my judgment, for God's people to shout when the Spirit fills them.

There 'was another church two miles northwest of our place. It was called Brushy Fork. That church was a Regular Baptist church, as they called themselves; but were known to others as Anti-Mission Baptist, and other nicknames. They were a splendid, plain people. Nearly all their members were middle-aged and old people, and, it appears to me, that every male member was bald headed. The preachers that came to feed the sheep, as I remember, were Henderson, Gouge, Coffee, Thomas, Spain and Lewis. The last was the most eloquent of them all. He was a Mexican soldier. And after he returned from Mexico he was out of his place in that church, as my mother said he told them that the Mexicans were so blinded by the priesthood of the Catholics that they ought to have the gospel, and he believed true Christians should send it to them. Information will make missionaries of all true Christians. He died in his early manhood. James Tate and Richard Fulkerson were later leading ministers among that people—especially the latter. He was an honest man and did not shirk the consequences of his theology as long as he lived. All the preachers took part each service, and everyone sang his own tune

at once. Their day services occupied from two to four hours every time.

In August, A. D. 1848, Henry Garner opened a subscription school in the log church house where the Brushy Fork church held their meetings. My mother subscribed one pupil at one-half price, amounting to $1.25, the regular price being $2.50. As a widow, she received a reduction of one-half. My brother attended twenty days and I attended forty. There were benches only one tier deep all round the house up against the wall. They were made of trees, one foot thick, split open in the middle, and the flat side worked off and shaved smooth with a drawing knife. Four large holes were bored with an auger in the under side and large pegs inserted for legs to hold up the bench. The house had one big fire-place, one door, and one window behind the pulpit, and a long window made by taking a log out of one side of the house in order that those who were learning to write, by turning their faces to the wall, could have light. The writing desk was a plank twenty inches broad, having the proper slant, just under the window. But few were sufficiently advanced to commence to learn to write during that term. Sixty or seventy pupils attended.

I dreaded to start to school very much, lest I get a thrashing the first day. I knew all my a-b-c's and my a-b abs before I started. My grandfather taught me them before he died. With my heart throbbing with emotion I entered the house the first morning and waited to be told by the teacher what to do. We were easily remembered, as our heads were nearly as white as the male goose, and we were known as the two little white-haired boys wherever we went. At last nine out of ten in that school had only "Webster's Elementary Spelling Book" to take lessons in. It was an open school. That is, one in which every pupil spells and reads as loudly as he pleases. Sometimes we would be among the last to arrive, and when we were within 200 yards of the house it appeared very much like a baby charivari, or a Babel of tongues, with all the tones represented from the deep bass to two octaves above. Each one tried to be first each morning, as the first to arrive was entitled to recite first. We had no classes, except that the two Jo Abneys recited together. We took our seats in the order of arrival till we reached from the teacher's seat clear around to his seat again. We leaned our backs against the wall and extended our feet toward the middle of the floor. When we saw the teacher grasp his long switch we rapidly drew our legs under the benches, for we knew he wanted to stripe someone, and many times he did it. Public sentiment demanded the frequent use of the rod by the teacher. We recited four lessons each in a day, but they were very short ones. The teacher worked all the time to get through his task. He used no bell to call us in, but he, being endowed with a strong clear voice, called us like he called hogs. He was a very good citizen and he did his utmost to earn his money and do us good; but his education was limited. He spent many recesses trying to assist the few grown young men who were "ciphering" to go through "addition." I do not believe they solved the most difficult questions. Perhaps getting the problems down correctly was what they were not able to do.

Happy? Yes. We did not know that we had a poor school and we played to the last minute the teacher gave us. He guessed at the time, for watches were not common. If there were any in the country I do not think I had ever seen one of them. My mother paid for all our tuition with jeans she had made and stockings she had knit.

During the next summer Mr. Beard taught a two-months school in a little old vacated building near where the Bankston Fork meeting-house now stands. He was an educated man and a Christian, I suppose, from his manner. His daughter—a young lady—gave me a little Sunday school book. I had never heard of a Sunday School before. The title was "Anson B. Daniels." It gave an account of Anson's long sickness and his patience and his readiness to die. It called him a Christian, though he was only a little boy. It made me sad to read it, yet I owed that duty to my lady donor and read it. From this school I never met anyone who could lead me in spelling.

In the early winter of 1850 I entered Mr. A. B. Pulliam's school at the Brushy Fork church again. He was a good teacher. By a little indiscretion on two different occasions I escaped whipping, as it were, by the skin of the teeth. I suppose my white head and saintly appearance were too much for Mr. Pulliam; for the others only as guilty got a licking. The best prize offered was a book worth fifty cents. I intended to win that book. I was leading the school and it was conceded by all that I would get it. But at the end of the first month the muddy condition of the long road and our poverty influenced my mother to stop me.

John Bond, a larger and a better boy, won the prize. The failure to secure the book, although no fault of mine, was a hardship for me to bear, yet I was glad John won it, as I could not, and he was a long way ahead of the other contestants. He died before coming to manhood.

In the summer of 1851 we attended Jonathan Abney's school at the same place one month. He was a nice man and a very good teacher. He had a large, happy school. But he committed what would now be an unpardonable mistake. On the last day, as was sometimes the case on the last days, he gave us all the sweetened whisky that we could or would drink. It was not long till the beautiful grounds were literally covered with drunken boys doing all kinds of things that boys could do. He stood around amongst us, perhaps to see that there was no killing done. Beside some getting bruised and skinned by falling against stumps and logs of which there were many and the loss of dinner and whisky and happiness by the determined and successful rebellion of the digestive organs, the normal health and judgment were restored sufficiently before night to allow us to depart for our homes. Some patrons regarded the practice as dangerous and immoral. Those six months were all I attended school in that community, and nearly half I attended in all.

During the first winter that we lived on the Brushy Fork, Robert Boatright set a day for men to come in and help him clear ground, and his wife invited the women and girls to come and help her quilt. They promised to give an old-fashioned frolic, or dance, at night. (I think that such antics are now called "balls.") The men and the women came in very satisfactory numbers and rendered honest labor all day. As our family resided less than 600 yards away, we were expected to attend. My brother and I were anxious to go, and we all went. At sunset we went home and immediately the heaviest hailstorm I have ever seen fell. But at our earnest pleadings and the urgent request of the host and the guests also, as we had promised that evening, we returned about dark. I do not remember that we had ever heard a violin before; and the sound of it thrilled me and enchanted me and intoxicated me till I thought of nothing else. I became used to it somewhat after a while and took notice of the dancers. I soon learned the names of several of both sexes beside

those I knew before. We remained till ten o'clock that evening and that was long enough to convince me that I would not only be a dancer and a genuine frolicker, but that I would also become a first-class fiddler (violinist) till I was forty years old, and that I would then become a Christian and get ready to die. For several days I could not get the jig tunes out of my mind. I think I sang the senseless words and the tunes so much that it was a real punishment to my mother for allowing me to go where the foolish exercises could be witnessed. However, being so happy at singing or sawing on a stick-fiddle or contemplating the future in those things for me, I was less annoying than I would otherwise have been.

The next year my mother took us to the same place and under the same circumstances and remained till near midnight. That time I procured a partner and took my place in the set, but so many eyes were on me that I could not proceed. I asked one to take my place and did not try to dance at all. I had not thought of the senselessness and uselessness and profitlessness that first began to dawn on my mind at the time, that I was soon to try to shuffle my feet about as the other dancers did. I could have danced very well, I think, if I had not had that thought which deepened my shame to a paralyzing extent. That little experience satisfied me. I observed that not one of the participants was a Christian, and from what I had heard of the character of the dance, if a Christian were to dance he would be thought less of than if he did not pretend to be a Christian at all. Even the dancers knew that dancing was not the best way to spend their time and strength. I deemed the dancer's pleasures like the drunkard's pleasures—intoxicating and deceptive. Ten years passed by before I ever for any purpose attended another dance.

The little creek near by was a lovely place for the boys of our size to fish and swim in. We had never heard of a Sunday school. Our parents knew no more of them than we. We had nothing to do on Sundays but play, and play we did. Our parents were willing for us to play on the creek in warm weather if water was low. We were not permitted to disobey our parents nor sauce anyone else. We were not allowed to use profane or vulgar words. If we did it would get to our parents' ears, and we were whipped severely for our conduct.

The one thing that detracted from perfect happiness, I suppose, was the lack of fishhooks. We could secure only pinhooks. There were fish of good size and sufficient variety in the creek but out of thirty lifted up, perhaps one might be landed. The loss of nearly all we saw made us sorry.

Late one evening mother gave me and brother permission to fish half an hour before going home from the field, and immediately he caught a large perch and I caught a large pike. We ran home and plead that it paid better to fish than to work. Of course our good luck was accidental. Each one ate his own fish and felt happy over our exploits for a long time.

The boys knew nothing about hunting, though there was something to hunt for then. I really hardly believe we would have tried to kill an opossum, a mink or a raccoon if he had presented himself as a subject of the chase. The squirrel, the turkey, and the deer were so common that we paid but little attention to them. We had no guns to kill them with, and, if we had, we would not have been permitted to use them. No boy lost his life from the discharge of fire-arms then, because he was not allowed to handle them at all. We caught quail in traps in winter, and squirrels in deadfalls in the Spring.

But we had great times in the water,

learning to swim. Every boy wanted to swim very much and almost every one succeeded. I did not learn to swim till I was past twelve years old, though I had put in four summers before that one. I had three narrow escapes from drowning while trying to learn. Each time someone reached me in time to take me out before I sank the last time. There was no need for me to be so long about learning to swim, if I had been told how. As it was, my learning was of use to myself, and enabled me in later life to save one man. Every boy should learn to swim in the presence of a grown person and then never to offer his life in vain effort to show out. Many good swimmers lose their lives in deep water because of cramps. It is foolishness to needlessly run risks, but I did not so understand things that way then.

Of all the boys that played together, I was the unlucky one. I had my left arm broken or cracked three times in the same place. I fell out of the walnut tree near our house and went over and over like a stick thrown, falling on my breast in such a way that no bones were broken, but three joints were sprained, and the breath knocked out of me till I thought I never would breathe again. That was in October, 1849. The tree is standing there yet, looking exactly as it did more than fifty-six years ago, and I think it never failed, even once, to bear its crop of walnuts in all these years, and its east limb, from which I fell that painful fall, still stretches eastward as it did then. I had many falls from horses and oxen, and, if I walked I fell as a matter of course. I had kicks from everything that kicked and was sometimes hooked. But some way, I escaped death from all. I do not believe I was a bad boy, but a venturesome one. Two opposite traits possessed me. Timidity and tenderness influenced me in one direction, and ambition and energy in another. They have served me as the centripetal and the centrifugal forces do the sun. The one has forced me out from utter uselessness, and the other has restrained me from utter rashness.

CHAPTER IV.

ON AUGUST 1, 1850, our uncle, who had helped to raise us, was married to Miss Julia Boatright, an excellent woman, and, began housekeeping in his new house, one-fourth of a mile south of our home. We then hired our house rebuilt one-fourth of a mile east of its former location, while we resided with our uncle and aunt. That move put us in possession of a claim on an additional forty-acre tract of land. But it was only a claim, and must be deeded to become our land in fact. When we were safely ensconced in our rebuilt home we were just as happy as we could be made, especially brother and I. We were located on a public road, and the woods were so pretty to us and every thing so friendly and clean looking. The next fall we cut small logs and hauled them to a place where we wanted a crib, and the men came in and put it up for us; and we put our corn in it as it was brought from the field. The men bragged on us so much that we obtained permission from mother to build a log barn for the sheltering of our stock. I was less than eleven years old and my brother about nine. I did things far beyond my strength. I did not dream of moving away for anybody or anything. It seemed that we never tired of work on the home place, but we could not bear to work on the old place. We actually felt afraid to work by ourselves where we had lived and was then so deserted and lonely. I, though I was so fond of work at home, did not lose my love for play. My brother was not as good a worker as I was, but he was a very good hand to play.

Sometimes mother had to go away from home to warp her thread or attend to other business, and she sent us to the field to pile brush and stalks. That was the one thing we could never love to do and never could make any progress at. Our sheep bell was in our hearing and we only waited for her to get away and the sheep were driven in to the lot and we did some tall riding till we feared she would come home and catch us. Then we hurried to the field and worked a few minutes. If she did not call us we came anyway as if we were very tired. To avoid the sheep exercises becoming monotonous, we varied the exercises— sometimes they were driven into the stable and opening the door after I had lain down along the front sill so they could not see me. If the sheep did not come out fast enough, brother punched them with a long stick. As they would start over the log or sill, after it was too late to draw back I would raise my back just under the sheep and the poor thing, being too far over to draw itself back again, would attempt to go skyward with a spontaneous bleat of surprise that was so funny to us that we repeated the project till we were tired laughing. We did not injure the sheep and the fun was worth a great deal to us.

When some good old woman came to stay all night with us we went out to the field to burn logs awhile, but we rode the sheep much of the time. No one who has not seen such fun as we had can estimate its worth. Our mother died without ever thinking of the deceit her little boys played on her. She was not hurt in any way by it, and they were greatly blessed. There is no occasion for boys to seek pleasure that way now. Outside of the hastening on of the inevitable and the mysterious future I was very happy. But I did not forget that I was coming closer to the river of death each day.

Our attendance at the Brushy Fork church on the first Sunday in each month was kept up, when the weather was good. Mother was anxious to learn the way of life, and we wanted to see the people.

On one snowy Sunday, while at the church, Ben Reynolds gave me my first quid of tobacco. I thought it would make me a little more like a man to chew tobacco. Well, I chewed it awhile, when it seemed to me that the world was turning round and round, and then the earth would want to fly up and hit my head. Then I found that I could not stand up. Then I became sick, and then sicker, still, till I felt like I would perhaps die. Meeting breaking, there was much interest taken in me and they all said I would live over it. I thought I would not taste tobacco again if I lived over that spell. I had a hard time walking home through that snow and I was too large to carry; perhaps there was not a horse at the church. But I tried the same foolish thing once or twice each year and suffered the same awful sickness and the loss of a half a day's work at each time, till I finally learned to chew tobacco at twenty-one years old. I learned later on to prefer it to my meals. I saw what a mistake I had made. Then I tried to quit the use of it but failed. It made me filthy; it kept me lean, and cost me money. Beside those hurtful things it did to me, by using it I set a bad example as a Christian after I became one. I could not consistently ask anyone to cease doing any foolish and hurtful thing. After very many efforts, at nearly forty-three years of age, I took my last taste of the stuff on November 1, 1882. I am exceedingly thankful to God that I was able to live to abandon the filthy, hurtful and costly habit. The boy who learns to use tobacco is a foolish one; but the boy who uses cigarettes is a criminal. He is destroying himself and those who love him. He is a physical, a mental and a moral suicide.

While the Brushy meetings did not attract the attention of the young people much, after we moved into our new home we often went to prayer meetings south of us a mile or two. The Baptists and Methodists held the meetings without a preacher. At every service someone would ask those who wanted to enlist in the service to come and offer themselves to the Lord in prayer. T. M. Cook, Margaret Cook, my mother, Hannah Pankey, William Smothers, and Gilliam Furgeson came regularly to the mourner's seat till converted or the meetings ceased for the season. I was a good listener to what was said and a good observer of what was done. But it was astonishing to me that I could learn nothing about religion. After my mother had been saved she informed me, or, rather, reminded me, of the prophecy that had been made concerning me at my entrance into the world, by my aunt, Jerusha Mitchell, a member of the Macedona church, and others present. They devotedly offered me to the Lord in prayer. My aunt believed her prayers would be answered to the day of her death. I lightly passed the subject by as an utter impossibility. She may have listened to me preaching a thousand times since then. Who knows? I thank God for that aunt and those who joined with her in that service.

We attended those prayer meetings and the occasional preaching services for two autumns and winters. I was so timid concerning the exercises, as not being prepared to take any part in them, that I would not sing unless in so quiet and unobserved way that I should not be taunted for my forwardness. I was always glad when the meeting seemed to be enjoyed by the people. We had James Canady, a Baptist man, who was gifted in crying in prayer and exhortation; Elias Weaver, a Methodist man, of great honesty and unselfishness, who preached often. I remember hearing him preach at the residence of John Smothers, one night, from the text, "In my father's house are many mansions." Berry Bush, another Methodist preacher, came around occasionally and preached as often as he came. I heard him preach one night at the same place from the text, "Master, we have toiled all the night and taken nothing; nevertheless at thy word I will let down the net." I was ready to enlist in the service of the Lord then, if I had known I was old enough. I craved so to enlist, but thought it impossible while so young. People seemed to think it a dangerous precedent for young people to seek salvation, lest they be deceived.

On a beautiful Sunday in 1851 I saw Elder Thomas Spain baptize a party in the shady waters of Brushy Fork creek, and in 1852 I saw him administer baptism to another group of candidates in the same waters. On one occasion those baptized were three sisters, Rebecca Henderson, Permela Howe and Mary Abney, all sisters; and on the other occasion those baptized were Nancy Stone and Polly Boatright, two sisters, of another family. The ceremony was a solemn one and it struck me as meaning something to see middle-aged women in the presence of 300 people perhaps, wade into the silent stream and submit to be buried in the water and raised out of it again, at the hands of an old honored man, just because the Bible gave them such instruction. I can not recall to mind which of the baptizings took place first. The candidates became members of the Brushy Fork church. They are all dead now, both minister and members.

On the first Sunday in May, 1852, our family attended services at the bridge across the Bankston Fork creek at the Vinson farm, where I witnessed baptizing for the third time in my life. A revival of religion at the Liberty church had been enjoyed, and on the aforesaid day the converts were to be immersed. The largest gathering I had ever seen was there. The singers rendered "How Firm a Foundation ye Saints of the Lord," in a new tune that day that became very popular afterwards. Those baptized then were T. M. Cook, and Margaret Cook, his wife; Wilson Huddleston and Jane Huddleston, his wife, Wilson Vinson, David Moore, Gilliam Furgeson, Leroy Gaston, Emeline Willeford, Martha Huddleston and Martha Cook. The first two live in the city of Harrisburg and are nearly eighty years old. The others are dead, I think.

The minister was named Edmon Vinson. He seemed happy at being privileged to baptize his own son. He was an earnest and fervent man. The good Lord had saved him from the gutter. He had not only been a drunkard, but a fighter of renown. Others of his kind went on to ruin while he was saved as a brand plucked out of the fire. Just as soon as he understood himself he went to work to persuade his companions to turn from their evil ways. He was ordained to preach as soon as his Baptist brethren regarded him as having the scriptural qualifications, and he labored faithfully till death claimed him for its own in 1855. He selected the place for a new cemetery and was the first one to be buried there, near his former home. The place is known as the Vinson cemetery. Some three months previous to his death I heard him preach one Sunday, in the Bankston church, from the text, "And these shall go away into everlasting punishment, but the righteous into life eternal." I thought if ever any man believed what he said he did. That kind of talk, I have believed for many years, was better than preaching one's self or quoting Socrates or Cannon Farrer, or some poet. He despised hypocrisy and formalism.

At a revival meeting in the summer of the same year at the same church, quite a number of the anxious came forward and prayers and singing exercises were taking place, when the shouting of a notorious drunkard and fighter was heard perhaps one-half mile away by those near the door. The man came on as fast as he could travel, and went into the house and to the seekers, exhorting and shouting as fast and as loudly as he well could. The people were awe-stricken. He finally told the sinners if they did not repent they would go to hell as slick as a fawn skin. Elder Vinson was seated in the old-fashioned pulpit and had not come to himself from the shock till then. He started to him with his walking stick, saying, "Let me to him." But cooler heads held him back and others took Abney, the noisy man, out. The meeting was broken up informally. The man went into a feigned swoon. The older men would wonder if he did do all that meanness on purpose, or might it not be he had been converted and in his awkwardness used his slang words. Morgan Dallas, a Methodist preacher, believed it was the spirit of God hold of him. But the men were much divided in their opinions. Finally John Smothers said he was convinced that it was the spirit working on him, but it was the spirit of the barrel. That settled the matter. He was carried into the house and a guard of three strong men detailed to keep him till an officer with a warrant should arrive to take him to court. The guard shut the door, put out the light and stood outside. I think they were afraid of him. When the officer came Abney had raised a puncheon, crawled out from under the floor and departed. He left the country, went into the 'Union army seven years later and died, it was said, for the want of whisky. Vinson soon discovered that he had come for mischief and he would not have it.

At that date the country was being settled up by persons moving in to it. And as soon as any one could raise fifty dollars he went to Shawneetown and deeded a forty-acre tract of land of his own selection. If he chose to deed the tract on which anyone had a shanty or a larger improvement, he was regarded as a very mean man by everyone in possession of the fact.

Jo Robinson, one of the very first inhabitants of the city of Harrisburg, an immigrant from some Southern state, having much money, caused much trouble and anger and ran great risks of assassination, for deeding lands settled on by persons not yet able to deed them. He had no children and when he died he left only a small estate to his widow. If his money had been used as not abusing it (1 Cor. 7:31.), he could have been of untold benefit to his fellowmen here and had a great reward in the future life. Occasionally some other person did a similar act at the expense of the ill-will of the settlers. Some who entered their neighbors' improvements paid them all they were worth or sold it to them at cost. Sometimes those entries (as deeding was termed) were done unintentionally; i e, the numbers were not what were intended, but the error could not be undone.

The close of the five years and one-fourth of my happy boyish life was drawing to a close, since we moved away from the old home near the Battle Ford, I loved almost everyone I knew, and it seemed that they loved me. Under all kinds of circumstances I was happy, with one exception. For if I was sick or hurt I enjoyed pleasure by anticipation. But every time my mind thought on the certainty of an early departure from the present mode of existence into a place entirely unknown to me I was fairly sick at heart. Life was yet to me incomparably more desirable than any other endowment or possession of which I had ever heard.

In the summer of 1851 we heard of the death of a middle-aged woman, five miles away, with whom my mother had been acquainted from childhood. That was the first death we had heard of that close to our home that I remember since we had come into the section. She was a Christian and a member of a Baptist church. People talked about her death and about her condition to meet death much for weeks, as the family was a prominent one and a death was seldom heard of then.

I studied of my own need of eternal life more than ever before. I was perfectly satisfied that I must be born again and desired to enlist in the Lord's service at once, if I was old enough and if I could only know how. It was a sad day. I remember it well. We heard how the loss of the mother broke the heart of the husband, and how the large family of children missed her care and love, and how the whole community mourned her death. The only comfort anyone could deduce from the sad occurrence was that she was taken from this world of sorrow and misery to a place prepared for her in heaven (Rev. 14:13.)

I dreaded nothing else that it might become my duty to do but to obtain eternal life. To become an educated man, I thought, would be an easy and enjoyable exercise. To become a rich man, I could do at odd times. To become famous, I regarded as possible to one who was willing to deserve it. Like Jacob of old, I was willing to labor seven years and joyfully add another seven years for what I wanted most of all. I did not speak to anyone of my great desire to become a Christian, and my continuous stream of mirth and play and fun doubtless led persons to think I was a very light minded and thoughtless boy. I am sure no one knew how happy we were in our new home while improving it and contemplating the wealth to be accumulated there.

CHAPTER V.

BUT alas! on the 17th day of June, 1852, we saw our dear mother and William A. Harris stand on the floor and be joined in the bond of matrimony by Elder Edmon Vinson, in the presence of the relatives and friends. We could not say a word that would effect anything, but felt that it was a great mistake on the part of our mother. Our prospects for doing great things on our beautiful place in the woods were blasted, and we felt a little like a Siberian exile feels when condemned to years of servitude in that distant and inhospitable country.

The man who became our step-father was a prominent citizen and land owner, residing two miles north of where the village of Carrier Mills is now situated, and half way back towards the Battle Ford. He had taught the district schools formerly, but had been an officeholder for many years and farmer beside. He was a Christian and a Baptist. He stood well wherever known for honesty, wisdom and sympathy for the needy, but he was a poor financier and was not competent, as a father, to develop those under his care into the best quality of citizens. He did not know that daily culture and restraint and direction and encouragement were necessary. He thought that the absence of very immoral and wicked conduct in a boy was proof that he was becoming an exemplary young man. He appeared to think that a small amount of literary education was sufficient.

Our farm was a good one and we raised a great deal of produce on it, but if we failed to use it all, or to destroy it, or feed to stock that was not worth keeping, others used it at our expense. There was not another citizen of his prominence in that community who was so poor a manager financially, but there were many who knew as little, and some of them cared less about raising their families well as he. And at this time, fifty-four years later in the world's history, I believe our country needs competent fathers and competent mothers much more than it needs houses, and lands, and gold, and fine raiment. It is not well understood that it is a greater work to give to the state a MAN or a WOMAN in the true sense of the term, than to present it with perfectly rounded horses or other domestic animals. Yet the first is a thousand times greater than the last.

When we arrived at our step-father's house we found eight children, ranging from two years old upward—only one little girl four years old, to help mother, except as the male force aided her. The family were moral and ordinarily peaceable. But nine boys, including her own, the two-year-old one sickly and troublesome for several years, furnished work enough to discourage an ordinary woman, especially during the summer, when they were working in the growing tobacco and scuffling on the loose ground. And the cooking! My! what eating! Unless the chills came among us. Then it seemed to make the boys more hungry when recovering. I do not think I knew what a chill or ague was till we moved there. It was expected that five or six would be down two months or less during the summer, with those periodical pests, each year.

We lived on the big road from Marion to Equality and much company called on us. The candidates for office made our home their place of rest and refreshment when in that part of our country. The preachers came to our house and were always welcome. And while one of them was there we were not required to labor,

except to do the things that had to be done. For we loved to hear the preachers talk.

But my mother was having the burden to bear and I knew it, though she did not complain. Perhaps she knew that we were learning some useful things which we stood in need of from those men. For we did not go to school except when we could find nothing else to do. In the six years and nine months residence there I attended school four months, in seven different schools. However, my mother's drudgery was almost breaking my heart, while it was wearing her out, though she was a strong, resolute woman used to hard work. Finally two boys were detailed— my brother and George, a step-brother of the same age to help in the house. They milked the cows, spun the rolls, washed the clothing, spooled the warp and quilled the filling that made clothing. That is, they aided in these labors. But they could not weave nor cut garments nor sew them. The patching alone was an item of dimensions. The knitting of about twenty-five pairs of stockings each year was a Herculean task for one set of hands and fingers. All these were my mother's burdens. We ought to have sat around the big fire till bedtime and knit, ourselves, but no one thought of it but myself. I suppose I should not have done so but for two long attacks of rheumatism. When convalescent I knit a new pair after footing an old pair. Those were of irregular softness, grading from the hardest of soft bacon skin to a stocking's ordinary pliancy. I drew the thread too tight at first. I was glad to help even that much. The boys worked in the house two or three years.

Matters were not always heavenly in our home. Elements of discord were infused into some of the smaller members of the family from without. My solicitude at the increasing burdens of my mother rendered me more unhappy. Yet in her life I did not tell her of my frequent repairing to the fields or woods to cry over her condition till I found temporary relief in my loss of tears. I sometimes dreamed of living in the little house on the Brushy Fork again, and was very happy till, waking I found it only a dream.

Four little girls were born to our parents in eight years. They were intelligent and handsome, and could sing tunes before they could talk. I loved them very dearly, for they deserved to be loved. I often cared for them on Sundays rather than play with the country boys. I would gladly have supported them and my mother at our old home if I had been permitted to do so.

If my step-father had been as wise as he was sincere and honest, our home would have been the most lovely anywhere to be found. A competent governor was needed. Not one member of the family was dull or incorrigibly mean.

In August, 1853, John Blanchard came into our neighborhood and began a series of religious services which continued several days. He was a notable man, for his size, his voice and his zeal for the salvation of the lost. No man stood better in the country and perhaps no man ever did more real good in Pope county than he. About twenty grown-up young men and young women were led to accept the Savior during the meeting, among whom was W. D. Russell, who later became a minister of the gospel and did honest and earnest work as pastor for country churches from 1872 to 1887, when consumption disqualified him from labor and ended his life in the year 1898. He, like most of the other Baptist ministers, bore largely the financial burdens of the churches, beside almost, if not entirely, giving them his ministerial labors. He was one of the very

best men I have ever known, all things considered.

A church had been organized three years previous, in the house where Elder Blanchard held the meetings, but had been disbanded because a minister was not to be had. The members had taken membership with Liberty church, near Harrisburg. That church was organized by Isaac Barbaree in 1832. The first church house was built of logs where the old Willeford cemetery is located. Elias Weaver, an uneducated Methodist preacher and a splendid, man, in passing the place one day about 1885 said to me, "These hands cut the hickory withes and twisted them and fastened the logs to the double trees of the teams of horses that dragged the logs to the place where they were to be builded into a house of worship." He said no chains could be had then. He doubtless told the truth. It was the way in that day and place.

Elder Blanchard returned about Christmas and a new organization was effected, composed principally of the members from Liberty. More than twenty were approved for baptism and church membership. The new organization was called New Salem Baptist church. I had been an anxious seeker for salvation privately through the meeting, and for eight months afterward; but made no progress. Seeing no chance for success, I could do nothing but turn to the world.

The first land entered in the territory of Saline county was deeded by John Wren and Hankerson Rude on the third day of September, 1814. Each of them deeded 160 acres in township ten, south, range seven, east, some eight miles southeast of Harrisburg.

February 25, 1847, an act was passed by the state legislature allowing a vote on the first Monday of the ensuing August, on the question of separating the west eighteen miles (ranges five, six and seven) from the eastern part of the county, to form Saline county. The majority of the voters casting their votes for the separation at that date, the final completion of the organization took place on December 10th of that year. By August, 1848, James M. Gaston had finished a court house, according to the previous contract in Raleigh; and in December of the same year a jail was contracted, which was afterwards built, two stories high, out of ten-inch square timbers, on a foundation of rock two feet thick. Later the officers believing the seat of the county would remain at Raleigh, advertised for sealed bids for a better court house, 36x40 feet, two stories high, to be submitted on July 18, 1853. Jarvis Pierce received the contract and built the house of brick and received therefor, $5,500.00.

The town of Harrisburg, six miles south of Raleigh, and one mile south of the center of the county, was surveyed and platted by Archibald Sloan on May 28, 1853, for John Pankey, John Cain, James A. Harris and James P. Yandale, each of whom contributed five acres in a square cornering on the stone which marks the half-section corner between sections fifteen and sixteen in township nine south, in range six east, of the third principal meridian. These men had been selected at a mass meeting, held at Liberty church nearby for that purpose, and each one deeded to the others an undivided equal interest in his five acres of land. Main street, running north and south along the section line between the two sections, and Poplar street, running east and west along the half-mile line between the half-sections, were deeded to the town. Perhaps other streets were deeded at the same time throughout the twenty acres. The beautiful public square was laid out for the

court house, which was expected to be erected there in the future. On the 16th day of the following July the lots were sold to the highest bidder. An old-fashioned barbecue was enjoyed at the place that day, and many people, men, women and children, came in ox wagons from a distance, or walked, or rode horseback. Not a buggy was there, and I do not think there were any horse wagons there. A small patch had been cultivated, but most of the twenty acres were in thick woods. The underbrush had been cut from a small place, and the snags left several inches above the ground were very unpleasant to that portion of the assembly who did not wear shoes. I remember that fact well. The dinner was bountiful and excellent. After dinner the auctioneer began his work. He began to cry, Lot one in block one, then lot two in block one. I did not understand what he meant; neither did I find out. I remember every piece he sold brought as much as five dollars, but nothing brought more than twenty-five. Soon small log frame cabins ornamented several of the lots and business began to thrive there. But saloons cursed the town from its beginning, with but one year's intermission, for thirteen years, and was the direct cause of several killings in the place, besides being the indirect cause of many more. Among the parties who lost their lives in drunken brawls were Carroll Stunson, Joe Feezill, Jesse Stiff and John Nunn. Long and expensive court trials followed each, at the expense of innocent taxpayers, all because there were men who preferred to sell intoxicating drinks to those who would buy rather than to labor for a living in some honorable business.

After a long and heated canvass in 1856 the voters at the regular November election said the county seat should be moved to Harrisburg. The matter was taken to the courts and the will of the majority was thwarted till the spring of 1858. The sessions of the court were held in the Cumberland Presbyterian church house, located on the south side of Church street, south of the square where it crosses Main street.

On the 20th day of July, 1859, Dr. J. W. Mitchell and Robert Mick were awarded the contract for building a court house in the city, and a jail, including a residence for the jailer, for $15,440. The jail was finished by August, 1860, and the court house was received by the committee not many months later. The jail was removed and a better one took its place perhaps ten or twelve years ago, and, after forty-five years of usefulness, the court house was taken away as being too antiquated in appearance to please the fastidious and refined generation of the present age of the world. So it happens to us all. A very beautiful and up-to-date structure adorns the square now amid the pleasant shade surrounding it of which we are all proud. Many conveniences are afforded that had never been thought of when the old house of justice was erected, and the most pompous of which is a thirteen-hundred-dollar time piece, mounted high in the cupola to remind us of the passing hours. The building was erected by J. B. Ford and Robert King, contractors, and cost about $30,000, besides the clock and furnishings.

During the same year the Illinois Central railroad was built from Galena, Illinois, southward, and the next year it was finished to Cairo. That was the first railroad to approach the south part of the state. It was considered a great and wonderful invention.

During the same year a caravan of home-seekers from Arkansas to California were led into the desert by Mormon intrigue and slain by Indians. The bodies

were left for the wolves, except the hair of the women and girls, which was cut off and plaited into ropes and bridle reins by the Indians. The children too small to remember much were taken and incorporated into Mormon families, and the teams, wagons and other property were kept by the Mormons.

In 1877, John D. Lee was taken to the spot and shot as one of the leaders of the conspiracy to kill the poor people from Arkansas. He did not deny his guilt but said the other officials were as guilty as he was. But they decided to saddle the blame on him as a scapegoat. He had seventeen wives, besides his mother-in-law, to whom he was married, for the benefit of her soul, he claimed.

Lieut. ——— of the United States army that year gathered the bones of the murdered people and made a monument of them.

On the fourth Sunday in April, 1854, the following persons were baptized in the Bankston Fork creek by Elder Blanchard, who had become pastor of the new church, viz: W. D. Russell, J. E. Russell, Martha D. Russell, Mary E. Russell, J. C. Ozment, Riley Spinks, Edmond Barnett, James A. Harris, Mary Fleming, Lucy Ozment, Mary Hannon, Lucinda Carrier, Della Carrier, and another whose name I have forgotten.

On the fourth Sunday following, at the same place and by the same minister, the following four persons were baptized: Elmore Barker and Ann Barker, his wife, Zachariah B. Russell, and Mrs. Margaret Harris, my dear mother.

At the next monthly meeting on Sunday, J. W. Adkinson, Martha D. Harris and Jo Allen, a colored young man, were baptized by the pastor.

During the revival in the fall previous I would have been very glad to kneel at the anxious seat for prayers and instruction, had it not been for two hindering causes. The first was that I feared I would be thought too young, and embarrass the leaders of the meeting, as I was not quite fourteen years old; and the other was that the boys would laugh at me for wanting to be a Christian. I concluded that I could seek the Lord successfully alone by learning from the instructions to others in my hearing. I began and tried every way I knew, not only through the meeting, but for eight months afterwards. However, the more I thought about the matter, the deeper grew the mystery of Christianity to me. I gave it up because I was making no progress.

The year 1854 has been known ever since by those old enough to remember, as the dry year. Scarce anything was produced that year except crops which matured early like wheat. But farmers had not begun to cultivate wheat to any great extent in our county then. Not one farm in thirty grew any at all. Old Mr. Cole, the colored man mentioned before, had a large crop that year. He let the people have for seed all he did not sow, at a low price. People were astonished at his magnanimity.

If we gathered five bushels of corn off our farm I do not know where it grew. One-half acre spot was considered worth cutting and putting under a shed. Men hauled corn next summer from Shawneetown, where corn grew in the river bottoms without rain, after paying one dollar per bushel as far west as Marion for bread. The winter following the dry summer was the lightest one ever known in our county. We kept a few cattle alive partly by cutting maple trees for them to eat the buds and twigs. Others did likewise in many instances.

The farmers put their best ground in wheat usually tobacco land.

During the dry year the land in Illinois not already deeded was divided into what was termed swamp land and ridge land. The swamp land was given to the counties for school purposes. Commissioners were appointed to appraise every tract of forty acres, and ditch it and sell it as fast as bidders were found for it. It was valued at twenty-five, fifty, seventy-five and one-hundred cents per acre. The ridge land was put on the market by the United States government at twelve and one-half cents per acre.

Any person of age, male or female, and the head of a family, could get a deed to any vacant forty acres of land for five dollars. But no one could legally enter more than one-half section, which would cost him forty dollars. The farmers went to Shawneetown and remained in rows to be listed, then returned home to await their turn, for the land, could not all be entered in a few days. I knew young men to loiter around and make no effort to secure any of the cheap lands which were put on the market expressly for their benefit. I was very sorry that I could not have any chance for a home, being too young. The land was all sold in a few months.

My step-father did not enter any, as there was none adjoining his land and he would not violate the law to get it.

Many persons furnished the money to poor men to enter land in their own names and later deed it back to the one furnishing the money. Our step-father said that was whipping the devil around the stump.

During the dry summer the Christian people often met and prayed for rain. Some excellent meetings were had at those prayer meetings. The preachers said if the Lord did not answer the prayers of his people in one way he would in another. So it was right to trust him.

At last the spring of 1855 ushered in. Everything was early and prosperous. The teams fed on green grass and the farmers rushed their crops. From twenty-five to thirty-five bushels of wheat grew on most of the acres sown, and there has never been a better crop of everything raised in the county. Persons who were able had bought flour previously by the barrel at Shawneetown and had biscuits on Sunday mornings only. After the good year wheat was raised to sell and to use at home every morning. Since that date wheat has been a staple article in Saline county.

Every article grown in the year 1855 was of the largest and most satisfactory yield except the tobacco crop which was partially eaten up by the worms. Excessive rains began to fall on the twenty-second of July and the wheat in the shock and stack was damaged very much and the people became too sick to save their tobacco. Our family was sick so long we lost all of ours, as we could find no one to hire to work.

Those who had produced wheat previously had beaten it out of the straw with flails, or trampled it out with oxen and horses. But a man by the name of Bill Keaster (who was killed in the Fort Donelson battle later) introduced a threshing machine in the settlement and the people thought it was a great invention. I did not get to see it, as I was very low with what was called white swelling. It was what people called a ground hog thresher. It left the chaff and wheat on the ground together. The wheat had to be cleaned by hand or a common fan. Such a thing, improved fivefold could not now, be given away.

Late in October I had recovered so far as to ride on a load of wheat to Carbondale to see the cars. W. H. Pankey, my cousin, with whom I went, had made one trip already and felt that he was so far ahead of me in information that he was an authority. He told me many outrageous tales as

we went on till I did not know what to expect to see. I first took a pretty good look at the ties and the iron tracks. Then I saw a handcar coming slowly along and, by remaining at a proper distance from it, I did not become frightened. But when a train of cars, hung to an engine, came puffing by, it was more than I could stand. By the time it was within two hundred yards of me my legs started to make tracks. I ran till the train stopped. I was afraid the boiler might burst and the pieces strike me. The train ran backwards and forwards while loading and unloading freight till I lost most of my fright and had the misfortune to see part of it run over a boy and cut him up. He was of my own size and was swinging on the cars. His father swore at the cars. But the other men told him it was not anyone's fault but the boy's. I do not know whether he died or not. His feet and legs and head and shoulders were awfully cut and torn. Some of his toes were left on the ground.

The next year was only an ordinary year for farmers. But as they had learned to raise wheat, a mighty impulse was given to farming. The next season, that of 1857, was almost as good for the farmers as 1855. As we had continued to open farm land, we had a good farm for that day.

Mr. Stephen Pankey, owning a section of good farm land, concluded to run a mixed store at his home. Every store was expected to keep whisky for sale. I was allowed to go to school and do his book-keeping in evenings and mornings. I tried it a few days and resigned. The drunk men would curse me and order me around as if I was a dog. The teacher weighed 300 pounds and slept most of his time. I quit the school and the store in a few days. The store broke up Mr. Pankey. He was honest and thought too many others were honest also. They secured his goods, but did not pay for them. I went home and began to cut and split rails. My step-brother, Hampton Harris, of my age disliked the teacher as being worthless, and joined me in the labor. The teacher's name was Willis, old Doctor Willis.

The following incident I relate only as teaching the habits of the mink: One Sunday morning during that winter, some of us were in the woods and found the tracks of an ordinary sized mink leading up a very large and tall wateroak tree. We had been taught to honor Sunday and would not cut the tree on that day if at all. Monday morning we found that the mink had been away during the night, but had returned to the tree again. We could see where its den was, in a hole under a limb, nearly horizontal only bending as it advanced from the body. The tree was four feet through, but we did not allow the pest to locate so near our chicken-house. About the noon hour the tree fell. The mink was easily caught and its skin brought one dollar. The tree now would be worth from ten to twenty-five dollars. We decided to cut into the limb of the tree to see what the mink had up there. Its bed was toward the body of the tree from the place of entrance in the limb, and beyond the hole were flying squirrels. Everyone had its throat cut, no other wound. The last killed were nearest the hole. The others were mildewed. There were seventy-nine flying squirrels in that hole.

The year 1858 was not a very good year for farmers, but better than the next one. We were all growing larger and, having the same routine labor to perform without any stimulating object held out before us, life was not so pleasant as desired. In view of possibilities, mother and I decided to have brother go to his aunt's, Mrs. Willis Russell, to live. He went there in June. Neither of us—brother nor myself

—had ever given one saucy word to the good man who was in the place of our father. We always honored him and to this day revere his memory. Yet he was not competent to develop those under his care into the best class of citizens, perhaps few, if any others, were. I would have gone away but for mother's sake.

CHAPTER VI.

ON the 13th of the next March I went to live with my brother. Of all the years I have lived, those six years and nine months just mentioned were the most unhappy ones. I believe it to be a criminal mistake to unite two families into one, unless the parents are as wise as serpents and as harmless as doves. God forbid that any should do so, as many have blindly done in the years gone by. We visited the family often and loved our mother and little sisters still.

We had a good home and worked together that year, but it was a poor crop year. I was not very happy, as I was nearing manhood and did not know what to do with myself. I had a poor education, was still a weakling, and was getting older every day.

About five years had passed since I had quit trying to find the way of salvation. I had learned nothing. I was without an objective point ahead. I entered the dancing ring as the only exercise at hand. I had a territory three miles wide and eight miles long. I attended almost every dance in that area for two years. I could stand the useless folly no longer. I knew no good could come of the dance, but harm, morally, financially and physically. I never knew of any of my relatives taking part in the dances, else I would have been very sorry, although innocent girls often do take part, not understanding the dangers generally surrounding them. I thought then that wise parents could not afford to encourage dancing, hopping, waltzing and like antics, among their young people. Now I know it. Those bring bad returns. I went to my Aunt Catherine Abney's to live about Christmas, and cultivated land there and kept my live stock there also. Although I had been an ardent devotee of the dance, I labored these two years persistently, and increased the little I brought away from my mother's home with me to about three hundred dollars worth of property. Every dollar I made at mother's was made while other members were doing nothing, doing anything I could find to do.

I went to a land sale on the 20th of July and bought forty acres for ninety dollars on one year's credit, except five per cent was to be paid in cash. Robert Dallas bought one tract at two hundred and fourteen dollars, and A. B. Bickers bought the other at one hundred and twenty-five dollars. They were older than I, but were single as well as myself. We could not raise the small amount for the cash payment. At last my uncle, William Pankey, loaned the money to me. I had nearly four hundred dollars worth of property at that date, but it was not money. I did not forget my benefactor. I know a friend in need is a friend indeed. Later in the year I bought another tract of the same size adjoining the one I owned, from Bevely Fleming, for one hundred and sixty-five dollars, nearly all of which was paid in trade, that is, personal property.

About the middle of December, 1860, I accompanied Stephen Pankey to Cairo, Ill., with a drove of beef cattle. The weather was cold when we started and remained so all the time we were gone. Some evenings we were compelled to travel after dark to find lodgings for ourselves and our stock. As we passed the little log residences with their new limestone chimneys, and saw through the single window the bright blazing fire and the happy young families snug and warm there, while I was out in the penetrating air, "shivering in the cold," I resolved to possess sometime a warm home, though it might be an humble one. The word, home, has been a sweet word to me ever since that time.

We arrived at the residence of Mr. McPhatridge, four miles east of Vienna, near eight o'clock the first evening, and found lodging of the royal kind. I thought I had never eaten as good a supper as we had that night. I thought if there was a McPhatridge to stop with at each thirty miles distance I would be all right. We drove the next morning to Isham Dunn's home three miles on, and stopped till the next morning. Mr. Pankey and Mr. Dunn were relatives.

When we reached the Ohio river near Calidonia, we saw that the river was very low, but the bank we were on was very high. I had never seen any watercourse larger than the Saline river, and the big Ohio looked fearful to me even at low water. I had never seen a steamboat and had no idea of such a spectacle, except as I drew it from the flatboats I had seen floating down the Saline. I waited with much impatience for one to come along. Mr. Pankey said the water might be too low for the boats to run.

After gazing at the river and the sandbars and other new objects with great interest for a good while, Mr. Pankey went on to see after some business and left me to ride leisurely along behind the cattle and see that none of them strayed off. Soon I heard a splashing noise that was a strange one to me. Looking in front and on both sides of me I failed to discover anything . But as the fuss came nearer and grew louder I looked behind me. Coming down the stream that I was so close to was an object, the like of which I had never seen. I was satisfied from the first glimpse of it that it was a steamboat. I was filled with excitement and my heart beat a tattoo in my breast, and the cattle showed signs of impending danger. That boat was moving slowly, as I later understood, but another appeared very soon behind it that gained rapidly on the first one and passed it as both of them passed me and the stock. All that racket was entirely too much for the cattle and they hoisted their heads and tails and stampeded into the woods out of sight. My horse and I would have lit out also if we had not been afraid to. I was very glad when the boats had gone on below, for I was afraid one or both of them might blow up and flying debris would strike me. Uncle Steve came back and anxiously inquired where the cattle had gone. I told him that when the two boats passed they ran off, and that I wanted to go very bad, too. We soon found the cattle and went on. The good man enjoyed the incident so well that he relates it and laughs about it to this day.

Arriving in Cairo, we found ourselves in a little town with only one street worthy of the name. The levee, on which the Illinois Central railroad is situated, was not as high then as it is now by a few feet. But the buildings on that street were nearly all there were in the town. The old stone depot was new then, and the Halliday House was the St. Charles Hotel then. It looked then much like it does now, to me. I had never seen so tall a building before. One or two other streets had been laid off and a few houses built on them. Sidewalks were built of plank, in front of the houses, ten feet above the ground. The lower story was meant for storage rooms in dry weather only; the second stories were the dwellings.

The sipe water filled the town with fluid when the water was high, and the high walks and high rooms prepared the citizens for emergencies.

The beautiful Cairo of today was only possible by filling in with millions of cubic yards of dirt. The prospects of war by the Southern states at that time crippled business so much that our cattle brought but half what they should have brought.

We lodged with the German butcher that night who bought them the next day. At supper I was handed a mess that tasted queer and thrilling to me. It seemed to go straight to the ends of my fingers and toes the first plunge. I thought it might be a mixture of pepper and garlic and parsley and dog-fennel. Perhaps it was horseradish instead of dog-fennel. I ate it, as I thought I could put up with what a German could. By the time I had finished eating, I liked the wonderful dish very well. I began to consider the propriety of seeking a Dutch wife sometime in the future. But I never did so, neither have I ever tasted anything like that spicy dish since.

When we were both in the same bed snug and warm, I quietly placed a Colt's revolver under my pillow lest I should not be ready when the robber came to rob us. When the morning came and we had not been disturbed I began to believe there were some people in the world who had some wisdom, if not principle, for I did not have anything to be robbed for; and the people guessed right, even if they had wanted to rob us. I had been made to expect all kinds of bad things when I had gone away from home.

The sun rose bright and shining next morning, in a direction I was not looking. I thought it would rise up the Ohio river. But it rose, down the Mississippi river rather on the Missouri side. I was so completely lost at what I saw of the rising sun, that it was forty years before I got all right on the matter, though I had been in the town many times.

The land beyond the Halliday House has

nearly all been deposited since those days. The Mississippi river ran near the hotel then. As we returned home we stopped at Mr. Dunn's again. For some reason I visited one of the young married sons and lodged there all night. The old man had kept whisky to sell for many years, and always furnished his guests liberally with the intoxicating fluid, not forgetting to imbibe freely himself. The hostess was a new one to Mr. Pankey, the former wife of Mr. Dunn's having died several years before. He had taken the hint from the words of our Creator respecting Adam that it was not good for a man to be alone, and had won another wife. She seemed to be in happy agreement with her husband in all things, especially in the use of the intoxicating cup. Mr. Pankey discovered that she was testing the beverage with dangerous frequency, through the night, as the door separating the rooms was left ajar. When morning came the good woman tried to prepare the meal, but gave up the task, complaining that she was sick. Mr. Pankey knew that the woman was drunk and put up with a comparatively short breakfast. The Dunns were good people of the old-fashioned kind, and the family passed away with its class more than thirty years ago. As to the woman referred to, I do not know where she went when she left here; i. e., this world.

I arrived at my aunt's on the day before Christmas. Passing through a large wood near the end of my journey, I decided to shoot the bullets out of my revolver. I selected a large tree, on which I fixed a small white spot, aiming to hit it every time I shot. I then took deliberate aim and fired. I was fearful that I would be heard, for even then it was regarded cowardly and unmanly to carry a pistol. I quietly moved to the tree and examined the spot, but it had not been hit. I then examined the tree, high and low. But no

bullet had entered its bark. I was astonished. I examined my gun thinking I had bent the barrel in some way. But it was all right. I then fired, time and again, till the chambers of my pistol were empty. But not even once did I hit the spot or the tree.

The handy cartridge of this date was not invented then. A proper charge of powder was put into the chamber, a bullet on a patching was forced down to the powder, and the percussion cap was exploded by the hammer which fired the powder, and the ball sent to the mark aimed at. I had used patching too thin when loading and in carrying the gun 200 miles in my bootleg, muzzle downward, most of the powder had wasted, only enough being left to send the ball into the barrel of the pistol where they were all found, mashed together. I traded that pistol off loaded.—i. e., the barrel was loaded. I did not inquire afterwards if the pistol was ever fixed for shooting or not.

I did not own or carry a gun of any kind after that experience till I carried a musket as a soldier. In two weeks the blister as broad as my thumb on the side of my heel, raised by the pistol carried in my boot, the long ride to Cairo and back had healed; and the elevated opinion I had of my own importance had been seriously shocked. Experience teaches a dear school but pays, etc.

Mr. Pankey was born Christmas eve, 1817, on the farm which he has owned to the present time. His wife and all the large family of children, except one son and one daughter, have gone to their long home; but he still lives, the same genial and generous citizen he has been all the many years of the past. He is the only person now living in the world that I knew when I was a small boy, except three or four cousins of mine. Possibly no other

person born at such an early day in Saline
county is alive today. He erected the first
frame dwelling I ever saw. Perhaps it
was the first in the county. The studding,
the rafters, the sleepers and the joists
were hewn out of logs or poles. The lath-
ing for roofing and for plastering were
split out of trees. The shingles were split
out of cypress trees and shaved with a
drawing knife. Such shingles will serve
fifty years. Proper repairs will insure another long service by that friendly old
landmark of a bygone generation.

Under embarrassing circumstances, I
joined in wedlock the first couple I ever
married, in that very old house, more than
thirty years ago. My ceremony was not
long, but longer than I use now. I did
not want to mimic some other person, and
made a form of my own. When I began I
found that my legs, especially my knees,
were drunk, my body became frightened
and my lungs gave out. I finished in a
mere whisper and was glad it was no
worse. That was the first time I knew that
marrying people was hard work. All the
parties present at that wedding except Mr.
Pankey have gone to the glory land long
ago.

It became my duty to baptize the old
man on a profession of faith in Christ as
his personal Savior, after he had been approved for baptism and membership by
the New Salem Baptist church on October
15, 1901, and he has lived a happy Christian life to this day. Indeed, he was regenerated and saved twelve years before
that time. His father died at about
ninety-five and his mother at ninety years
of age, the week preceding Lincoln's
second election to the presidency. One of
them, if not both, were members of the
same church as Uncle Steve is now. I
have written at length of Mr. Pankey because the old people are nearly all gone

and will soon be. He is an authority on
many things now.

Having disposed of all my property by
March, 1861, I went to Mr. Vernon's school
one month, in the New Salem district. He
was so much better a teacher than had
ever taught in our county before that his
school was crowded with grown-up young
people. It required a month for me to get
into the study habit. I was alarmed at
that. I tried to find a select school, but all
were suspended. The war clouds were
gathering and gloom pervaded everybody
and everything. Then Mr. Vernon began
a select school at the same place. Many
grown young men and women came in at
the beginning. In three or four weeks the
call to arms was too loud, and the school
closed. I had labored on my land at convenient opportunities while waiting for
school to commence.

I kept a violin in a hollow tree, and intended to keep my fiddling a secret. I
was an apt pupil and soon made the woods
ring so sweetly that I was soon found. I
tried to get into the army all that summer,
but failed each effort I made. When the
weather grew warm, as if my ax and violin
were not enough to employ my time, I
took my Brown's grammar with me, and,
at intervals between work and fiddling I
memorized the rules and digested them.
The foundation of my knowledge of grammar was obtained while laboring in the
silent woods.

The war was progressing, with the
Southern army, who had the start, coming
out ahead in most of the battles, as the
idea with them was to make so great headway at the start as to encourage the European nations to recognize the independence
of the Southern states. It was evident that
an opportunity to go to war would soon
come. Though elected constable to fill
out the term of G. J. Empson who had resigned to become a soldier I continued to

fiddle and clear ground and study grammar. I would not have gone to another dance for money. But I was not happy. I cleared one acre and put it in cultivation; fenced ten other acres, and girdled the trees on ten acres more. I made such progress with my violin that I could make very sweet music for the uneducated ear. I digested that 'Brown's grammar till I earned a certificate to teach a district school by August.

But the subject heaviest in my heart was whether it was the thing to do to go to the war without first becoming a soldier of the cross. I knew if my mother and other honest people had been regenerated, as they claimed to have been, I was not ready to be killed. If they were mistaken, then I was ready to go and be killed; for it would not make much difference. I did not know what to do about it.

I boarded at W. D. Russell's and labored enough for him during the summer to pay a small board bill. He was a warmhearted man, but did not know of my troubles. In July I decided to go at once, anyway. I concluded to risk the future and go to some place where I would be received, as I did not seem to be doing right, while married men were going, for me to stay at home, though I had no one to support but myself.

At that time John A. Logan began to organize what was later the thirty-first Regiment of infantry. I was among the first to enlist in the company which T. J. Cain was organizing. It was lettered "B." My friend Lewis and many other neighbors went in that company. I was pretty certain I should go to the front and let the husbands and fathers take care of their families. Then I had the spirit of adventure and presumed I'd get along all right anyway. However, if I had possessed any fixed plan of belief or knowledge of the great beyond, my course would have

been ordered strictly according to the demands of an immortal soul or a mortal being as the case might be.

At last a meeting was held in Harrisburg and the day fixed on which we were to go to Carbondale, thence to Jacksonville to be mustered and receive clothing, arms, etc. The company was almost full and in three days we were to go. My brother was larger than I and much more active and strong. He had been perfectly silent about enlisting till that day, or only one or two days previous. He announced that he was going at all hazards. To have both her boys go into the army and they unconverted seemed more than our mother could bear. During the interval I agreed to stay with mother six weeks and teach school and then join the company with my friend, Joshua Medlin, who must need wait till that time.

I went with the boys to Carbondale and returned home a very sad boy, for I wanted my brother to stay near our mother and let me go. I was examined and received a third grade certificate to teach in one district only. I think now that if I had an aptitude for any business in the world, it was teaching school. I had a great time in my school of twenty-six days. My wages was $1.00 per day.

Determined to enlist, as I promised to do, I closed just before the first Monday in October the end of the school year, much to the sorrow of pupils and patrons, and drew twenty-six bright, old-fashioned silver dollars for my work.

I do not know why I did it, but I took an extra suit of clothing and hastened to Cairo to meet my brother and other friends, to be with them in their great undertakings. Our mother had consented to my going for my brother's sake. When I found him he was very sick with measles. I stayed and gave him all the attention that I was allowed to. The doctor seemed to me to be very unfeeling and esteemed life very cheap. We both remembered to have heard that pure whisky was a specific for measles. Yet the physicians would not let him have a drop of it. It seemed more and more that he would die. I went out and bought one quart of the best rye whisky that I could find and smuggled or slipped it in to him. I feared that the waiters or doctors would find it and punish me but I would have done what I did if I had been sent to the penitentiary for it. He improved slowly and, after two relapses, recovered. But he would not have me to try to get into the army, and I returned to my mother and to my school again.

My friend Medlin was mustered in and made a good soldier. However, his services terminated in a few months. On the 15th of February, following, in the Fort Donelson battle, he was shot through each thigh and the left arm. He would have frozen to death had not a kind Confederate rolled him in two blankets, where he lay for two days and nights. The Union army had been driven back and did not recover that ground again till the Confederates surrendered. I had the account of his experience from him while he lay in the hospital in Mound City several days later. Pneumonia developed a short time after I left him and he lived but a short time. His grave is one of the many thousands marked "Unknown" in the National cemetery there. He was a strong, brave, manly young man, and he was mourned by all who knew him. I dearly loved him and mourn for him to the present time. He was the baby boy of his parents, who many years ago descended the tomb in sorrow because of his tragic death. The physicians said his fatal sickness was contracted while he lay on the cold, bloody battle field so long and so chilled, though not frozen.

On Friday, after the mighty struggle at Fort Donelson on the fifteenth and sixteenth of February, the rumor of a battle became news. Those of our neighbors who had been killed or wounded in the battle were numerous but their friends had not been able to learn all of them. That was the first fight near us where very many casualties had occurred, and all was commotion among us.

I received a letter from my brother that he had arrived at Paducah and that he wanted me to come to him. I dismissed my school that very evening and started to Golconda the next morning. I was teaching in the Cain district then, on account of the largeness of the school. From Golconda I went by boat to Paducah. Many of our citizens hurried to their wounded or sick or to bring their dead home for burial. They all went by way of Carbondale and Cairo, then took a boat for the city where their friends were in hospitals; or to the battle ground for the bodies of their dead. The eighteenth, the twenty-ninth and the thirty-first regiments were all hotly engaged in the battle and our neighbors were in those three regiments.

Anxiety to go to the aid of those in need was so great that the train could scarcely be waited for. John Berry, of the eighteenth, was wounded, and, the news having reached his father, John Berry, senior, he hastened to Carbondale to take the train to reach his son. The train not coming immediately, the old man, in his excitement, started on foot as fast as he could walk, declaring that he could not wait for a tardy train. He reached the next station, by a very close race, in time to get on the train with his neighbors bound to the same destination. He had gained no time, but he had the consciousness of knowing that he had done his best. His son lived to fight again and again and to see many years of peace after the war was over.

The eighteenth Illinois regiment in that battle reported sixty killed and died of wounds in a few days afterwards and 140 others wounded. The twenty-ninth regiment reported thirty killed and seventy wounded, some of whom died of their wounds later on. The thirty-first regiment reported twenty-six killed or wounded. Among those who were killed or died of their wounds were G. W. Cain, Harmon Abney, Samuel Willis, Edward Barnett, Dick Thompson, David Tyler, Robert Fagg, James S. Roberts, Lieut. Geo. W. Youngblood, James H. Dunn, Alfred Reed, Eli Willis, Joshua Medlin, James W. Allen, F. M. Allen, James H. Estes, John W. Ferguson, James E. Kieth, James McIlrath, Edward Odum, Thomas F. Owens, William F. Keaster, and a few others whom we knew.

When I arrived at Paducah I found the city in a bustle with strangers from the different states searching for sick or missing soldiers. I saw bodies of tall men placed in coffins a foot too short for them for transportation and boats so full of the sick and wounded that it was impossible to give half attention to the suffering ones, and I saw bereaved ones of both sexes unspeakably disconsolate because they could not hear of their own or could not recover their bodies.

I searched the thirteen hospitals over twice. But not one word of information of my brother could I get. I was cursed and bemeaned and ordered off, time and again. I tried to be as winsome as a man could be, but the scoundrels cared nothing for that. I was a little, weak man, but if I had had a dog's chance the big head of a few of them would have been punctured with a brickbat. In all my life I have not seen so mean a set of men as I found there.

I went to all the cemeteries but I could not find his grave.

I then found where Captain Cain, his commander, was, and called on him, at the officers' hospital. He had been shot through the body from the front, through the hip, but was improving. He knew nothing at all of my brother. I, failing to learn anything of him, turned toward home with no comfort for my mother or for myself.

The boat started up the river near the noon hour, with many sick soldiers, besides wounded ones also; and, to my very great dismay, it did not nor would not stop at Golconda, where my step-father had waited for me with the horses to take me home. The officers of the boat gave me to understand that their business lay to the north; that I must look out for myself. As we passed we could see the people looking and wishing for us to stop and my step-father said afterward that he was satisfied that I was on that boat and only waited till the next morning for me and then started for home.

I did not know whether the boat would stop before it reached the headwaters of the Allegheny or the Monongahela rivers. So I purchased a gray blanket from one soldier and a red blanket from another, both of whom were discharged and did not want to see them any more and asked ninety-five cents and one dollar for them, respectively. I thought I might be in hard luck when night overtook me without bed or blankets. I had not finished the purchase very long before we were in sight of Elizabethtown. To my joyful surprise the boat began to turn in. I gathered my two blankets and made ready to get out some way. The river was pretty full but I knew I would go no higher up even if I went down in trying to get out. I had the good fortune to get off easily, though I had on pants of exactly the same pale blue of the soldiers pants, but of much finer texture—made and worn before the war began; and carrying two blankets, I did not know but I would be arrested as a deserter. I did not stop one minute. I had never been in that place before; neither have I ever been in it since. Yet I lit out as fast as my legs could carry me.

I could make little headway, however, as every one I met wanted to know all about the battle, thinking, of course, as I wore blue pants and carried two soldier blankets, that I had been in the battle and could tell them all about it. I told each one that I was not a soldier and that I had bought the fine blue cloth in Marion in the summer of 1860 and had it made and wore it long ago and had bought the two blankets from two discharged soldiers who were needing a little money and did not need the blankets any more and that I had thought I might not be landed under 1,000 miles and might need them.

My story was so unreasonable, though true, that I did not believe one of my listeners believed me and if I could know that my brother was alive and could come round all right I would be glad I had belonged to the most distant regiment in the United States army, where I would meet no one of those Hardin county folks till the war was over.

At last I walked about a mile without meeting anyone. The sun had set. I decided to change my story. I met another man. He plied me with the same questions and I told him about the great battle as briefly as I could and got off pretty well.

A few more repetitions of the lie to a few more honest inquirers brought me to a Mr. Gazad's residence, where I was compelled to seek lodging as it was dark. I soon, at his request, repeated my lie and received his sympathy and kind treatment. But he came near stalling me when

he asked me which side of the river the town and battle was on. That, I had not once thought about. I told him, however, that we moved so many ways that I could not certainly decide but that I thought it was on the north side. Next morning I tried to pay him, but he said we soldiers had hard enough time without paying our way when out. I felt so hateful that I did not know what to do. I begged him to receive pay; when I saw that he would not I tried to give a child a gold dollar that I had, but he watched me and would not let anyone have anything. I felt worse than if I had stolen from him; yet I could not afford to undertake to correct my story there and then.

I started as quickly as I could and traveled as fast as I could. I met a man every little distance and repeated my lie till I thought Mr. Gazad would not find me out. Half way to Mitchellville I traveled two or three miles without having to repeat my story. Then I began to tell the truth again.

Traveling as fast as I could I came to my uncle, D. J. Blackman's home. After dinner he took me to my mother's home. My step-father arrived at dusk from Golconda, where he had waited for my return from Saturday evening to Wednesday morning. I arrived one hour ahead of him.

We were all despondent over our failure. John Owens of Harrisburg had seen my brother in Paducah after he came there, as we heard. The next morning I went to see him and learned that it was true. He told me the hospital he was in then, but he had no idea that he was yet living, as he was a very sick man then. I hurried home, and together with George W. Russel, started in search of him again. The next day we arrived at Golconda and put our horses away for time indefinite, and made ready to take a boat for Paducah. After waiting till evening we took our horses out and started through to Brooklyn.

We lodged with an Irish family and there learned that some people wear wooden shoes. We heard from our host that they were much the better kind of foot garments. In the forty-three years past I have not tried them nor seen another pair.

Before noon the next day (Saturday) we were on the ferry boat trying to go over to the city. It was a dangerous journey, as the wind was blowing a gale from the south. After taking our dinner, we easily found the place where my brother had been, but he had not been there for several days. The only word we could get was from a negro servant there. He said that he knew he had been taken to the river with a lot of other sick men and put on a boat, but could not tell where they were sent. He said he was not mistaken, for he so much resembled myself. That word we believed and took courage.

The packet came before noon Sunday and we went on it to Mound City on our way to St. Louis. But to our surprise, the Mound City hospital people constrained us to stay with our friends who were there sick or wounded, and had us to eat there. They said it was worth much to the boys whom we knew.

There we found Medlin, of whom I have previously spoken, with three bullet holes through his limbs, but he was cheerful and full of hope, not suspecting that an early death awaited him. Hez. Morgan was there with his arm amputated to the shoulder joint. I saw the physician dress it. That was my first acquaintance with surgery. I do not remember all we saw there as my mind was on my absent brother. However, I remember to have seen a man die there by the name of Dunn, who belonged to the twenty-fifth Indiana regiment.

The next day while waiting for a boat to carry us to St. Louis, I read from a list of soldiers who had arrived at Cincinnati on a certain boat at a certain time, the name of my brother with his company and regiment. Some thoughtful person had seen it and cut it out of a newspaper and pasted it on the door facing. The boat coming toward home was about to start, and we did not have time to go back and tell the good news to those who knew him. They knew that I was so interested in him that I could not be the lively company for them that I would otherwise have been.

We boarded the transport Tycoon, which was loaded to the guards with pig-iron, the first I had ever seen, which was in long rows all around. The old craft traveled so slowly that it was near midnight when we landed below Brooklyn. Our tickets called for Paducah, but I gave the captain five dollars in gold to put us off on the north side. They threw out a gang plank under a blackjack bush, and I ran out all right, but as George plunged into the brush from the stage it fell into the river. If we had fallen into the river I do not believe they would have reported a mishap, much less would they have tried to save us. We believed that we were very fortunate in getting away from the rascals alive.

We went to the house of the kind man who had kept our horses and slept sweetly and ate the best meal next morning I had ever eaten away from home. I remember that the host would charge us only one-dollar each for lodging and breakfast and keeping our horses from Saturday morning till Tuesday morning.

We traveled hard, and, as the sloughs were level with water we plunged in often enough to keep us wet all day.

Wednesday at 10 o'clock a. m. we were

at home telling mother the good news of our discovery. She had still later news, however. Two letters had been received from a Mr. Medock, formerly a partner of my uncle, Bennet Blackman, in a large lumber mill in old Barnham, four years previous. He, seeing the name in a newspaper, thought it was my uncle and hastened to aid him in any way he could. Finding his mistake he wrote to us and declared that every want of brother should be supplied. The last letter stated that he was mending.

In a few days my brother wrote, in answer to our request for instructions sent to him before I arrived home, for me not to come till he had improved sufficiently to come home with me. I began my school on Monday after a vacation of two weeks, and taught two weeks and dismissed.

On Sunday morning, March 23, I started to Cincinnati by way of Shawneetown. At eight o'clock, p. m. I went aboard the John H. Doane, a very slow moving craft and a very antiquated one. Forty-eight hours later we arrived at Louisville, her destination, 265 miles distant.

At one o'clock Wednesday, I started on the boat "Superior" for Cincinnati, 150 miles, where we landed at sunrise the next morning. I soon found my much-hunted brother.

It was interesting to see the other boys' enjoyment at our meeting. Each one was glad to know of good received by the other.

I was surprised to learn that Mr. Meddock had never returned after writing the second letter for my brother. Some accident befell him, perhaps. Our old school teacher, Mr. Vernon, had called to see him once. Rules of the hospital authorities may have been issued preventing their coming again.

I visited other hospitals to find other acquaintances, and during the day found John and James Simonds, who were suffering of wounds, and others of our neighbors. I managed to procure a furlough for my brother, and we took passage on tne boat Sultana, for Shawneetown as the sun was setting.

I can truly say that I was in the city from sunrise to sunset, March 27, 1862. It was a beautiful bright Thursday. On Saturday a man came aboard and poured out on a table piles of gold and silver. Men began to bet with him. Some won all the time and others lost. Finally an old brown jeans-clad gentleman from Kentucky, who seemed in a fair way to lose all he had, asked me to throw once for him. I did so, and, without any art or science, won him two dollars and fifty cents. I do not remember why I did not continue to work for the old man, unless I ran off from fright. I had not brought much money with me and we feared we might not have quite enough to pay all our bills home.

We consulted the propriety of trying the gambler once. As I had been lucky in throwing for the old man, it was agreed that I should do the throwing for ourselves. So we walked out from our berths and I put my one dollar down and threw whatever it was, expecting to win about $5.00. But I lost it as easily as I had won for the old man. Not quite willing to give up the game, after several hours consultation we decided that my brother should try his luck, and he did with precisely the same results as myself. We had less than one dollar left, and it began to dawn upon us that the old brown-clothed Kentucky corn-cracker might be a goat in sheep's clothing. I then wished I had not bought fine boots and other goods on my way up.

We left the boat at Shawneetown in time to lodge at Equality Saturday night. I had paid up all bills so far. My motto for fifty years has been, "Where there's a will there's a way." Harvey McCaleb, the hotel and liveryman, credited us, and we were at home Sunday noon, March 30.

That was another bright warm day, and our neighbors came as the news spread that "The dead's alive and the lost is found." When the thirty days furlough expired brother could not return, but before the next one was out he would go back to his regiment at Shiloh, where the great battle had been lately fought.

We feared that we would never see him again alive, as he was so feeble. But he would not be restrained from returning at once to his command. His regiment was at Shiloh and he arrived only a few days after the great battle there. My mother was mostly troubled about his future state. She said there was no chance for heaven if one died without repentance toward God and faith in the Savior of sinners. Like my mother, I wanted him to live the life that now is, and, as well as I knew how, I wanted him to have the life that Christians claimed.

Our step-father, being a member of the court, was away from home, and to keep mother company I remained with her some of the time. About the tenth of June, after talking till late at night, we were only commencing to sleep when we both heard a footfall on the porch. Jumping out of bed, I cried out, "It is Ben." Sure enough, it was he. We had not heard from him since he left home. But I seemed to know who it was at the first sound that greeted my ears from his first step, though I had not thought of his coming. I do not understand how I knew the step was that of my brother, yet I was as certain of it as I was after he came into the house. There was great joy there that night. We had another supper and talked and rejoiced till wearied out, and slept the last part of the night. His discharge was dated May 30, 1862.

I then declared again that I was the one

who should have gone at the first and, that I should enlist before the year should close.

I attended Mrs. Chase's school in Harrisburg seventeen days then, and that was my last attendance at school. She was the best teacher I ever had. She corrected my faulty grammar, to my shame, but to my very great benefit. I'll continue to remember the debt of gratitude I owe her for her interest in me. She said that I was a great student. Seven young ladies attended the school, but I was the only young man in attendance. Their names were Ann Warfield, (now Mrs. Ann Baker), Miss Kate Glass, Miss Sarah Roak, (now Mrs. Sarah Bellah), Miss Jennie Wilson, (now Mrs. Dr. Rodgers), Miss Helen Davis, Miss Kate Bruce and Miss Eliza Bruce. The last three went away before the war closed and I have known nothing of them since. But the others are still living.

Mrs. Chase taught the round-note system in music. That seemed philosophical to me and I determined to study it some time, but could not spare the time then.

The girls were hard up for gentleman company and could only accept such as were at hand, or have none at all. The number of young men was soon reduced to less than half a dozen, as the Riley boys, Joe Wear and myself went that August, and left only Joe Towle, who was too lame; and Mose Stiff, who was too fat; Robert Ware, who was too consumptive; Jim Willeford, who had epilepsy, and Tom Jones, who was too lean, for army service.

Courting was the rage then. One thing I have not forgotten, however; the town girls knew how to make a short walk seem long by taking short steps. I had been used to walking, as my life depended on making good time, but they lengthened our period of conversation by shortening our steps.

At the close of Mrs. Chase's school, I re-

reived a second-grade certificate, and began a three month's school two miles northwest of the town. I boarded in the town to avoid the loneliness I felt and for the exercise of walking. I grew more lonely and sicker, till a weeks vacation was indispensible before I could teach the last week of the term. During that vacation week I was sworn in as a soldier and then finished the school.

That was almost the gloomiest period of the war. Many hundreds of thousands of Union men had all ready gone into the army. Many bloody battles had been fought; many prisoners had been captured by both armies, and many thousands had been killed in both armies, and money to bear the expenses of the war was only greenback, which was opposed by a great part of the people. Beside all those things there were great reasons to fear that some of the European nations would recognize the independence of the Southern Confederacy and thus encourage that section and prolong the war.

The young men of the country were nearly all gone and I was so dissatisfied that it seemed I could not bear the loneliness any more. On Saturday I drove a yoke of oxen to a wagon to Crab Orchard and back for our family, that a good supply of breadstuff might be left on hand. The youngest boy went along also. As I passed each point of interest I remembered that I might never return that way again.

Resting with mother and the rest of the family and the neighbors who came to be with us all day Sunday, not withstanding the dangerous venture before me, I was glad when morning came, that I might get away from the unpleasant solitude I had borne for several months. I had no knowledge of experimental religion, I had no doubt of the honesty of many Christians that I knew, but I could not see into their joy or hope. I could only trust to my good

luck as to all future good,—blind and dangerous as that was. But I never was sorry I took the venture, even in the darkest day of my experience.

CHAPTER VII.

ON the Monday following, Captain Roark's company and Captain Horning's company encamped at Shawneetown, on the Ohio river. I was the orderly sergeant of the latter company. If muster-in-day had come soon I was likely to be rejected, as I had not yet recovered from yellow jaundice, which had necessitated my vacation week. But I intended to go anyway, in some arm of the service.

I supposed my age and experience were guarantees against weakness as that brings most persons to tears at solemn separations. I embraced my four little sisters and kissed them good-bye. Then I intended to merely bid mother good-by and to move lightly on. But when I read the inexpressible anguish depicted in her countenance at seeing her sick and weakly son start on so long and so dangerous a mission, my heart felt more like bursting than it had ever done before. I had to hurry away and try to forget the burden she felt for my sake. Nearly forty-four years have flown away since that parting, and mother went to glory and to God more than five years ago; but that silent but tender parting and the solicitude I knew she had for my welfare, both temporal and eternal, is as vivid in my heart now as it was then.

Joe, a step-brother, went with me. He was nearly five years younger than I. Though he, like the other younger boys, was a kind of burden on my hands; he was a brainy fellow and made very good company.

We had quarters in O'Pool's great packing house, one mile north of the town and on the bank of the Ohio river. While there, the officers went back home some of the time, and I acted in several capacities beside to draw and issue rations to the men. The variety of business and the outdoor life from the first day were conducive to my health.

The Peoples of Ridgeway company tried very hard to hire me to engage with them in business, as I was slim material to become a soldier, and they regarded me as a promising future business man. That opportunity would have been eagerly accepted some years earlier, but no reasonable salary multiplied many times could buy me off then. I craved to go to the defense of the Union, not because I loved it better than other men, but I was ashamed to know that men left wives and children at home who needed them and I was in much better condition to go than they. I hated for another to bear my share of duties and responsibilities. It is the same way yet. I abhor the lazy or the stingy or the selfish thing in human shape that is willing to leave another to bear his burden. Such excuses have ever been stenches in my nostrils even in my most wicked days. During the few days that we remained there, I had a dangerous experience in saving a man from drowning. One afternoon about twenty men went down to the water's edge, intending to go in to swim. But when they found that it was a long way to deep water, only four would go out to it. Steve Brothers, Jim Nolen, Joe Harris and myself were the four. I think we went one-third the distance across before we found deep water. I had gone ahead and had floated thirty feet down stream when I heard the cry of Nolen, saying the others were drowning. I looked upstream and beheld Harris, under to his chin, holding to Brothers, who was under to the tops of his ears. I urged Harris to hold on till I arrived. With all my might I went upstream. I felt that if one drowned the other would drown also.

When I reached them I took hold of the hair on the top of Brothers' head and bade Harris to get out himself. He was nearly colorless and almost under by the time I reached him. But he managed to raise himself and swim to shallow water. At no moment of my life had I been confronted with so momentous a task. Outside of superhuman help there was none to save Brothers from death but me, and in trying to save him I was most likely to lose my own life.

I remembered that a drowning person caught anything or any person regardless of consequences, and I looked for Brothers to catch me if he could. I told him I would take him out if he would not catch me, but that if he touched me I would let him drown. I was towing him landward all the time. But he was too deep in the water to breathe, or, perhaps, to even hear me. I saw that he might still grab me, for his hands remained, as at first, about six inches apart and the same distance in front of his neck. It had been some minutes since he had drawn breath at all. I determined to change tactics. I whirled him around and put each of my hands under one of his shoulders. I then raised his head and neck clear out of the water and kept them so. Every time I kicked I carried my burden landward and then went under, head and ears. But I saw that I was going to save Brothers, as I breathed while above the water. And I had found that Harris had succeeded in getting to shallow water. So I was already happy.

Harris says that if he had ever let his feet get under him another time he could not have raised them again. I continued to move on till I reached for the bottom and my great toe touched it. I was so tired that I welcomed the presence of the rocks so near me. In due time I came to shallow water and delivered my precious charge to Harris and Nolen, who had waded down stream in the water three feet, while we floated with the current in the deep. I was so tired and weak that I did not go out till they had rolled him and taken him to camp. He was never well afterwards and died in the following February, four months later. The men on the bank heard Nolen's frantic cries, but thought he was at his usual antics. He was known as a very untrustworthy, hateful boy, and the men paid no attention to him.

If Harris and Brothers had been drowning I could have saved both of them, if I could have known they would not touch me, more easily than I saved one, as it was. No one, save my own self, knows how glad I have always been that I did not let Brothers go, when it seemed I could not afford to hold him when I knew he was drowning, and thought he certainly would try to catch hold of me. I now believe he was unconscious all the time I had hold of him; hence his inaction. I went without seeing after I whirled him, for I had no spare hand to wipe the water out of my eyes. When he saw that he was sinking, he said, "Joe, I am drowning," and Joe, being close to him, caught him and held him till I relieved him and sent him out. Brothers might have become insensible at the moment of his calling for help. It was my inexpressible love of life and my extreme hatred of death that caused me to save the man at my own peril.

If persons would retain presence of mind in emergencies, much benefit would be derived therefrom. It is a pity for one to drown while it is easier to swim than to sink. However, knowledge is a requisite as ability to accomplish difficulties. The one danger to be dreaded by swimmers is the cramps. They undo the best of swimmers, in spite of all his arts.

I did not appreciate the danger I underwent, and the greatness of the accomplishment of my successful feat in any fair measure, for nearly forty years afterward. I do not know that the family ever did appreciate my efforts as none of them ever did ask me any of the particulars that I can recollect.

Two other of the boys were killed by horses, and the good old man and woman went to their long home many years ago. Two others have died, and but a remnant is left to remember the accident.

About the middle of October, 1862, the six companies belonging to the 132d regiment, as ours was to be known, were shipped to Cairo on barges towed by a small steamer. That was a new experience for us, but not a bad one. But at Cairo we were loaded on to boxcars, with temporary rough seats wide enough apart for two men to lie between, if they lay on their sides and spoon fashion. I had a full grown man for a partner and we filled our space so full that we had to rise before either could turn over. The train traveled very slowly and we were glad to get off.

We had been at Camp Butler only four days when a swindler came along with a deck of cards, wanting to bet that he could turn up the ace from the top, but permitting some of the men see the ace on the bottom. I did not know one card from another, so I had no inclination to bet, even if I had wanted the man's money. He continued to banter till Matt Horn, an honest farmer, became wearied at the man's boasting; and, having seen that the ace was on the bottom, bet the man ten dollars that when he turned up the top card it would not be the ace. Now, Matt thought the man did not know that the ace was on the bottom; and as there is but one card of a kind in a pack, the man would lose his ten dollars. The money was staked, and the man holding the twenty dollars was made to understand that if the top card was the ace the strange man was to have the money; but if it was not the ace, Matt was to have the money.

Much interest was aroused at the issue. Those who had seen the ace at the bottom of the pack thought the man had forgotten that he put it there, and that Matt was sure to win. But others who had seen it there, thought the man too smart to bet against his own trick, and felt sure Matt would lose his money.

When everything was ready the card was turned up, and it was an ace. Without any ceremony the man took the money and walked off. The humbug was understood when it was seen that the man had used two aces. Matt had been initiated, and the rest of us had received a much-needed lesson. To avoid the danger of punishment, the man returned half the money.

Hardy's regiment, from Vienna, was at Camp Butler, where we went. It had only seven companies. A union of the two pieces of regiments was formed.

Pemberton's company left ours and went to the 128th, Waters' company left ours and went to the 118th, and Horning's company, of which I was orderly sergeant, disbanded. Neighbors and some of my late pupils and relatives had enlisted with me and depended on me to decide what we would do.

Waters' company, which had gone to Col. Fonda's regiment, wanted me to take my boys into their company and keep my office, as they had no fit man for the place. I studied over the matter for a few days and refused to accept the flattering offer. The man whom they did secure in the place I was offered, was mustered captain, as all those elected were absent, being sick at the time of muster.

I should have certainly have been mustered captain if I had accepted the place. The reason I refused was that the regiment was strange to my men. The company Roark was captain of was from our place,

and I placed most of my boys in that company and the others in four different companies of our regiment. I was given the office of corporal. I never had a chance again to receive promotion, except to a sergeant's place. As I could look the mothers in the face after I served my time out and returned, and say I had sacrificed my own chances to care for their boys, I am satisfied with my choice.

After drilling and marching from place to place without any apparent purpose for several days, and sleeping on naked-floored bunks when it was too cold to snow, till we were all sick with colds, we were mustered into the service on the 29th of October. The officer merely passed by us as we stood in a row, and the evening was dark and the hour late. That is the way I was received into the service.

The three companies of the regiment from Shawneetown were "C," "F," and "H." Geo. W. McKeaig was mustered colonel, and Bluford Wilson of the same place, adjutant. Hardy was mustered lieutenant colonel, and S. B. Floyd, major.

The regiment was numbered the 120th Illinois Infantry. We did service at different places, especially guarding the railroad at Jimtown, not far away. It was wicked to have us sleep on the green oak plank in very cold weather, when straw could have been had easily. But when men are sworn to obey their superior officers there is no way to do but to obey or desert. When the commanding officer is a MAN, all is well; but if he is a dog, all things are wrong.

On the ninth of November we went by the railroad train to Alton, and thence by the steamboat "Decatur" to St. Louis. After waiting part of a day we were sent on down the river to Memphis, Tennessee. It rained and snowed and the wind blew. Part of us were on the top of the boat, part around the middle deck and part were on the lower deck. We were taking our primary lessons.

We drew little tents after we arrived there, each man receiving a piece large enough to cover an old-fashioned oblong square table. Four of them when buttoned together made an enclosure. The rain came down on us till we were glad to be out on picket duty, where we could stand in the rain with our oil-cloth over us; for it was better than to have to stay in the mud in the camp.

On November 26, we were detailed to relieve the thirteenth regulars in Fort Pickering. While doing duty in the fort, smallpox, measles and pneumonia smote the men, and there were more than one hundred deaths before we went down the river the May following.

While at Memphis many expeditions were made into the surrounding country and into Arkansas to break up camps of the enemy or to head off their intended raids. On one of these Arkansas trips the boys captured two pet bears, together with quite a number of prisoners.

During the long and sickly winter our company lost ten by death and twelve discharged. Yet numerous incidents occurred to break the monotony of the doleful surroundings. Card-playing was the general exercise. Come sang old sacred hymns to pass away the time, and some of the men would try fist and skull fighting.

Enoch Gaither and Bill Robinson, of our company, and neighbors at home, had a fight. They were strong men.

Every man, however, who was not sick, or on duty was getting acquainted with as much of the city as he could. I was studying both my grammar and the army tactics, some of the time. I expected to get through the war and see home if I could, and determined to do my duty in every way I could. I kept myself as clean as I could, and cheered our men as well as I could. Sam Dallas was our company wag, and did a great deal of good by his funny expressions as long as he lived.

I concluded it would not be very degrading to play cards for fun, and finally undertook to learn the game. I was an apt scholar. Nearly every one of the men played with a zest long before our regiment was sent down the river to Vicksburg, Miss. I soon became a great lover of the pastime and an expert at playing. If we played for fun, I usually won with my partner. But if we played for a stake of any kind, we lost every time. It was never otherwise even once. My experience taught me not to risk much at a time, and that amount but once or twice. It was the same if I threw dice or shot at a target. I am now glad it was so. For success only led men on to ruin.

I had two comrades named Bill Washam and Jo Murphy, each of whom had a streak of luck and won from fifty to seventy dollars each at throwing dice. I begged each of them to stop and send the money home to their families. Other comrades also tried to persuade them to do so, but they said if they could win that much they could win more. Each went on till he lost every cent he had and came to me for money to start again. I loaned each two dollars and informed him I would loan him no more, as it would do no good and only enable him to lose his next payment. Each lost his two dollars and had to quit.

No gambler will set up in business unless he has largely the advantage. Gambling has a fascination for men which continual losing only will squelch. But in my case it was somewhat different; and I did not care for the amount I lost. I deemed it so low a habit in one to want to get something for nothing that I thought no man ought to degrade himself to do so. That principle in me, braced by my inability to win at all, and my natural repugnance to the taste of intoxicants of every kind, mightily assisted me against degradation and profligacy. I deserve no praise for the possession of those traits of character, for they were and are natural to me.

President Lincoln issued his Proclamation of Emancipation on New Year, 1863, as he had promised if the rebels did not lay their arms down and take their places in the Union again. A great many soldiers deserted on account of misunderstanding the true intent of the president.

One of our company had already deserted from general meanness and did not return. Four more went off soon after the proclamation but they were all brought back and three of them made splendid soldiers. Three others came to me one day and told me they had decided to leave that night if I would go with them, as they were not willing to fight to free the slaves. I told them that our great men were doing all they could to save the Union and that the proclamation was a necessary war measure only. That the South had been given four months to accept the terms, and had not only refused but had declared nothing would bring peace but their success. I reminded my comrades that the Confederates had much the start and the North would not believe they meant to go to war. But they had continued to brag that one of the Southern soldiers could defeat four Union soldiers. I told them that I saw no way for the President to do but what he had done. I stated my friendship for them, and told them that the war could not last always, and, if one deserted, he would at best be disgraced by the act as long as he lived. They agreed that I was correct in my reasoning, and abandoned the idea. They are all dead now, but I would not tell their names, as they were good soldiers. Two of them died in the service and the third died more than thirty years ago.

The destruction of property, the waste of wealth and the loss of life I saw, or was informed of, during our stay in Memphis and vicinity, lead me to question the origin and the control of all things. I really thought if the author of all things was ever needed anywhere, he was needed there and then. I was astonished that an enlightened nation should be left to destroy itself so.

I learned my being a soldier was not enlightening me as a Christian. I improved in health all the time, was industrious and happy in a way, and did my comrades all the good I knew how by teaching them to write and helping them when sick and in many other ways.

CHAPTER VIII.

WE started to Vicksburg on the ninth of May on some boat, and landed near that place on the thirteenth of same month. The enemy, knowing where the boat would come close to the bank of the river on either side of it, ambushed us several times, but succeeded in killing only one man and wounding several others. Those intending to fire on us would hide behind trees and logs near the river where we had to pass, and at the right time fire on us without danger to themselves. One time they were not cautious enough and lost ten of their men from our return fire. A gunboat reported the fact afterwards.

Our first service down the river was to carry verbal messages from the mortars, three miles above the city, which fired once every 15 minutes from a point just opposite the city, informing the cannoneers of the damage of each respective bomb. The men stood several hundred feet apart and called out the effect of the shot to the one next westward till the news reached the gunners on the mortar boat. By the information thus received, they regulated their aim and the length of the fuse.

During the darkness of the night it was a rare but solemn sight to look at the burning fuse in the shell as it sailed from the big gun which had set it on fire to the city over which or in which it was expected to explode, scattering destruction and death to all things in its reach.

The main streets from the city to the river were dug through a steep bank and the people dug large excavations in the earth from the sides of the streets. Those sheltering there were thought to be safe from the shells. I think the shots were estimated at a cost of twenty-five dollars each. They often burst over the city, and at first looked like a hornet's nest as large as a half bushel, rapidly increasing to the size of a small house, then vanishing from sight. I often figured out the distance from me to the boat, and from the boat to the place of the exploded bomb, and from me to the same place, for I had eyes in my head, and a watch to measure the time with, and ears to decide the distances from the reports.

Our line of communication lay through a swamp of densest underbrush. Every bush that I remember was an elbow. If a horse, or a cow, or a person could traverse it, I do not know how. There seemed to be one or two feet of water covering it.

There seemed to be more toadfrogs and turtles in the water than could be listened to. Beside the ordinary and extraordinary kinds, there were some that barked like dogs. Ten thousand croakers of many different kinds at once throughout the dark night made a poor lad think of his quiet home far away. Our walk was on a levee, through the thicket. We were glad to get away from the sickly, noisy place.

On Sunday morning, the seventh day of June, our regiment was hurried onto a boat and carried fifteen miles up the river

to save a little detachment of soldiers there from extermination or capture by General Price's army. When the boat reached Miliken's Bend its stem ran into the bank, and the men poured off it and up the embankment to find that a gunboat had appeared in the nick of time to save the day for our forces and that Price had left the place without taking his dead or wounded. The weeds were high in the intervening field from the river to the woods—two miles away, perhaps—and, as we had no cavalry, we had no way of knowing how far the enemy had gone.

We hurried off the boat and up the bank unceremoniously, not knowing what a minute might be worth to the little band there. Fifty yards above the landing place we came to the scene of the battle. A negro was standing in the attitude of a guard. The dead were still untouched on the east, north and west of him. One wounded lieutenant colonel of a Texas regiment was east of him, with a shot or a bayonet hole through the thigh. The soldier repeated his story as we passed him over and over again.

The levee was located forty yards west of the river. One hundred feet west of the levee grew a splendid hedge, and between these ran the public highway. Some of the fighting was done through the hedge, as most of the rebel dead were lying there. But some had come through an opening in the hedge and over the levee; and several of the enemy's dead were found there. The negro said that as the enemy came at him he drove his bayonet through him, and, before he had time to dispose of that one, another came at him and he stuck his bayonet through him also; and he immediately threw them both over his shoulder behind him and pointed to the colonel as proof of the statement. We supposed the other man had risen and crawled or walked away, else he died, as only one wounded man was there. I suppose, in his excitement, the man thought he had done as he said he had, but we had our doubts.

As we did not know how soon Price's army would return, we hastily made breastworks out of cotton bales, two feet high inclosing an acre of land. It was extremely hot and there was no shade in the fort; yet we did not dare to go out to a shade even for one minute.

We next began to bury the dead soldiers inside of the little fort, and finished the work by nightfall. We did not observe the regulations in their burial, as we could not do so.

Learning nothing of Price through the night, we went out and gathered the dead bodies of the Confederates and buried them as decently as we could by noon Monday.

I am satisfied that among them were twin brothers, lying behind the hedge dead together, as much alike as two men could possibly be. Another one had deerskin pants on. Before I noticed what was going on, one of the men had cut a strip two inches wide from the front of the pants, and I protested against their further mutilation; and all agreed that I was right.

The view of those decaying bodies brought from my lips the open declaration that I believed the resurrection of the dead to be an impossibility. Doubting that doctrine of the Scriptures all else to me stood on the same basis.

We bore the steady beating of the rays of the shining sun all that day waiting for Price to attack us. On Tuesday before the noon hour, as we had nothing to indicate Price was near, we went out to an orchard two hundred yards away. While resting under the welcome shades I lay down to sleep. A negro roustabout had been out beyond the pickets and was riding in on a horse. Another negro, seeing the top of his head just above the tall weeds, took him to be the enemy's cavalry. He started to the fort crying at every breath, as loudly as he could, that Price was coming. As he passed by us he swept us like the wind. I did not take time to wake up, for I was at my gun in the stack ready to make for the fort by the time I was awake. I told Stricklin my bedfellow, who had been shot through the thigh and could only hobble along, that I would have to leave him, as I could do him no good there, but could help to save all if I reached the fort. Never did men run harder than we did and were ready to meet five times our number if they had come. Stricklin and other ailing ones had plenty of time to gain the fort. The enemy never did come. It was only a foolish negro's mistake.

Our next funny episode, that I remember, was in the rear of Vicksburg. We had been moving from one position to another almost every day for several days, and on that particular evening posted in an entirely strange place in the besieging line. An hour after dark, suddenly, perhaps fifty guns or more were fired, in quick succession, between us and the Confederate fort. Our captain soon had us in line and, commanded by a higher officer, we were creeping silently up the slant, cityward. I judged there was thick brush on both sides of the path, a short distance to an open field. We could not see anything in our front. However, we supposed we were not far from the enemy. In obedience to orders, we stretched ourselves on the ground, guns in hand, with our heads toward the enemy, to await results. There was a deep ditch in the rear that we had gone partially round.

Two of my company were known as profane men. John Farmer and Jo Morris were the men. They cursed from day to day without any respect to anyone or to themselves. We were so tired of their useless streams of oaths that we welcomed any circumstance that could abate the nuisance.

Well, John Farmer rose during the night and fell into the ditch headlong. The reader doubtless has heard of the irresistible force coming in contact with the immovable object. Well, there was a swearing man filled with rage and swear-words surging forth to his lips seeking freedom, in the presence of an alert foe, who must not hear him at the peril of all our lives. He grunted and moaned just above his breath and swelled and puffed till perhaps every man was awake, and most of us were happy at John's predicament. We were removed before daylight and only know that we were told that we occupied the place of a company captured at the firing early that night. Poor John enjoyed cursing as well as he did his tobacco, to the end of his army service. His grave is in Old-Gully cemetery, near Mitchellville.

On the thirtieth day of June our regiment was sent to Lake Providence, seventy-five miles up the river, to protect that place and the Union interests there, from Price and other commanders of the opposing army. That was four days previous to the surrender of Vicksburg and all thereto belonging, to General Grant and his army, including 25,000 prisoners.

By that time our men were beginning to get sick from long exposure in the hot sun and in the sickening swamps. In a few days nearly all were considered too sick for duty. But as we were threatened with an attack by Price's army, we were obliged to make another fort of cotton bales of the same height, but of less dimensions, than that we made at Miliken's Bend. The east side was protected by the river. As we had no artillery we valued our little fort very highly. If Price had attacked us the fight would have been on or across our camp ground, with each tent containing one or more sick man.

When the attack seemed inevitable our colonel resorted to strategy, which was successful. He stationed every man who was able to walk, out a short distance, in a row from twenty to thirty feet apart, and everything available resembling a flag was hoisted at intervals of two hundred yards apart to indicate that there were many of us and that we were hurting for a fight. The weeds were so high that the enemy could not count us.

My share in that fiasco was anything but pleasant. I was stationed at the extreme outer end of the line. We were to remain till all hope of fooling the enemy was lost, and to fire on them when they came, and to run only when we saw we could not drive them back. Now I knew I could run as hard as any other soldier in the whole army, but I was only a very slow runner. I preferred to fight rather than to have the enemy run after me and shoot at my back, or to be captured and have to go to prison. So I was glad when we saw that we had deceived them and they were moving away.

When they decided that we were many and saucy, they set the country on fire, destroying corn, cotton, and dwellings, driving off stock, and scaring the negroes into spasms as they left. Thousands of those poor creatures came in from the South, and we passed them on to their camps north of us.

Women came riding on both sides of antiquated animals, with small drayloads of the family belongings packed on, and then as many children, and sometimes sick persons, hung on as was possible; the woman talking to us, was amusing, if it had not been so pathetic. They thought if they could get under the care of Uncle Sam's troops they were safe. But we knew they might still be captured together with us.

A gunboat came to us about that time, and stayed close by until all signs of an attack had passed away. The next day those well enough were sent down the river to a beautiful home adorned with a mansion-like residence. I was the last one to go out from the boat. I met others coming to the boat, but I hoped to find a good book. As I was looking through the different rooms I found a box full of rags, or clothes, on fire. The only other person there was our hospital steward, whom I consulted as to our duty, and he consented to drag the box out of the house and we emptied its contents on the ground. By that time the boat bell was calling us in board.

I rushed riverward and passed two soldiers who were looking intently at the house, and heard one of them curse the mansion and declare it would burn very soon. I had a very different opinion, which proved to be the correct one. I always believed it foolish and mean to destroy property, when such destruction could not aid our cause. Afterwards I had information that lead me to think that house was in all probability the residence of the father-in-law of General U. S. Grant. It was to our great advantage that Price left that part of the country.

The men of our regiment died during the time we were at that place, at the rate of one each day. Thirty-one men died in thirty-one days. I was sick, but went all the time, because I was not as sick as most of the other men.

One evening when it was nearly dark, I went up to a darkey meeting, where a congregation of perhaps a thousand had gathered to worship God. I do not remember having been at one of their meetings before. Of course, their singing was very odd to me. It appeared that every songster consecrated himself, including his nerves, his blood, his voice, and his brain, together with all else that pertained to him from his thick skinned heel to the skin of his curly head, to the singing. Their earnestness was emphasized by the swaying of the body and the impromptu groan and the unceremonious ejaculation. That suited me pretty well. I can allow ignorance, but I always despise formalties or hypocrisy.

Then a man rose to preach who was more like a baboon than any other one I saw during the war. He had my sympathy and my attention as long as I could stand him. I could not find out what he was talking about. He hollowed, and screamed and jumped, and scolded, and I thought perhaps he was cursing some of the time. Before I had gone many yards away the listeners began to jump and shout, and I judged, from what I saw and heard, that at least seventy-five were shouting at one time. I went to camp and told Riley that I had been worsted pretty badly by my visit to the meeting. He reproved me for expecting anything of them. I had been pleased at their earnestness, but displeased at their shouting at such a tirade of nothingness. They could more reasonably have shouted at reading the Declaration of Independence or at the singing of America. It was a stunner to me. It has been said that where there is little known there is little required.

When we had been at the sickly place a few days, and the men were dying so fast, I became deeply solicitous about their future state. I suppose I commanded the squad of six men that fired the salute over the grave of every man who was buried there. It was a sad duty at best, and when repeated so often it became a very unwelcome one. As we were on the river, we had coffins for the dead. When the grave was ready the six pall-bearers bore the body to the grave and laid it down. Then I marched my six men by the foot of the coffin to the left side of the corpse as it lay face upward. I commanded the squad to "Halt, Left face! Reverse arms!". At the last command the men placed their guns on the toe of their shoes and their chins on the butt of their guns, and reverently remained in that bowed condition till the coffin was lowered into the grave. I then commanded as follows: "Attention! shoulder arms! Ready! Aim! Fire!" At the word "Aim" all would aim across the open grave, and at the word "Fire," all would shoot a blank cartridge exactly at once. That ceremony was repeated three times at each funeral. Then I would say: "Shoulder arms! Right face! Forward march!" At that command we marched away and left others to fill the grave of our comrade.

Bill Escue, a good-hearted but very vulgar-mouthed boy, was sick in his tent, and his sufferings aroused my sympathy for him more than for others less neglected. I nailed the staves of a wrecked barrel crosswise to two fence rails and put legs to the rails and put him on the improvised cot. He was glad to be raised out of the dirt but was too sick to talk except to ask for what he wanted. I soon saw that he would probably die, and went to Lewis Stricklin and asked him to do something for him if he could.

Lewis was a member of the Baptist church at home, and I had heard him pray in meetings and had seen him instruct inquirers often; hence I thought he might instruct our dying comrades. He said nothing could be done. I then told him that if I was a Christian, I could benefit our dying men. That if I had a Savior, I would know how to please him, and that I would have power with him. That if I had a God I knew I would use him every day. He appeared so confused and discouraged that I left him and went to the sick again. The next morning we removed him to the little hospital, where he occupied the cot made vacant by the death of another. He died in less than twenty-four hours.

James Banks, John Shrum and L. D. Riley were the others of our company lost by death during our month's stay there. D. L. Riley, an older brother of the one that died, lived to receive his discharge after the close of the war and to the present.

My astonishment at Stricklin's weakness and timidity led me to investigate religion anew for myself. I understood the 'Baptists, the Methodists, and Presbyterians to have the same kind of faith and to experience the same joyful sense of pardon, and I thought if any person or persons were in truth possessors of eternal life they were the fortunate ones. I went to a barrel which was nearly half full of Testaments, and, selecting one, I determined to fairly digest it. I believed if I could get at it right I could understand it as easily as anyone else. I had no confidence in the false religions of the heathens, the Mohammedans, the deluded Mormon, nor the priest-ridden Catholic (either Greek or Roman), nor an immersion in water for salvation, nor a salvation for all as taught by Universalists; I did not know that I had confidence in any at all.

I craved to find whether there was in reality, real salvation anywhere. I believed our dying men were being lost forever if the Christian faith was founded on truth. I believed that most worshipers were honest in their way, but I knew but few of them could be right. And if nearly all were surely wrong, then all might be wrong. The inestimable value I set on life in childhood held its place in my heart still. And as I knew death must soon be the portion of us all, I desired above everything else to know if the Christian religion was what it was claimed to be.

I began to read in Revelation, then in the Romans and Hebrews and the book of Jude and Peter. I quit before I read half the Testament. The reading was to me dry and unintelligible. I think I could understand what a strange language meant as well as I understood the letters of the apostles or the Revelations. I do not know why I did not begin at the Gospels. I suppose I did not think of it. I did not speak to anyone of my desire nor of my attempt to learn of the truth of the Scriptures. I had come to depend on no one, as I thought it a dangerous business to trust one's welfare in another's keeping.

I was very much depressed. I could see nothing in the future for me but eternal oblivion. I hated eternal nonentity with all my heart, and still searched for something better than that for my soul to delight itself in. I had no desire to sin against God nor man. I knew that sin degraded the sinner in the scale of being. That it had not paid in the long run, even once, in the ages of the world. I knew it was suicidal to anyone, too, but I had to do something and be something. I wanted to possess something that would last forever. The condition of our dying men was an awful case. If there was to be a resurrection or if there was not to be one —I was not willing to accept either way. I knew some people believed in Jesus and were happy in believing. But that I could not advance in the subject of Christianity while I had tried to do so with all my might, and having known so many persons who earnestly declared they had positive knowledge that God had pardoned their sins and that they had a principle of love in their hearts, and light and joy that the world could not give, could not be accounted for by me except on the theory that they were honestly deceived, as the devotees of other systems of worship were.

While much preferring that the Christian religion be as I knew the best people in the world accepted it as being, I could do nothing else than to look to other sources for food for my hungry mind to digest. I solemnly but sorrowfully laid the book away where I found it, saying, as I turned from it mentally or perhaps vocally: I'll never read you again. I don't believe there's anything in you. If there is, I can't find it. I know that if Christianity is true I'll go to hell. If others can endure that place I can do the same. If I can not, then annihilation awaits me. I know nothing further. I can do nothing else. So good by. I'll get whatever of pleasure that I can get out of the present life while I am alive, as the best and only thing left in my reach to do, and when death shall come I'll lie down as the beast of the field forever and forever. Wonderful, mysterious Testament, I bid you a final farewell.

I actually thought that I would never more read one page in the Bible nor think any more about the future, nor of the origin, control or destiny of things visible or invisible as I regarded such time and talent uselessly expended. If there was one thought passed through my mind during the ensuing ten months regarding the merits of the Bible, the Creator, or future existence, I do not remember it.

I had the same kind heart I had possessed since I could remember and enjoyed sacrificing my time and talents for the good of others. And in my expectation of enjoying the world in the future I intended not to do so at another's expense.

CHAPTER IX.

ON JULY 29 we left the sickly place and landed at evening at the water's edge in Memphis, Tennessee, August 1, 1863, and camped where we landed. The next day we were put off the cars in Corinth, Miss. I suppose we were the sickest and dirtiest regiment that ever came north to recuperate. Two regiments who had been doing provost and guard duty there, and had been kept well and clean, wondered at us as if we were of a different race of humanity. Many of our men were left at Memphis, as we passed through, sick and nearly all the rest of us were unable to clean our guns and equipments and our clothes; we were really fit subjects for the hospitals like those we left at Memphis as we came by.

Four more of the sick of my company alone soon died from their sickness contracted down the river. Their names were Elijah Keith, George W. Gully, Francis M. Bourland and John M. Ward.

The last was a young man of great promise. He and L. D. Riley, who died at Lake Providence, and myself were a kind of agreed trio, having many similar tastes and ambitions and education. But they were taken and I was left. In large letters I cut in a broad popular plank the name, the company and the regiment of Ward and placed it at the head of the grave. I did the same for the four who died at Lake Providence. The other three died at Memphis.

Our company had lost eighteen men in one year dead, and nearly that number discharged and deserted. I do not know how many the other nine companies had lost. I think it was a month or more before our regiment had sufficiently recovered to relieve the ones we met there to go with Sherman to Chattanooga and to the sea.

N. B. Forest was the terror of the country, including western Tennessee and northern Mississippi. I think it was near the middle of October that an effort was made to meet him toward the Yazoo river that kept our regiment out on foot some

weeks. But he and his men, being mounted, and we, being on foot, escaped, after wearing us out to cut him off. He was similar to the Dutchman's flee,—"when we put our finger on him he was not there."

We ran out of provisions on that trip; but a day or two previous, when our colonel saw the impending situation, one morning he lined us up and, in a good, loud voice, said, "Men, you must live on one-fourth rations and be economical with your coffee." The men thought it all right to live on one-fourth rations till we could do better.

But that new word was a poser for them. "Economical." Only a few of us had heard it previously. But it served a good purpose. I think it roused more fun than two jugs of whisky would have done if it had been taken by the men. They all soon learned that the colonel wanted them to be saving with their coffee.

When we were hastening back toward Germantown, if I do not forget the place, we halted for some purpose, and my captain, who was regarded as extremely strict on his men, asked me if I would catch him a chicken. I told him I would, as he was sick. I went out and in a few minutes brought him a hen nearly grown. Then I asked the privilege of catching one for myself. He could not quite deny me, though he knew there was no pressing necessity for me to do so, and if he had denied me I should not have thought hard, as he was living what he understood to be a right and honest life. I always respected an honest conscience, though it be an erroneous one.

When I returned to the yard it was fairly full of men and chickens running in all directions. The women were on the porch telling the chickens to run, and laughing at some of the men who had turned a stand of bees over and were

having an awful battle with the brave little
warriors. Those who were silly enough
to go for the honey caught the comb and all
that I stopped to notice ran away as hurriedly as they went in, but some of them
brought a pound or more of the honey with
them. I could not pay such a price for
the honey and left it for those who could
afford it. There was not an unkind word
uttered by the men nor the women that I
heard.

I soon hit a beautiful hen and was
reaching for her, when a man, crossing my
way three feet in front of me, lifted the
hen as he went by. If I had been three
feet ahead of the place where I was, one
or both of us, might have been crippled or
killed. I was glad he had the hen. The
next one I tackled was a small rooster of
the dominecker variety. He was very old,
according to the looks of his spurs, which
were long and frazzled. I struck him and
sent him under a large bunch of roses or
other kind of briars, and I lit on the briars
just over him. I suppose no one else
wanted him and I managed to take him
out and I slew him. That happened near
the noon hour, and, as we went forward
without anything to eat except what we
captured, there was no reason for stopping.

At one or two o'clock we met the com-
missary teams, within seven miles of some
railroad town, and camped and ate and
rested till morning. Bacon and coffee and
crackers were distributed to the men at
once, and they satisfied their hunger and
were all right.

However, those of us who had fresh
meat of any kind had work to do. I discovered a number of white bunches near
us, and, on inquiry, found that they were
the skins of geese. The wings were cut
off and the tail feathers removed and the
skin all removed in one piece. It rolled
itself up like a white snow ball.

Well, I could get no vessel to boil my
rooster in till dark, and I was of the
opinion that he was past the proper age to
fry. I boiled and parboiled that same
rooster till eleven o'clock. Judging him
to be ready for food, I went to sleep all
right. Sure enough, I had put the proper
amount of salt and other seasoning in
and boiled him in the proper number of
waters and had boiled him long enough.
I ate most of him myself, as the best
friends I had were supplied with goose;
and my fowl was of the small kind. I
have never tasted any flesh of the chicken
variety, since that one, as solid and tender
and good as that little old dominecker
rooster was.

I think it was on the last of November
that we came on the cars from Corinth to
Lagrange, Tennessee, to guard teams and
wagons back, in order that they be sent
east to General Sherman. We waited a
few days for them to come to us.

We had no place to stay except under a
large old shed, open on all sides, and it
was very cold for the time of year. The
worst part of it was that we were getting
nothing fit to eat. When the boys of my
regiment drew old ox tongues and quarters
of beeves lean and blue with poverty, or
age, they hung the stuff to the tallest tree
or telegraph wire they could find handy.
We were really needing rations badly several days, I think, before we received
them.

As I intended to live through the war,
if I could, I usually kept from forty dollars to fifty dollars sewed to the inside of
my underwear for hard times. But, as
we were to draw our pay in a few days,
and hard times were on us then, I opened
my safe-bank and let the boys have one
dollar each as far as it would go.

There was a restaurant 400 yards away
that gave a splendid breakfast for fifty
cents. Then one could make out the re-

mainder of the day. One morning the first men that went to the Arcada, the name of the restaurant before mentioned, after eating all they wanted and waiting a while for W. S. Butler, one of our company, came to me and reported that he was likely to kill himself by overeating. Butler was rather young, of pretty good mother's wit, tender-hearted, caring nothing for money, except to use, had been kicked round as an orphan, sometimes proceeded to act wrong as a mental satisfaction. I was not uneasy about the man, knowing him as I did. But I was at a loss to divine the mystery of his continued eating, for by the time I arrived he had been seemingly eating an hour.

One article of food that we were very glad to have for our breakfast was first-class biscuits, hot and soft from the oven. We were used to bad light bread.

I suppose the proprietor had been advised to counsel me about the man. As soon as I walked in, before I took my seat at the table, he came to me and asked me if I could get Butler away from the table. He said he did not care for what the man ate, but he did not want him to kill himself at his table. I told him that I would get him away at once. I walked to Butler, who motioned for me as I went. He handed me the dollar bill I had loaned him and bid me pay for his breakfast lest the man keep the whole dollar if he paid him. I agreed to do so, and Butler began to move out. He had prepared himself for the business intended by putting on plenty of underwear and fastening the lower end of his blouse close to his body. As the proprietor would turn his back, Butler would appropriate the biscuits in sight and stowed them away in his bosom.

At last the biscuits were supplanted with lightbread. Then Butler was ready to leave, but he feared to let the man get hold of the whole dollar. He waited for

me to come to help him out of his fix. The proprietor was so glad to get rid of what he thought was the biggest eater in the world that he did not look toward him as he left. Butler looked much like a large black bear as he waddled away with perhaps a peck of biscuits in his blouse, and doubtless they were as hot as he could bear them. He took them to the boys in camp and distributed them. After Butler left, the hot biscuits came to us again. If the proprietor is alive today, I suppose he thinks Butler ate all the biscuits he took out. Butler is yet alive and remembers the little trick he played on the biscuit-maker. But he has never been known to relate the story.

I think it was the next day after the foregoing episode that George Clark discovered a fine, fat hog in a stable at the southwest corner of the town. It belonged to an old German, who, I have heard since, was an uncle by marriage of Doctor Rawlings of Eldorado, Ill. Job Ingram, Joe Morris, Bill Baker, Frank Pankey, Frank Ingram and myself were selected to go with Clark for the pig. The stable was on the street, the door opening out into it. But there was a scantling firmly spiked across it, requiring much prying to remove it. The dwelling was a two-story frame building, forty feet back, and the negro cabins were still further back and somewhat to one side. I did the guard duty that night, and used a piece of plank, five feet long and four inches wide at one end sharp at the other.

The rebel general, Chalmers, was not far away at the time, and my excuse for being there was that we had Chalmers in the town and were going to capture him. We had been at the barn five minutes, myself standing ten yards to the south, facing the west, when a fourteen-year-old boy came out of the dwelling toward me. As he approached me, I halted him and informed him that no person would be allowed to leave his premises that night as we were determined to capture General Chalmers that very night in that very town. I told him to go in, and inform the family what we were doing and that they must not come out our way. Soon a negro man came, and I halted him and instructed him as I had the boy. He also meekly obeyed me and everything was as still as death to us in those houses.

After a long time the spikes began to move, and, it seemed to me, that the squeaking noise arising therefrom could have been heard two hundred yards. The door was opened, and the pig was among the horses and all in perfect darkness. In his anxiety to do the killing himself, Clark, the discoverer, struck and made a bad lick. Then the horses began to crowd around, the pig began to squeal with all his might, and our men put forth extra efforts to stop the racket by killing the pig and removing it to a place of safety.

The landlord could stand the confinement to his room no longer. He was a German, and in all the excitement of which he was capable, after coming on to his high porch, he cried out, "You are killing my hog." I bade him go back into his house—that Chalmers was in town and that we must get him. That the horse had only kicked the hog. He called as loudly as he could for the guard, and hearing the noise in the barn still going on, he ran out as if to jump the fence, but I met him with my board bayonet, declaring that I would kill him, and he quickly turned and fled to his porch. Turning around, he called repeatedly, rapidly and loudly, "O guards!"

The guard was a detachment of the ninth Illinois cavalry, and they had extra orders at that time. We knew they could soon overtake us, as we were only footmen and could not afford to be captured

by them, as a trial for disobedience of orders by a court martial would be a serious matter under the circumstances.

The old man, hearing the stir in the barn, could not remain on the porch, but came bolting out as if he intended to jump the fence. But I sent him back as rapidly as he came. The point of my board bayonet coming toward him always had the desired effect. It would be too much for anybody who thought it a steel one. I did not intend to hurt him at all. I was really enjoying his antics, while doing my best to secure his fat hog. He, although in his night garments only, made four attempts to get outside, but was sent back to his porch each time, where he called for the guards again.

The hog, having been drawn from the barn and started down the slant northward, Morris waited to see the outcome of my strategy. And we heard the sound of the tread of advancing horsemen as the old man came at us the last time. In the great emergency I told Morris to hand me the ax and I would kill him, and he ran one way while we ran another with all our might. I only wished to scare him away till we could get a start. We overtook the pork and the butchers at the foot of the hill. I ordered the men to roll the hog off the road into a gully, at its edge, and single to escape capture. The order was obeyed, and one after another left the road and made his way through the sage grass and shrubs, then the alleys of the town, back to the old shed and quietly to a conference and to sleep. I was the last to leave the road northward, as I could see the cavalry as far as they could see me, and the woods was at my left hand. I ran till my breast seemed to be on fire.

In two hours all were in conference at the old shed. We decided, as I remember, that four of us should quietly approach the dead hog sometime before morning, and, if the soldiers were not there and the hog was, we would drag it in a place of safety and use it. If the men were captured the other three, who were to be in sight, were to come up and pretend to be hunting the four that they might be severely punished, and get possession of them. It began to rain at midnight and two of the seven slipped away to find the hog had just been hauled in from the place we left him. We supposed the guards watched for us to return all night, and deciding we would not come, appropriated the meat to themselves, or returned it to the determined old German. We came nigh being captured, and missed our pork after all our hard work. But we knew that one never knows what can be done till an effort is made. I never suffered much sorrow for our act, as we were being shamefully treated in the matter of rations. We were not gratified with information as to whether the cavalry or the German ate the hog. However, we knew that we did not.

Pankey was killed later on; Clark died while in the service; Morris and Job Ingram died soon after returning home. The other three are still living, but are not in the business of foraging for food because we are hungry.

In a day or two we drew two months pay, twenty-six dollars each for corporals and private soldiers, and thirty-two dollars each for sergeants. We then started to drive and guard about seventy-five six-mule teams through to Corinth, Mississippi, that they might be sent on east to General Sherman for service as he marched and fought from Chattanooga to the sea.

The men were divided up so that each wagon would be protected from probable attacks by General Forest's cavalry or other parties of marauding guerrillas. One swamp of several hundred yards breadth was crossed by our road, the like of which I suppose there never was one before, nor will there ever be one like it in the future. It was regularly irregular. The wagons of former expeditions had tracked one another till the ruts were deep on both sides, at intervals, the distance of the front wheel from the hind wheel. As the left front wheel and the right hind wheel went down the other two rose to the top, and as the right front wheel and the left hind wheel went down the others rose to the surface. The drivers rode on the saddle mules, but all the soldiers guarding the train walked through the swamp, as it was out of the question to try to ride in one of the boxes of the wagons though they were two feet high.

However, this statement does not apply to John I. Capel, one of my company. He had confiscated a kettle somewhere and he did not want to lose it. We had nothing to boil victuals in, and he liked boiled dinners. To save the bushel vessel, which could not remain in the wagon-bed a minute, he determined to hold it down in the bed. As he was on the kettle sometimes the kettle nearly on him at other times, applauses and jeers greeted him from start to finish. But he went through and saved his kettle, anyway.

Our headquarters continued to be at Corinth, Mississippi, where we did provost and picket duty with occasional expeditions to some town or into some section of the country, where we might find mischief brooding, till the twenty-sixth day of January, 1864. On January 1 the weather was much colder than any we had seen in the South, or that we saw afterwards. I learned that it was colder in our home land than had been witnessed by the people there in their lifetime. (On January 1, 1884, another similar cold period came.) The Irish potatoes belonging to the hospital corps froze and we got them. They were as hard as bricks, but they were all right for us, and we were glad they froze, for they were a great rarity there. A week previous (I think) we had some good news from another part of the army, and the colonel, after dress parade, had strong men carry barrels of apples, with one heading knocked out, pass along the line and the fruit which the officers had bought poured out as they went, and we had more enjoyment in picking up the apples and knowing that it was the officers' treat than in eating them. The officers enjoyed the treat as well as we did.

On January 25 the forts were dismantled and the next day the place was evacuated, as all the men were needed elsewhere, and the enemy was not able to set up business there any more. All were drawn to Memphis, Tennessee.

Our regiment had gained the friendship of the citizens when there, as we went to Vicksburg, at first, and they requested that we be detailed to fill the place of another regiment as provost guard and as picket guard in and about that city. The request was granted and we were located as the exigencies of the case required. Removals were frequent, but our duties were mostly in and around the city till June 1, 1864.

I had not incurred the enmity of but one man, and that was because I was a friend to him when no other one would befriend him beside myself. He had been a deserter and, after he returned to us after light punishment, he seemed to hate all of us and me in particular. I soon thought he aimed to kill me, and I decided to be first to fire. I watched him, for I believed then and I have never changed my belief, that he wanted to kill as many as he could and be killed in the melee. One night he was given to me as one of my relief, and we started on the rounds. He commenced to slur me as we came to the first post. I ordered him to relieve the man at once and left him. I think he was not looking for so sudden an end to his intention, and I

have seen him no more since that time. He took small-pox that night, and was taken to the small-pox hospital next day and he died there. He was the first man that I ever rejoiced to hear was dead. He was named Samuel McIntire, and he had been a steamboat hand for many years. I am glad he died to this day. He hated me for my kindness, and did not even charge me with any wrong. I did not want to have to kill him, and the good Lord saved me the job.

The opportunity to try again many of the pleasures of the world was afforded me in Memphis. I was competent to do any business that came up, was popular among the men, and was liberal-hearted and full of fun; and was devoid of any hope of anything good or bad after this life came to an end. Yet I was craving everlasting existence and enjoyment, and was determined to get all of the pleasures in sight that were possible then.

Lieut. A. O. Hill was my especial friend, and often accompanied me in my excursions into the different places of amusement, wickedness and danger. Our captain was a Christian man, very strict, and not of a popular disposition. But Hill's friendship secured for me liberties that other men could not have. And the captain died less than three years ago in ignorance (as I suppose) of my riotous living at that time.

At the end of four months I grew tired, and began to take an invoice of my profits and my losses. I was four months nearer the end of my life than when I commenced my wild career; had spent much money that I could have educated my little sisters with and saved my dear mother, my one never-failing friend much hard labor by paying for help for her during her hard lot in this world. The profits were as blank as blank could be. The pleasures that I had expected I found to be delusions.

They could not satisfy my hungry being.

And I remembered that I had escaped death by the assassin's knife once and by another's pistol once, and that only by great calmness and presence of mind on my part in either case was the sad tragedy averted, unless I saved my life by destroying another which I was prepared, though unwilling to do, if it could be avoided. I made no threat; did not indicate that I apprehended any danger from any source, or that I was armed, or that I was at all alarmed. Yet I had my hand on my pistol and my finger on the trigger, with my right side turned away all the time in each case, and could have shot in one second. I could not have been so cool and have acted in so deliberate a way if I had not been prepared to save my own life. I was not to blame, only for being in bad company. I suppose those men never knew me, nor their danger.

At another time I had an escape, that had a very sobering effect on me, from some men who had planned to rob and doubtless to murder me also. Only a few days before I was passing along not far from the place where I was attacked, and came upon a large spot of coagulated blood on the ground, and the track of the object which had been lacerated.

I followed, less than ten yards away, to an unused well, where I found the body of a man with his throat cut from ear to ear. His legs and arms and face were under the water, but his back was out of it. The distance to him from the surface of the ground was not more than eight feet. The well was a large unwalled one. The water in it was so shallow that the hands and feet of the dead man may have rested on the ground. I gave the alarm and when the corpse was examined it was decided that he had been decoyed from a notorious house, 200 yards away, by pals (as they were called) and while one from the rear of him had suddenly drawn a silk handkerchief around his throat and pulled him backwards, another one had cut his neck half off, it was thought, with a razor. No alarm would be given if he was destroyed in that way. He might have been destroyed for his money, or from a fear that he would betray the clan, or from mere jealousy.

The action of the woman who was responsible for the conduct of the house when she viewed the remains of the man, convinced the hundreds who had gathered there that she understood all about the tragedy. I do not know whether the murderers were ever punished or not. But we were taught by that circumstance, and others somewhat similar to it to be prepared to defend ourselves if in that territory and alone after night fall.

I was coming to camp at 10 o'clock, p. m., and as I entered a vacant square, advancing toward the southeast, I had to cross a ravine at right angles; and ten yards to my right the ravine suddenly became a gulley three feet deep. I was carrying my pistol in my hand by my side, the hammer pulled back so that I had only to pull the trigger to shoot. A man, dressed partly in citizen's and partly in soldier's clothing, rose from that deep gulley and advanced as fast as I was going to the path that I was traveling, so as to come in contact with me. I ordered him to stop; but he came on, claiming to be an acquaintance by the name of Martin. I told him to stop, else I would shoot him, and bade him keep his hands down. He obeyed, but he was so close to me that I walked around him and kept my pistol pointed at his heart till I had passed him ten of fifteen yards. I looked every way for his accomplices and would have run like a Turk, had I not been afraid of running into some of them before I saw them, for there was a row of trees along the south side of the square that made a shade so dense that I could see but little there.

I think that man deserved to be killed, but I did not want to kill him if I could avoid it, and I was afraid of his partners, whom, I felt sure, were near by; and of being court-martialed if found to be out against orders. I walked rapidly and watched every way till I made the distance of a mile into the camp, convinced that it was unwise to go out into that part of the earth alone.

The next morning, Lieutenant Hill, being relieved from duty, accompanied me to the scene of the episode, and, as I had believed before, there were tracks of different men in that gulley. No doubt that, if I had permitted one to embrace me, the others would have cut my throat as they had that of the man whose corpse I had lately found near the same spot. They were, literally, a set of cut throats and murderers, and it is probable that they killed many a lone traveler after dark that none but the All-seeing Eye alone to this day knows of.

I concluded it was not paying me to endanger all the life I had in so reckless a way; that others might continue to attend theaters, balls, billiard halls and any or all other places of evil communication, if they preferred to do so, but that I had seen their emptiness, costliness and hurtfulness, to my own satisfaction. I took a farewell drink only, another card was never thrown by me, and I abandoned at once and forever those foolish and dangerous and costly expedients resorted to in search of happiness.

From my early boyhood I had intended to become a wealthy man some time. As I turned away from the excesses of sin, I turned to the consideration of wealth as the means of the satisfaction that I was so hungry for. I did not consider the means of getting it, for I had no doubt that I could accumulate wealth at my leisure. By anticipation, I added farm to farm; orchards, meadows, palatial residences, surrounded by beautiful groves, adorned with statuary and marked off by graveled drives, sprinkled by beautiful fountains, cared for by loyal attendants; fields of herds, blooded teams and costly carriages; wife and children, friends and money. I believed the procuring of them would as certainly come to pass as I should find that they were what I needed. The one great question with me was: Will their possession give me what I really need?" or "Will they make me happy?" I think I estimated their value then as if I had the wealth of John Jacob Astor. But all by anticipation.

I believe now that the spirit of God opened my understanding to estimate the whole matter. I sat as in the possession of them all. I realized truly all the pleasure their possession could give also the care and weariness those joys involved, and finally the creeping on of old age and the leaving of all my possessions at death to, perhaps, a wise party, but more apt, to an ingrate or a fool, and I should lie down, as the serpent, or the dog, or as the murderer, forever.

My experience along these lines during the forty-two years since flown away have wonderfully verified the correctness of my judgment when I at that time, ceased to hope that great worldly wealth could or would make me happy or supply the wants of my craving heart. I felt in the very depths of my nature that riches brought only vexation. (At that time I did not know any thing about the Christian use of wealth, as not abusing it.) 1 Cor. 7: 31. All desire for much wealth as affording pleasure or satisfaction to me thenceforward was as completely eradicated from my mind as though I were dead, as I verily believe.

Yet I was in fullest confidence that at the proper time I should easily ascend the ladder of fame. Then I would be happy. Others sacrificed time, money, friends and often principle also for office and certainly it would be the merest folly if, after all, the possessor did not revel in the enjoyment of that which had cost him so dearly. I had no hesitancy in starting in pursuit of the coveted prize if I should live a few years longer; for I estimated that I possessed ordinary talents, an indomitable will and a conquering industry.

The only place of which I had heard that held out any hope of enjoyment, to compensate me in any degree for being at all was that supposed to reside in the prestige, fame and honor that accompanied the occupancy of official position in a noble country like ours. But before deciding that I should rest my entire trust in that expectation, I began an investigation of the realities of these supposed delights. I did not want to go very high in those places open to every citizen of our great country, however.

When viewed from a human standpoint and at long range and for time only, the honor of a county or state office seemed very inviting to a young and ambitious mind. But that I might probe deeply in the fountain of the greatest worldly honor that could be bestowed on any man in the world, I selected General George Washington as my subject for exhaustive examination.

He had been useful to the country in his youth; he had led the Revolutionary soldiers to victory; had filled the highest office in the gift of the American people, and had died in honor, mourned by nearly all his own nation and the civilized world beside. Yet when I considered thoroughly the responsibilities of Washington as an officer and the uncertain tenure of his office, among a fickle-minded people, my confidence in finding all I needed, taking Washington even as an illustration, melted away as snow. But I followed him to the grave.

He had been lying still in the embrace of death sixty-five years. And I realized that his glorious past, the praises of all people in all time, and the monuments of stone built to his memory the country over, could not affect him for weal or woe. He was as impervious to their influence as a stone would be. His ear would be deaf to the praises of a grateful people forever and forever. He would be, so far as I could know, as if he had never been at all.

I decided that as a means of the gratification of one's vanity, men intoxicated with that light and foolish article might thrust in the cycle. But to one who lives higher up and broader out, no earthly office or honor could fill the vacuum in his bosom. I was willing to do my duty as a man and be a blessing to my kind as I knew all should.

In view of the fact that there was no way to avoid our future eternal destiny— that I knew of—after absolute failure in life to be happy, I could find no just or adequate reason for being at all.

With sadness of heart I turned away from sensuality, the prospect of wealth and fame as means of enjoyment, to nothing but a blank, a blank —so sad. I was at sea without any compass or rudder or pilot—if any one could be.

On the last day in May, 1864, I had occasion to visit a squad of my comrades who were on duty a few miles north of the city, on the Wolf river. As I returned I looked, from a high place, over the city, where I saw several places entirely devoted to the destruction in one way or another of humanity. I remembered my desolate condition and how I had been deceived by the offers of satisfaction by projects that were incapable of doing more than to delude and destroy.

I abhorred every opiate, for the longing life, that I had ever tasted. I did not dread futue punishment. I dreaded future nothingness. I had loved life and everything in nature that was innocent— the air, the water, the land, the plants and trees; the birds and animals and the people. I craved to live forever. I dreaded not hardship nor labor nor losses.

Standing there alone in the anguish of my heart I cried out, "Oh,that I did know that Christianity is what honest Christians believe it is. Then I could be happy all the rest of my life. There is nothing else worth living for, seeing that all must go hence forever."

In that minute of despair I seemed to get some relief. Of course, I had no confidence that my earnest wish for such knowledge would ever be gratified. If I had thought one time in that direction, since the reading of the testament in Lake Providence ten months previous, I have no remembrance of it. Ten days later my mind was exercised in a divine direction again, for a minute only. I said nothing about my desires to anyone, for I knew of no one I could believe unless that one could show me so that I could understand. I was utterly without hope except during the few days I might live on the earth. It was only from a sense of duty and the desire to help save the Union and the remote possibility that something might come to pass to my benefit, that I could act in my normal easy and lively manner.

CHAPTER IX.

I WAS sent with another squad of our company to the north of the city at midnight, as an attack on the lines was expected any hour. But before noon the next day, June 1, we were relieved, and in the afternoon took the cars for Colliersville, fifty miles away, as a start in the disastrous expedition into Mississippi under S. D. Sturgis.

I'll copy an article published in the Harrisburg Chronicle in December, 1891, when we were encouraging the voters to keep saloons out of that city, which they did for twelve years at once:

Whisky the Cause of the Guntown Defeat.

I take up my pen to narrate an experience which many thousands of us had at one time during the war of the great rebellion; an experience of so sad a nature that not one who participated in it can forget the event while he shall remain conscious of anything in this world. However much space I could command in your paper, I should be able but feebly to express the horrors of that event; much less shall I be able to give a proper detail of it in one column. It was the complete overthrow of the Union army under General S. D. Sturgis, near Guntown, Mississippi, on the tenth day of June, 1864. That old slave auctioneer and sly fox of Fort Pillow massacre notoriety, N. B. Forrest, was in command of the rebel forces. I should not, after a lapse of more than twenty-seven years, call the attention of your readers to the incident but for the fact that "whisky did it."

No one among us ever heard of Sturgis until we were marching in his command, and each one of us soon learned to be sorry he was ever born. His very name when we first heard it sounded suspiciously in our ears, and for more than twenty-seven years it has been more nauseous to the souls of the still-living victims of his meanness than even the effluvia from the stomach of the whisky bloat, or the nasty mess of India berries and swollen tobacco plugs in the bottoms of the barrels of "bust head" whisky we used to see.

On June 1, 1864, an expedition started out from Memphis, Tennessee, to operate against the rebel army under the aforesaid Forrest. Said expedition was composed of the 4th Missouri, 2d New Jersey, 19th Pennsylvania, 7th, 8th and 9th Illinois, 7th Indiana, 6th Iowa and 10th Kansas cavalry regiments, and the 84th Iowa mounted infantry, under command of the cavalry general, B. H. Grierson, the 9th Minnesota, the 81st, 95th, 108th, 113th, 114th, and 120th Illinois, the 93d Indiana, the 72d and 95th Ohio infantry regiments, the 1st Illinois and 6th Indiana and Co. E. 2nd Illinois batteries, the 55th and 59th U. S. colored artillery, Col. McMillin commanding.

There was along with us a supply train consisting of two hundred and thirty new wagons, each drawn by six good mules; also twenty ambulances, each drawn by two good mules. Those wagons were for the most part loaded with the best quality of bacon and hard tack that a soldier ever met, and an abundance of sugar and coffee. The other wagons were loaded with ammunition for the army.

It was our lot to move some days through rain and mud, and, of course, left our provisions so far in the rear that we frequently had to wait without anything to eat until the middle of the next day when the teams would catch up. The moving of such an army, including twenty cannon and these two hundred and fifty vehicles, cut up the roads on such a day till traveling was not going to heaven on "flowery beds of ease," but a very unpleasant thing, especially if, as was sometimes the case, some of the foremost wagons got mired down or turned over in the road at a place where those behind could not pass.

There was no necessity for such a proceeding on the part of Sturgis, as the enemy had not been located by the scouts.

What was very strange to us all the time was the entire ignorance that prevailed among both officers and men as to our mission. The preparation made indicated a long march, but our seeming want of plan militated against such a thing. However, the new general kept his own counsel, and, as we afterwards learned, drank his own whisky. In the meantime we had moved in a zig-zag way to the southeast more than one hundred miles by the end of the ninth day.

On the morning of the tenth we got up out of our wet beds, for it had rained a good portion of the night previous, and after breaking our fast and throwing away our damp ammunition and replacing it with forty rounds of dry cartridges we started off like we meant business. At about eleven o'clock we were ordered to double-quick. We started and trotted at a lively pace for about two hours in the middle of that June day, while the hot steam was fairly smoking from the ground, until we were run into the enemy's line endwise, not being allowed a moment to rest before engaging them.

General Grierson asked General Sturgis to form his army in line of battle and let him draw the enemy out to them. But no. He would do no such thing. Notwithstanding that one-fourth of the infantry had fallen out of line from sunstroke and exhaustion, he rushed the remainder on until they struck the enemy in their well chosen position, fully rested and under command of an able general.

Fighting commenced at once; as the tired troups came up they fell in on the right, which was the south. Our left was flanked by the rebs, and we fell back three or four hundred yards, where we were hotly engaged until our ammunition was about all gone, and, as we were being surrounded by the enemy, we were compelled to retreat.

All this time we were in much worse condition than if we had had no general. Any one of our regimental commanders could, in all probability, have gained a victory, but Sturgis was on a drunk. We had to give up our batteries and retreat to Tishomingo creek, about one mile back, where to our disadvantage Sturgis had hurried the wagons and ambulances into a corral in a kind of pocket at the side of and across the road between the creek and the hill in such a way that they could not be gotten out, nor could the men get by them except by wading the creek to the north or the south of the bridge.

The rebs now turned our own batteries on us, and gave us hail Columbia till we had passed over a timbered hill out of their sight. They then came up and took peaceful possession of our wagons and provisions, our killed, wounded and completely exhausted men.

About two miles from the battlefield a stand was again made by those of us who still had any ammunition but the rebs had learned the worthlesness of our commander and continued their policy of flanking our troops. Our forces, seeing that they would soon be surrounded, gave up all hope of saving anything except by retreating. Sturgis, having ordered Grierson to surrender his cavalry forces, had started with his body for Memphis, about 115 miles away, an hour or more before. Grierson was not drunk, and of course saved his cavalry.

Just after dark the enemy came to Whackerdam bottom, a marsh about two hundred yards wide and two feet deep in slush. Every vehicle not already abandoned was lost in this bottom, save one ambulance, which carried the dead body of Colonel Humphrey of the 95th Illinois. Besides the loss of all our wagons, ambulances, provisions, ammunition and artillery, about six hundred mules were lost.

It was reported at that time that about 3,000 men were killed, wounded or taken prisoners.

The men, in getting through the mud in the darkness, lost their shoes and stockings, and many a man cut off about two feet of his pants to rid himself of the mud on them that he might better continue the long retreat to Memphis.

Next morning our rear was overtaken at Ripley, twenty-five miles from the scene of battle, and another engagement took place in which our Colonel was shot from his horse and left for dead, together with several killed and wounded. This was the last effort made by us to fight. Our guns had become useless for want of ammunition, and many were bent around trees to prevent their use by the enemy. The cavalry and those of the infantry who had secured mules, got into Memphis Monday morning, while the rear guard and stragglers, numbering about 1,000 met the cars at Collierville, Tennessee, about thirty-five miles from Memphis, on Monday evening. The rebs had followed, scared and shot at us until after dark the night previous, (12th), and would have captured us but for a few Indian scouts and the guns and ammunition about 100 of us had saved.

Those of us who reached Collierville, got a little rest while waiting for the train. The rebs could be seen not far off, but did not attack us. When the train arrived those who were able got aboard, and those not able were carried on by fresh troops who met us.

What a scene! A thousand men! Most of them hatless, shoeless, sockless and partially pantless, with feet black and swollen, half-asleep, half-starved, not having had one-fourth of a meal from Friday morning until Monday evening, traveling night and day in continual dread of the horrors of a rebel prison.

Just at this time we heard firing in the

south, and we knew that some of our men were being murdered; and so it proved to be. Seven men, including Frank Pankey and John Parks of our company, were captured, set on a log and shot like dogs.

Those on the train reached Memphis that evening to their great joy. Little squads of two or more continued to come in for ten days. The 10,000 well equipped soldiers had dwindled to 7,000 refuges. Our own regiment was in such poor condition that it was excused from all duty until July seventh.

Sturgis, having lost his whisky, got back but wore citizen's clothes to keep from being shot by the boys he had wronged. He was court-martialed and found guilty of drunkenness and cowardice, but by some hook or crook was never punished.

Yes, through the drunkenness of the brute, Sturgis, which could not have been but for the rum traffic, many of our comrades were killed outright, or died a slow death in a rebel prison. Can any comrade, who shouldered his gun in defense of his people so far depart from the exalted ground he occupied then as to aid in any manner the rum traffic? If I should decide on doing such a thing it seems to me that the blood of Pankey, Clark, Mitchell, Summers, Orr, Bean, McCool and many others would cry out against me. No! Rum slew them; and I shall oppose rum in all its forms as long as I live. Unite with me, comrades.   CO. F.

CHAPTER X.

TO relate the operations of those days as I saw them and felt them and knew of them I regarded as pertinent to the mission of the book, as my own turning from death and regeneration by the spirit of God to be his son was effected in time which includes every one of the transactions herein named.

As I remember, the command began to march at the double-quick at eleven o'clock a. m., and we kept it up till one o'clock, when the 113th Illinois came to the skirmishers in an open wood and staggered a moment while my regiment came up and formed to their right, when both regiments started eastward whence the skirmishers had retired. In fifty yards our regiment, the 120th Illinois, came to an open meadow. The enemy had his battery of field cannon planted southeast of us, and commenced to fire so rapidly on us that we were ordered to fall to the ground. We obeyed the order immediately, but we had scarcely struck the ground when three men out of each company were commanded to run forward to the woods at the east side of the pasture.

The captain called Blackman, Dallas and Sweat, to make the advance. We were on our feet and running to the woods with all our might at once. By the time we had fallen and looked around, all the two regiments were coming on the run. We were immediately ordered to advance under Captain Pillow. A short distance south of us there was no woods at all. The 108th Illinois soon took their places, touching our regiment on our right, and were hotly engaged before we returned from the skirmish line. The woods we encountered there was a thicket of extraordinary denseness. We knew the enemy were concealed close by and rested in places of their own selection, while we were very hot and tired and could not see them in their position.

We moved slowly on till they opened fire, when we dropped and began business. One bullet hit a stump in front of the head of Dallas and my legs. He had seen the danger and fell, but as I was crossing over to the left of him, I saw a large tree fifteen feet in front of our line and I aimed to benefit by that tree if I lived long enough to get to it. I knew we could not advance much farther. At the very first fire I made for that tree on my hands and knees; but I found I had made a mistake. It was on the east side of the old road in the open sunshine, where no air was stirring. There was a brown coat behind another large tree ten or fifteen yards in front of me who was industriously firing at our pickets, or rather, our skirmishers. But nearly all the firing was done obliquely as we were too close to expose our heads if it could be avoided. Every man on both sides lay behind something or sank as flatly on the ground as he could. Many bushes along our line in sight of me were cut by the bullets that went over the men or beside of them. But the enemy in my front soon ceased to fire. One comrade to my right who could see him by rising to his knees and quickly firing and dropping again, had laid him out. Not even a zephyr moved. But the sun was pouring down his rays on my back without mercy. In that hour of prospective death by the sun's heat in case the enemy did not kill me I thought of my extreme need of help from some source. As I was not very confident of help at hand of a finite nature, I thought of the God my mother believed in and worshiped. I said, "Oh, that I had a God that could help me." Of course I meant only the God of the Bible. That was all I said and it was all I could honestly say. At that the left retired, as the rebel general seemed to know all about the situation he continued to rush fresh troops north of the 113th, the regiment on our left, and compelled them to fall back and soon the skirmishers of the enemy were aware of the advantage they had and as soon as they advanced westward to the road, they commenced to give us the benefit of their attention from that direction, also. Our regiment, thirty yards in the rear, were obliged to lie and wait while scattering bullets fired at us were killing or wounding some of them and the 108th

Illinois just on their right where there was no woods were having a hot time and other regiments still on southward were being engaged as they came up and formed. When the skirmishers commenced to shoot southward as soldiers nearly always do they did not shoot low enough to hit me, in the old road. The road was perhaps eight inches lower than the other ground and I was pretty flat on the ground in the road. The skirmishers did not draw low enough to hit me as most of the shooting at that time had to be done at haphazard way and their bullets flew down the road over me as I lay on the ground. In that interesting time Captain Pillow, who was commanding the skirmishers, ordered us to retire to the regiment. We found that the bullets that missed us had killed and wounded a few of those we left in line while we had advanced as skirmishers. The fighting to our right had become heavy and on our left the flanking movement kept the 113th retreating to avoid being surrounded. That fact compelled our colonel to fall back across the open field. The men marched back in two ranks and in perfect order.

The main body of the enemy had not come up and only the skirmishers could see our movement for the timber. Comrade Denning of Co. E was by my side and we were crowded out behind the column with the sergeants and a bullet passed through his breast from the rear and he said, "Boys I'm killed," and went down. He was touching me on the right. I could not stop to care for him as the whole enemy I knew would certainly be able to kill me if I did.

When we reached the west side of the field the different regimental commanders were frantic at observing the lack of generalship and signs of treachery on the part of the drunken general whom we were sworn to obey.

Col. McKeig had us to fix bayonets preparatory to driving the enemy back and regaining the ground we had lost. Just as we were on the point of moving eastward again our bayonets gleaming in great beauty the brigade commander came on the ground and countermanded the order. After cuss words and prospects of a duel between the two commanders we retired fifty yards where we held the enemy in check till our ammunition was exhausted. The 113th gone, the north companies of our own bent back facing the enemy from the north and the inevitable retreat began. Ten or fifteen minutes before that event Lieutenant Hill had moved the men of our company still with us thirty or forty yards south, declaring that the battery must not be lost. I went forward to a tree behind which I saw K's orderly standing and shooting. I need not have done so as the left side of a tree is no good to shoot from. But he called my attention to perhaps 100 men coming from the northeast. They must have been crawling. I faced that way and loaded and shot as fast as I could. At that moment I heard my own orderly say, "Boys, Im killed," and he went down as Denning had done. He was shot through the breast from the placing of his hands there. He was six feet to my left, and I had unconsciously moved four feet to the left of the tree. I have no recollection of any sense of fear or danger at that time.

I heard the voice of a man call, very loudly, three times, from behind me, before I looked around. It was an artilleryman warning me to get out of the way. I glanced around as I moved south in front of the four field cannon; for I had been fully as far to the front as the muzzles of their pieces, and only five yards to their left, all the time I had been there.

Jones was gone, so was my company. Some of the artillerymen were turning the cannon toward that dangerous company of brown coats; others were putting canister into their cannon. One wounded man was slinging his shattered hand. Horses that I supposed to be wounded were rearing upon their hind feet.

Those noble men had been left without support, to die or be captured at their post of duty, because the old traitor and drunken sot had made it impossible to procure ammunition for the infantry.

I do not believe that there was another man in fifty yards of that place, when I left the spot, except the artillerymen. If I had known that they were all going I suppose I should have gone too. But I had my mind riveted on that creeping company and I was trying to stop them. The battery men doubtless thought I was too brave to kill with their cannon, when really I may have been temporarily insane. After I was relieved from the duty of shooting at those dangerous men I passed toward the south till clear of the battery and turned west.

My company seemed to be the last, and it was 150 yards toward the northwest. I was so worn out that I could move but slowly and went directly west, down a slant 300 yards to a little basin of rain water, which I intended to sit down in. But if I did so I do not remember it. Before I went far I met Billy Tuttle going toward the southeast where he would shortly be captured. I prevailed on him to come with me. He was partially insane, I think. He had one bullet in his shoulder and one in his arm between the elbow and wrist, which last was giving him great pain. I do not remember when we parted. I continued westward to the woods, 250 yards further, where I met with three of my company. I rather think they were some who had fallen out during the trot from eleven to one o'clock that day. I laid aside my gun and accoutrements and my oilcloth, and said I would die if I did not rest. Frank Pankey, who was killed three days later, declared that I should not do so. He and another placed themselves under my arms and the third man carried my gun and accoutrements and they pressed forward to a point where we met the wagon train, wedged in so it could not get started out again.

I rested on a wagon five minutes and found that that would not do. I started on foot again, but could not carry my gun and I left it in the wagon. After walking about one-fourth mile I felt refreshed and picked up some other man's gun, abandoned, perhaps, because the man had no ammunition.

About two miles away we made another little stand. But we had nothing much to fight with. The old scoundrel that had butchered us so cruelly had fled toward Memphis, 110 miles away. We were soon outflanked again, but I could not start with the company on the retreat. I was sitting against an oak, not being able to control the muscles of my limbs, I was shaking as if I had the ague.

I saw the rebels coming leisurely along, and I knew they would soon have me as a prisoner. In that important moment I discovered a wagon nearby, that the saddle mule was still hitched to. I shuffled along on my feet and hands till I reached that mule and cut it loose, and, by the aid of the tongue or hub of the wagon, I mounted the mule with all my belongings and rode away in the presence of my friends, the enemy.

As I advanced northward I felt better. About 300 yards from our last fight I came across Comrade Stricklin, unable to go on. I bade him get on my mule behind me, and if he would carry two we would let him do so. The mule raised no objections and we went on.

Six hundred yards further on we came upon Lieutenant Wash Canady of Co D, who said he was unable to go further. I do not know why I did not have him get

on with us, for the mule was large and strong. But I came down and gave my mule up to the two men. I had recovered much strength and became a helper thenceforward.

It was growing cooler as the sun was about setting or clouds had hidden it. As I found much to do in aiding the others, I continued to feel better every hour. After dark overtook us we came to the "Whackerdam" bottom, which was a slough 200 yards wide and two feet deep, filled with thin mud. Those who let their pants get into the mud had to cut off the legs of them at the upper end. I was wearing a new five-dolar pair of kip shoes, their first trip, and a new pair of hose that my mother's own fingers had knit, which I had just received, and I pulled them off and rolled my pants as nearly to my hips as was possible and started through. If it had not been dark I do not know how I should have done, as there were others I would doubtless undertake to help. But I could not see them and took care of myself only. My pants did not get much muddy, as I was five feet and nine inches high and my legs were lengthy enough to keep me out of the mud, but I lost one of my hose in some way.

After we had traveled a few miles our colonel stopped and called out to us at intervals, and in that way he collected most of his regiment that were not killed, wounded or captured. I slept while he collected the men. I had been on foot while he had ridden and commanded and raved and cursed. When all had passed that we supposed would, we started on again. There I left my other hose, which I had used as a pillow on the top of my cartridge box, while I slept. I forgot it.

Then the old traitor had taken time· in his flight to safety to send orders back for our regiment to hold the rebels in check till the others were safely away. We formed across the road to do our best. But few men had any ammunition. I thought that the only way of escaping the horrors of the wretched Andersonville prison was to be killed; for it seemed to me that the Southerners gloated over the success the prison had attained in starving Union men to death, or of having some bigoted boy to shoot them down as if they were beasts, if for any reason they came near enough to the dead line to give him any kind of pretense for doing so.

But just before the rebels came in sight General Grierson sent word to our Colonel to come on; that he would hold the enemy in check. That was joyful news to me. For it would have been impossible for 100 men, and the most of them with little ammunition, to successfully meet a victorious army of many thousands.

The enemy were not yet in sight and the retreating Union forces were too far ahead to be seen by us. Yet we went on as fast as our poor condition would allow. It was about eight o'clock, a. m., when we came to the little town of Ripley, Miss., twenty-five miles from the scene of the conflict of the day before. The colonel collected us together there, and was dividing two or three pecks of broken crackers among us when the enemy was seen coming. Not one of us had tasted food since early the morning previous, as the traitor seemed anxious to have us butchered, and hurried us out earlier then common that morning; and as we went into the fight, all were ordered to discard their canteens, and haversacks containing the food and water they had along. But we never saw them again; so we had been destitute of food for twenty-four hours.

Those who had guns went back on the double-quick to the south street of the town and formed in the street. The ground descended toward the south and the enemy were coming up the slant 150

yards away. By lying down we could get at the approaching foe by shooting under the dwellings, which seemed to be on pillars two feet high. But it did not take them long, on the east and on the west of the town, to advance so as to fire lengthwise of the street and rout us in short order.

Our colonel, while on his horse directing our attention to a most dangerous squad to the east, received a ball through the breast and right arm, breaking it in two and bringing him to the ground. Our condition seemed desperate. The colonel was thought to be dying.

Lieutenant-Colonel Floyd, the next in command, at the request of Adjutant Mc Murty, gave the soldiers orders to retreat, as they saw we had no chance to stay the progress of the enemy; and he therefore ordered us to retreat and save ourselves if we could.

Two or three men carried the colonel into a dwelling at hand, where the lady promised to treat him right, and they left him, reporting to us afterwards that the man was in the throes of death when they left him.

We passed between the houses in the rear of us and retired to a fence of rails 150 yards over, where we thought it best to stop behind it for the moment. By the time we were there, the enemy were ascending the stairs and shooting at us in a promiscuous way through the windows. I shot three or four times, not at the windows, but where I supposed the men were while reloading, two or three feet to one side. A little ravine ran under the fence where I was kneeling, and I thought I was so low that I was well out of danger; but a bullet from them struck the lower rail, which was a large one, exactly in front of my forehead, but did not go through it. We did not stay long. Retiring northward through a field, we fared rather rough. I saw Lieutenant Joe Jennings of Co. D shot in the middle of the calf of the leg; Private Hahs through the thigh, and A. J. Spears through the right shoulder. I do not know how many others were shot there. Those were near me. Spears was at my right side. I was especially interested in him. His case was as follows:

He was a boy of seventeen years large for his age, who lived in Yellow Bush county, Mississippi. His uncle was a Union man. To avoid furnishing the rebels with horses, he had the boy stay with them in the ravines and thickets, somewhere in that county. The Southern soldiers caught him away from the horses, and, to compel him to reveal the horses' whereabouts, they hung him till he almost died. He did not tell them at all. When they let him loose he cleared out for the Union army, and after a time we took him into our company and began to drill him, but we were loth to go into battle with him lest he fire the wrong way. But he soon proved that our fears were groundless. In the hottest of the battle the day before, when a bullet hit the hammer of his gun and knocked it away, he gathered one which was lying there and with fearful threats and oaths concerning the enemy, began to fire again in the right direction. When the ball struck him that time he was in no condition to curse.

He kept along with me and those who remained with me. We entered a pine thicket less than a half mile from the outskirts of the town. Nearly everyone bent his gun around a tree, as the supply of cartridges was entirely exhausted, and the men did not want the rebels to get their guns and they could not afford to carry empty ones. After an hour or more we finally went east to the big road leading toward La Grange, Tennessee.

We could hear much firing to the west, and rightly guessed that the rebels were after those who had much the start of us.

We started northward on our perilous tramp of ninety miles in an enemy's country, not more than one man in ten of our number having a gun, and that one with only very few bullets, with several more wounded and more worn out on our hands, and all perfectly destitute of food. As we moved slowly on, other men joined us, and before noon we came up with 150 colored troops, with their white officers who were bravely staying with their men and leading them, notwithstanding the danger they were supposed to be in, if captured, for belonging to a regiment of colored soldiers.

At noon we came to a short turn in the road toward the west, and we fell behind and then went down into a deep gorge to the north and lay down to rest. Colonel Floyd, Captain Pillow and I were the only ones that were not sound asleep in a few minutes. I sat bathing my feet in a little running stream, ten-yards from the other two. There I could hear them talking solemnly, and I knew that they were devising a way of escape. That was the most lonely hour that I ever experienced in my life, I really believe.

A report of a large gun, in our very midst startled us, but did not rouse one of those sleeping by our sides. I met the two officers half way as we all asked the same question, "What was that?" Of course we thought the enemy had found us and we were theirs. As nothing further was heard indicating that we were fired on, we looked around for the cause, and found smoke issuing from the scabbord of the colonel's holster pistol and the torn blackgum chunk where the bullet had entered. We were glad it was not the enemy, and hoped that none of that tribe of mortals were near enough to hear it.

I had no disposition to sleep, but I helped my feet all I could. After an hour's rest, the officers requested me to arouse the men. I bathed my Southern boy's shoulder often, and solemnly promised him not to leave him.

We started on our wearisome tramp, looking all the time to be overtaken and captured if we could not slip out to the roadside, as they were corralling the others.

Captain Roark succeeded in collecting his company at the rear of the others, and proposed that we take off to ourselves and try to make our way to Memphis alone, as we were almost certain to be captured with that defenseless band before we could reach the relief expected. I objected and we went on.

At sundown my wounded man became so sick he could go no further. I plead the most eloquently that I had ever done to that time with a beautiful young lady to care for the boy and bring him to the Union lines when he was recovered, and promised her all the money her conscience would let her ask if she did so. She promised me heartily to do so. John Capel says he stood by and took notes of the words of the girl's mother, who continued to repeat the question, "What are you'uns doin' down here a fightin' we'uns for?" She looked tough. But I was not dealing with old sour-looking women then. I knew that if I could win the girl the boy would have a friend there. If she had succeeded in carrying out her contract, I would have carried out mine sure.

The enemy came and took him and Edwards of company "C," whose feet had worn out and who was left also, in one hour. In a short time they were taken to Cahaba, Alabama, and they were afterwards exchanged.

Our party numbered about seventy-five men all told. We traveled until ten o'clock in the night, and came up with the 150 colored soldiers and other white soldiers, including the 9th Minnesota regiment,

commanded by Colonel Wilkerson. The pickets were colored men, who were so wearied that only one of them could be awakened at all.

We put out other pickets and went to the main body and rested till morning. We rose and started, for we had nothing to cook. There were nearly 1,000 men in our party that cloudy morning, and about 100 of us had guns. Every time I found a cartridge after I picked up the gun in the road I appropriated it, so I had eight or ten in my box, and I hung to my gun. I asked if my mule was in the gang, and found that Stricklin had not left him to others. I mounted him in front of Stricklin.

But when we were ready to start I looked back and saw that Dallas was not able to walk at all. I put him on my mule with Stricklin, and I felt like I could hold out a week longer.

About noon we were attacked, and, to save the helpless men, ten of us who had arms guarded 100 who had none, and every time the enemy attacked our remnant appeared as if we were glad to meet them. We shall never know, however, how many of our men got away in small squads that day, as many were captured and shot by guerrillas. Two devices saved us. The Indians of the Minnesota regiment were put out as skirmishers, which the rebels did not understand, and Marion Harris of Du Quoin and his brother, J. Carroll Harris the minister members of the 81st Illinois, were captured and were taken to a Southern colonel whom they knew and they made him believe it very dangerous to assault us with the expectation of capturing the whole command.

Captain Roark, Matt Horn and John Capel left the main body and found that they were nearly surrounded, and Capel laid his gun and ammunition in Wolf river, seven feet under the surface, and they swam the river, the captain holding his pistol out of the water. They arrived in Memphis the following Friday, nearly naked and nearly starved, after thrilling and exciting adventures, which space will not permit me to chronicle here. Roark and Horn died in June, 1903, just thirty-nine years after their hard experience.

Capel recovered his gun afterwards and he has kept "Rachel," as he called it, all those years; till lately he had it deposited in the museum in the state house at Springfield, with other relics of the Civil war. He is still living, and relates with thrilling interest those hardships and dangers.

By perseverance and almost superhuman exertion the men went on till pitch dark, when our friends the enemy stopped. Then we took renewed courage and went on. At ten o'clock that night I called for my mule, for I thought I deserved to ride, and I knew that he could carry three of us better than I could walk further. I was told that three men were already on him and that not one of them could walk at all. Vinson said that his partner would let me ride on his mule, as he could then walk awhile. I mounted in front of him and Dallas, who still rode the mule I saved, carried my gun. I was so sick and dizzy and sleepy in fifteen minutes that I could not sit there. They put me behind Vinson, but I could do no better. They then tied a twisted oil-cloth around both our necks and he took my arms under his and held me on at all hazards. It seemed to me that we crossed a gully every two minutes, and each crossing jolted me most unmercifully. I slept and I gagged and I mourned that I did not continue to walk. I wanted them to let me stop and take my chances next day.

I was nearly in the same fix of the man who started across the ocean. He soon became so sick that he feared that he would die. But after he suffered awhile and grew unspeakably sick he feared that he would not die.

I suffered on till one o'clock next morning, when Colonel Wilkerson gave orders to stop till morning. The grass was four inches to six inches high in the old field where we halted. I got down some way and lay where I fell, not able to walk one step. I rolled over on my gun, which was given me, and slept a sound, sweet sleep without one minute's waking, till roused to start again as light was appearing in the east. Again we did not have a breakfast to cook. I had passed my hungry period.

The day before, at ten o'clock, we were passing a wealthy man's residence, and I thought a small piece of bread would be of great service to me. I stepped out of the road to the door and knocked. A negro woman came to the door, and I told her I was starving for food and asked for bread. She declared that there was none in the house. I assured her that there was, if she would look well. She went away and brought a piece of long cornbread as large as a large biscuit. I praised her goodness and requested some meat. She assured me there was none. But I assured her that there was, if she would search the place well.

My crowd of one had increased to a dozen beggars by that time, but none of us offered to open the door, which she was careful to shut each time she retired. When she returned she brought the crooked bone of a hog's hind leg that was endowed with an antiquated smell, but seemed to have been rid of meat since the war began. It had been saved to make soap. But it was the best she had. I divided the bread and passed the bone backward that all might see the prospect. I did not suffer any more from hunger.

We were not molested much on that Monday till we reached Collierville. We looked for an expedition of relief to meet us, but we were growing uneasy. The enemy evidently did not know our desperate condition, else they would have tried more energetically to do us up. While waiting there awhile we could see dangerous signs of an attack, as the numbers of the enemy in sight of us increased in all directions.

We piled the wounded not already left and the wornout men on the mules again, and made our weary way along the railroad two miles before help finally met us. We had heard shooting at intervals and believed that our men were being murdered as they were captured.

We heard twenty or thirty guns fire at once and then scattering shots, after one o'clock, more than a mile away toward the south. Those, we afterward learned, were the shots that Dick Davis and his guerrilla band of murderers fired at Captain Somers of the 108th Illinois, and six others, three of whom belonged to our regiment and two of whom were members of my own company. The particulars will be given later.

At two o'clock p. m. the much-wished-for train appeared. But we were too weak and weary to cheer.

The first action of the newly arrived regiment was to throw good, brittle crackers out to us in every direction. One fell near me and broke diagonally into two pieces. I took one piece up and ate it; that satisfied me. The rested men were, in the meantime, carrying the wounded and wornout and foot sore ones on to the cars and placing them there preparatory to returning to Memphis.

We could see the Southern soldiers on their horses in all directions, and we feared they might tear up the road before the train could return. I was as happy at the coming of the soldiers as I had life to be. We had been so long on the retreat and heard the enemy's guns for seventy-five miles back, and they had become to sound

so loud to us that I had more confidence in the ability of ten fresh men than I had in all of our 100 men who had guns. I felt safe, and if we had been attacked then, I felt like I could lie down and let the new men shoot over my body as breastworks to aid them. But I had no confidence in ourselves.

When part of the new men had taken charge of the mules and the only wheeled vehicle that escaped—a hack carrying the body of Colonel Humphrey of the 95th Illinois regiment, killed the first day of the fight—and started on the way to the Union lines at Germantown, our train started out. It stopped less than one mile away to take on one of the 113th Illinois, who had escaped from the Dick Davis massacre an hour before, and reported that the other six men with him were all killed. One of his arms was shot so nearly in two that it was amputated as soon as practicable.

In two hours we were in the city of Memphis, from which we had started on the first day of the month. It was on the thirteenth that we returned. The men who had thrown away their guns, after all hope of receiving more ammunition had gone, were not detained in the Riply fight, and had improved every opportunity to escape, had returned to Memphis the day before we did. I think the cavalry men aided them, as it looked as if all those left would be killed after the general rout. They met us at the train and aided us to camp or hospital whence we should go.

We did not resemble the clean, well-disciplined regiment that went away on the first day of the month, any more than the track of a tornado resembles the country before it came along. Most of the men were without shoes; some were without legs to their pants; nearly all were without coats; many were hatless, and I was without shirt or stockings. I put on a calico shirt to make the trip in, and it came to pieces and was discarded the Sunday before the fight, and I was without a shirt afterwards and was, therefore, compelled to wear my coat. It was a blessing to have lost my hose. I wore my soft shoes thirty minutes and walked barefooted thirty minues on the damp ground, and thus partially avoided scalded feet, which were such a calamity to most of the men. Yet with that advantage over others, the skin came off the bottoms of those parts of my feet that bore my weight, and my toes. My little toes lost all of their skin in one piece, except a little on top! Nearly all the others were in worse condition than I was.

Till the seventh day of July we were not assigned to any duty whatever. After I ate the half of a cracker at the coming of the relief train for us, I ate less during the next three weeks than I ever ate in any other three weeks in my life, if well. I did not once feel hungry.

The first thing I did after getting to camp was to send my mother a short letter, telling her of a little skirmish we had been in and that I was all right. My letter, from some cause, did not reach her, and, as I did not arrive with the first of our men, the news was sent home that I was among the missing. She thought of my unprepared state to meet death, and therefore she could not be comforted. She slept neither day nor night, and was on the verge of collapse or insanity when a letter was received from me by a young lady, who had heard of mother's broken-heartedness. A messenger was at once dispatched to her, conveying the news that I was alive and well. Her grief gave way to great joy, which rendered her unfit to talk of much else for days. Her neighbors, who had deeply sympathized with her before, came to rejoice with her now that she was happy. I sorrow to this day on account of the accident that caused her inexpressible, though needless, grief for three days and nights.

The next day John H. Parks came in and brought the sad news that the guerrillas had captured six others beside himself, including Captain Somers of the 108th Illinois; and, after having them sit on a log, shot them all to death except himself, who alone rose, running, and escaped. Frank Pankey, one of our own company, and James Mitchell of company E, he said, were among the killed. The particulars of the killing will be told later on.

The men who escaped death or capture continued to arrive for six or seven days, one or two at a time. They had to do most of their traveling by night, through thickets and byways, and without anything to eat; for none could allow himself to be captured if he could avoid it. Andersonville prison was too bad for any civilized soldiers, unless it be such cowardly traitors as S. D. Sturgis, who was the whole cause of all our misfortunes. If he could have been confined there and died in the pen, instead of the innocent men whose death he caused, justice would have been subserved.

CHAPTER XI.

ON the seventh day of July we were shipped to La Grange, Tennessee, to drive away guerrillas in the rear of General Smith, who had gone to punish Forest and to keep open communications with him till his return.

Comrade Vinson passed me, with a book in his hand, which I borrowed. That was on the day of our arrival there. I read on the back, "Nelson on Infidelity." Opening the book on the title page, I read, "The Cause and Cure of Infidelity." I was a great lover of books and especially of those which seemed to come in my line of business. But I did not know what the word "Infidelity" meant. I had never heard anyone say anything about it, nor had I read one word about it, nor agnosticism, nor atheism, nor deism, nor any other ism in all my life, that I could remember. Yet, some way or other, I suspected that it was unbelief in the Bible, the truth of the God of the Bible, or the religion of the Bible. If I was correct in my surmisings and an infidelity, and that the disease could be cured, of all the anxious students that ever investigated any subject, I would be one of the most fervent while examining his propositions.

Only twice in nearly twelve months had

JOHN H. PARKS,
Who escaped the Dick Davis massacre.

able and honorable man could show me the cause of one's complete ignorance of truths the most important ever uttered, and the cure for such a state of ignorance could be effected; and it should turn out that I was afflicted with the disease called my mind turned toward God, religion or the 'Bible. Those times were, as said before, on May the thirty-first and June the tenth previous. I borrowed the book and read it with as much avidity as a hungry man ever ate his meal. From the first page I began to see, and my astonishment increased from hour to hour. The thoughts were as new to me as the scenes of nature are to the one whose eyes are opened for the first time after a life-time of total blindness.

It seemed like I had been dreaming when I closed the book after having read the last page. It appeared incredible that I should never have thought or heard of any of the ideas that I had read about in the book before me, and I remembered that the author had, according to his own words, been fully as much in the dark regarding the things which he set forth in the book so convincingly as I was myself.

I was very glad to believe what I had read, but still, I was afraid to believe them lest I should build up high hopes that must be shattered at last; for I had for nearly one year been entirely without hope of any enjoyment of any kind except what little I could find in the present life; and I would prefer to stick to that, unsatisfying as it was, than to embrace what later should prove to be a delusion. This world, however, even at that early stage of the investigation, was not sufficiently alluring if I could have it all to purchase my interest in the things about which I had just read.

I had been detailed to perform the duties of the first or orderly sergeant for the time being, as there were some who doubted that Clark was dead, as no one whom we knew of at that time had seen him shot and fall except myself and I had not examined him after he fell. Yet I had not the least hope that he was yet alive.

I was an apt scholar and did my duty so easily and satisfactorily that I had much time to read, and I improved it. I eagerly began to read the book again, determined to carefully weigh each and every thought, and if it came out as it looked at my first reading to be pointing I surely would be the happiest person in the world. For I put an estimate on the life to come, if there was any, ten thousand times more highly than I judged most Christians did.

At the end of eight days, at one o'clock p. m., July 15, having read about half through the book the second time, I closed it, and said in my inmost soul, "It is enough. It is the truth. I see it all now. I am happy in view of the salvation that is for me and that I shall seek till I find it." I had turned away from the practice of the sins that enchant others when I had nothing to turn to. They did not have the weight of a feather to allure me away from the way I judged to be right then. And I cared even less for them, now that I saw plainly, as an honest intelligence could see, that my mother's faith was well founded. I realized that persons with the evidence of pardon that I now believed Christians have, must be happy even in the hour of death.

I was so glad of the reason I had for believing the things I had read that I wanted to begin to seek my pardon at once. That very hour I decided that I would commence. I did not know what to do but to pray. I had prayed in my boyhood and it did not seem to do any good. But others had prayed and had been heard, and I could not see how God would make any difference. I could not afford to live without hope any longer if it were possible for me to obtain life. I thought the Lord would in some way lead me if I asked him to do so. I remembered many things that were useful to me that I had not accepted at all before.

I might have been truly converted and regenerated that very hour, so far as I have ever been able to understand, if I had only been taught then by a living loving gospel teacher. I did not know that the Old or the New Testament could give me any light on the subject of conversion. While I was not at all broken up with pungent conviction as I had desired to be when I was a boy and had heard of others who said they had been and that I would gladly be if I could, yet I could only be what I was and I could not wait for something I might never receive. I believed that salvation was free for me if I could find out how to get into possession of it.

I was was encouraged by Heb. 11:6, which I some way remembered or read or heard, viz: "But without faith is is impossible to please him for he that cometh to God must believe that he is, and that he is a rewarder of them that diligently seek him." I knew that I believed intellectually without a doubt that there was one great God, the Maker of all things, the Redeemer of sinners and the Preserver of us all; that the Bible was his own word, and that the Christian experience was a reality. Yet I knew that I was an unsaved sinner, in ignorance and Spiritual darkness, and destitute of spiritual fellowship and happiness.

I remember that the Scriptures said that with the heart man believeth unto righteousness, and with the mouth confession is made unto salvation. I did not know how to believe with the heart. That was exactly what I wanted help to do. I fully believed it must be done, yet I could not see how to do it. Therefore, I thought the right thing to do was to pray to God for what I needed.

There was one hindrance, perhaps, to my conversion, then, even if a Moody or a Spurgeon had been teaching me. That was my determination never to profess to be interested in the salvation of my soul till I had been a Christian long enough to try myself and know that I could walk so as not to be regarded as a hypocrite. I abhorred the shallowness of the religion of anyone who wanted to engage, or who did engage in the foolish things that I had found to be delusions while they professed

to love God at all. I knew that I might be so silly as to be like them, but if I did I thought I would never tell anyone that I had a hope at all. But I did not believe that I could put so low an estimate on Christianity as to love worldly pleasures that way. From those considerations I started out without a cross. No man living had seen me bowed in prayer. I did not intend that anyone should till I could know that I was saved and could prove it by a perfect walk.

Our camps for three weeks were in the vacated store houses on the east side of Main street. The west side was vacant for a distance of 500 yards. Weeds covered the ground thickly from two to five feet in hight. I chose the place where the weeds were highest to bow in prayer to God. I found that place 250 yards west and, so far as I had discovered, no one had noticed me as I retired to that weed patch. It had been a delight to learn of the things pertaining to religion that I had lately learned, but to bow on my knees to God in that secret place was an experience altogether new and unpleasant to me. I had come there for that purpose, and, having gone so far away from God when I ought to have served him from my earliest youth and having been saved from danger and death so many times during those late years, I thought I ought to be glad to bow on my knees there and ask for pardon. It was not that I had any high opinion of my physical or mental or moral worth, that I demurred to facing God on bended knees, but a sense of my unfitness to do so and shame for that unfitness deterred me. But I knew no other way, and, after again assuring myself that no one was near to see me, I quietly bowed on my knees. Then I tried to find a suitable request to make. Every time I was about to ask for what I supposed I ought to ask for, I would conclude that I was not in earnest and therefore God would know that I was acting the hypocrite and my case would be worse than to say nothing. I was sure that God was there and knew all about my needs, but I could not feel like I was at that time able to pray right. I do not remember whether I uttered one word or not. Yet I had advanced in experience so far as to realize that I knew very little about the way to pray. I rose and went away. That was my first effort to pray.

More than forty-three years have gone by since that time, but I pray to God yet as the only one I have ever known who is an able friend at all times and under all conditions.

I was compelled to turn away from my excessive fear of acting the hypocrite because I could not become more honest and earnest to save my life.

One dark, cloudy evening I found my way into the Protestant Episcopal house of worship and knelt on the floor of the choir's stand in the rear of the building, several feet above the floor of the main audience room. It was a very lonesome place. I think it had been vacated as a place of worship for some time, perhaps on account of the war. I was trying to talk to the Lord very earnestly, but I could see that my prayers were worthless. I either had my eyes shut or my head bowed low. For when I looked in front of me I saw in large letters the words: "Thou, God seest me." The solemnity of the scene was increased so much that I evacuated the place to return there no more to this day.

Whether in camp or on the march, hurrying to meet the foe or retreating to a better position, whether on guard with all the company or drawing or issuing clothing or rations, the one desire of my heart was to know God in the pardon of my sins and to have eternal life.

Smith's expedition returned, having gained a great victory over the men whom Sturgis had betrayed us to, including the recapturing of most of the 200 wagons and the batteries, the provisions and ammunition and prisoners being out of his reach.

We grieve over the death of the wise old Colonel Wilkins of the 9th Minnesota regiment who lead our squad to safety at the late Sturgis disaster. He died from a shot in the neck by one of the enemy in the battle in the Smith expedition. All honor to his memory.

We were again returned to provost and picket duty at Memphis, late in the evening of the 31st of August, 1864.

On August 4, Josiah Nickolson of company A of our regiment rejoined it, after an absence of fifty-four days, and made the following report. In the interest of truth I asked him to write me the story for my forthcoming book and the letter follows:

"Eddyville, Ill., July 22, 1905.

"Comrade W. S. Blackman,

Harrisburg, Ill.

"At your repeated request I write you of my experience in the hands of the rebels after the Guntown defeat, which you are at Liberty to insert in your book if you think it suitable.

"On the morning of June 11, when we were routed for the last time, our Colonel and many others killed or wounded, our ammunition exhausted and the men left to escape captivity or death if they could, I was with a squad that was so sorely pressed that it was not long till everyone but myself was killed or captured. That I might escape the Confederates and the Bushwhackers, I lay concealed most the time, day and night, till I became so hungry that I went in search of food at all hazards. I saw a man go into the barnyard, but I went directly to the residence. The landlady was clearing the table after the morning meal.

"I told her that I was very hungry and asked for something to eat. That was June

15, just five days since I had eaten anything. She gave me all I could eat. The man came in and volunteered to watch while I ate my cornbread and drank the buttermilk, with becoming relish. I thought I had never tasted anything better. I appreciated that fortunate meal. I asked the woman if I might take the piece of bread along which was left after I had done. She consented for me to take that also. I then started on and in a little while came to two little boys working in a field, I felt so weak and wearied that I did not keep the road around the field, but crossed over the fence to go through it.

"A short time afterwards six Rebs came to the boys and inquired if any Yanks had passed that way. The boys pointed toward me, and they started after me in a hurry and commanded me to stop. They had to stop to pull the fences down while I was making for the woods, and they lost sight of me. They then went for bloodhounds and returned with an increased force. I expected to be killed then. The dogs soon brought me to a stand and the Rebs came running up and calling out, 'surrender, you —— Yankee!' I tried to surrender, but a musket ball went through my uplifted hand.

"Then I asked them if they would not let a man surrender. They then took me to a citizen's house and kept me all night there. But the next day they made me march all day in the rain. I received some good out of that, though, for I held my hand under my hat brim and the water ran off on my wounded hand and reduced the fever in it, and it became cool and pale.

"We stopped that night at another citizen's house and remained two nights and one day. The next day they took me to Holly Springs, Mississippi, and put me in prison. The next day, Sunday, two Rebels or guerrillas came to the prison, pried the door down and took me away. When we

had ridden five or six miles one of them asked me if I was prepared to die. I told him that I was, and that I lived that way. I also told him that they intended to kill me, and that I would as soon be dead as to be in their hands. One of them said I was —— bold about it.

"We had not gone far after the foregoing conversation between us when one of them, named Jack Hood, lagged a little behind and shot me in the back of the head. The bullet entered low enough to miss the brain and far enough to one side to miss the spinal cord, and lodged above the roof of my mouth. After I was on the ground, he walked round me and shot me through the head, the bullet entering just in front of one ear and going out in front of the other one. I fell over from the sitting posture which I was occupying, in a helpless heap. I had not lost consciousness, though I could not speak nor move. They then took me by my feet and dragged me to a fence and threw me over it into a thicket.

"They then dragged me into the thicket and Jack Hood said, 'Give me a chunk. He breathing too easy. I'll knock him in the head.' The other man said, 'Come on. He will die anyway.' Jack Hood then pointed his pistol at my forehead and pulled the trigger. The cap burst but the ball did not leave the pistol. They then left me there.

"In an hour afterwards two little boys came along the road and seeing the track of blood, followed it till they came near me. They were not much surprised at seeing me except that I was not dead as they had heard the report of the pistols.

"They went back and told their father that they had found a wounded man in the thicket, not far from the road. The good man then came with them to me. I was sitting up against a tree. The man took me to his home and washed me and cared for me as well as he could. His name was Farmer. He had a wife, a daughter and two sons. The name of the daughter was Julia. 'Julia Farmer.' The names of the two little boys were Thomas and Willie. Yes, 'Thomas Farmer' and Willie Farmer.' They were all very kind to me except the landlady. She was a full-blooded rebel, and could not enjoy my presence there very well. The good man took down his Bible and read some of it that night before retiring and then led the evening prayer. The burden of the prayer was for me.

"Whatever fear may have lingered in my mind of treachery on his part, was dispelled then I understood that I was not in the house of a dog but that of a man; and I felt safe in his house. He was a minister of the gospel of the Baptist denomination.

"That blessed family cared for me for four weeks and I mended from day to day. Then six Confederates came and took me to Coffeyville, on a mule, where I passed one night in the guard house. The next day I was removed to Grenada, and was cared for in the hospital one week. I was then taken on a train to Jackson, Mississippi, to join a squad for exchange. Thirty-two of us were taken to Vicksburg, Mississippi, in two wagons, a distance of sixty miles, and exchanged. That was on the 28 day of July, 1864. On August 4, I met my regiment at Davis Mills, Mississippi.

"(Signed) Late Private Company A, 120th Illinois Infantry."

The foregoing strange story is a true one.

Comrade Nickolson is yet living in Eddyville and is a Christian gentleman, well known in his county for truth and honesty. The bullet in his head was about to kill him and would soon have done so, but twenty-one years after being lodged there, he sneezed and it flew out of its place to the ground, and a life was saved. He has not been able to open his mouth more than a part of an inch since he was shot, but he still lives mainly on liquid food. He wishes he could return thanks to the Farmer family for their great kindness to him, and would do so if he knew of them.

Perhaps Jack Hood and his fellow murderer never knew but that their victim died. Perhaps he is now reaping his reward. But God can save his children anywhere if he is not ready to let them go. The comrade carries the bullet as a relic of his suffering in his pocket.

I was acquainted with the circumstance at the time and have known Comrade Nicholson all the years that have elapsed since that time.

On the 23rd of September I had a chill, from which the fever fastened hold of me, and I grew weaker all the time. On the 30th my regiment left on boat for Eastport, Tennessee, by way of Cairo and the Tennessee river, where they were engaged in scouting, fighting some, nearly a month, before returning. The captain was left a prisoner in the hands of the enemy and it was thought that he was killed.

That was the first time I had ever failed to be with our men in all our experiences, and actually tried to get out of bed to go that time, but could not hold my head up. I was left in charge of the sick and lame of the company, however. I took thirty-seven broken doses of quinine and grew steadily worse. Hospital Steward Samuel Gardum recommended bathing thoroughly in hot water and drinking tea, then wrapping in blankets to induce sweating. I tried it and improved from the first day.

When the boys came back they were glad to see me, and declared that if the captain was dead I should be their captain. It was not many weeks, however, till we had word that he was a prisoner.

On the fourth of November those old

enough to vote, if they could be spared from military duty, started home on a seven days' furlough.

I met my dear mother and the sweet little girls for the first time in more than twenty-five months. I was not strong and was so much interested in the pursuit of everlasting life that I did not visit any. My family tried to have me eat many good things they prepared for me, and were much surprised that I did not enjoy them What I ate kept me half sick while there.

Great excitement possessed the people as to the result of the ensuing election. Our people were war Democrats; but had been made to believe that if Lincoln was elected that there was little hope for peace. I heard one good old woman say that she wished that Lincoln would die, as that was the only hope. I did not let her know that I heard her. I went to the polls and cast my first vote for president for the Lincoln electors. I was three months too young to vote when he was elected the first time.

I turned away from the old party that was dominant in our country when I was little, on account of their attitude on the slavery question. When men in our community would form a cordon across the road and capture the negroes that were runaways from Kentucky or other slave states and carry them back to be sent to Louisiana to wear their lives away, as they said, and gloat over the gold brought back for their trouble, my heart beat quicker, my blood ran faster, and my brain grew hotter over the wickedness that could fellowship the chattel in human beings.

Lincoln received four votes in my precinct in 1860 and forty-nine in 1864. McClellan received 100 votes in 1864.

I advised our people to be quiet; that Lincoln would be elected, and that the union would be maintained, and that the war would close before long, and our country would be prosperous, and our people happy again.

I was at home seven days and eight nights, but I did not let even my mother know anything of my seeking the salvation of my soul; for I could not know what was to be the outcome of all my anxieties. I learned afterwards that my acquaintances were surprised to see me so changed. Yet I was as sociable as I could be among the younger people, but liking the company of the older ones best.

Our stay was short, but it was long enough for me. If the war had lasted many years longer I think I should have stayed in it, as I did not want to experience the loneliness I did before I went in. I promised mother that we should be home again after a while to stay with her; and that we were having less excitement in the army than the people were having at home. I was glad to get back.

CHAPTER XII.

SOON after our return to camp a one-armed man came to our regiment and inquired for John Parks. I went in search of Parks, in company with the man. We soon met him. The man asked Parks if he remembered him. Parks said, "I have seen you somewhere, but I cannot remember where." "Well," said the man, "Did you see me when Dick Davis set us on the log to shoot us?" "Yes," said Parks, "but I thought that all were killed except myself." The one-armed man, who was a member of the 113th Illinois regiment, said, "They shot this arm in two and I rose running and came to the train in time to get on and come into Memphis on the same train that brought so many that were still struggling to avoid the dreaded Andersonville prison. With other wounded men, I was hurried away to the hospital. There I was informed that I must suffer the amputation of my arm, which I knew could not be avoided if I was to live. And I was very glad to be assured that I was likely to recover and have even one arm. I was fortunate in recovering rapidly, and as soon as it was considered best I was sent to my home in Chicago. As Dick Davis was captured lately by a squad of cavalry, being surrounded while eating breakfast, at a citizen's house, I was sent for as a witness against him. The man the soldiers captured denies that he is Dick Davis, as I am informed; and I am expected to know whether he is the man who was known as 'Dick' by his men, and who ordered them to shoot us off that log after commanding us to sit on it, or not. He is to be tried for his life. I accidentally heard that there was one more man of the seven that made his escape. I began to inquire and gained bits of information till I came to the 120th, where I found the man. I am very glad to know that one more man lives to testify to the horrible murder which I have related. And if I see Dick Davis I shall know him anywhere, I believe."

Then Parks related his escape to the one-armed soldier in my presence as follows:

"A short distance before we came to the big log on which we were placed to be shot, I was walking before the man with the old white hat on his head, and he civilly asked me my name. I told him that it was Parks, John H. Parks. He remarked that our names were nearly the same. Parker, he said, was his name. As we were a little way off and he seemed kindly disposed I asked him what they were going to do with us? He said that if he had his way we would be treated as prisoners ought to be treated. I knew then that we were to be shot.

"When Dick ordered us to sit on the log Captain Sommers of the 108th Illinois, squatted on his heels with his back against it. Dick ordered Parker to give the cap-

tain his old hat and to take the captain's hat himself. Parker passed from my front to my extreme left hand, and, after exchanging hats, returned to my front again. Dick then ordered the captain to sit on the log as the other men and he obeyed. Then Dick said, 'You must all go by the board, boys,' and as they all turned on us, Dick commanded his men to fire. Parker being in my front, I suppose he missed me from nervousness of from pity. As they turned to fire, we all expected to die there.

"Sergeant James Mitchell of Company E of our regiment was next to me. He was weeping from the certainty of being taken from his loved ones, perhaps; and he was shot and pitched forward before I moved. He was a member of the Baptist church in that country and was known as a Christian man. When he pitched off forward I knew it was time for me to be going backwards.

"I think I was the last to fall because I was not hit. But I was not much behind the others, else another bullet would have got me. When my back struck the ground I bounced and ran for dear life. They fired at me many times, but the bushes were thick and my dodging by them may have caused them to miss me. I fell once and thought that a bullet had gone through my thigh. But I ran on my hands and knees till I found that I was not wounded, and then I rose and ran on till, coming to an old field with many spots of briars, I saw two of the guerrillas galloping forward on my left side intending no doubt to shoot me down like they would a dog and leave me when they came up to me. But I saw them first and I fell and crawled into one of the briar patches and lay there till two o'clock next morning, for I thought they were watching for me.

"The train that was rescuing our other men perhaps attracted their attention so, they did not think so much about me. I did not dare to look at the train, for I did not know how many were watching me nor how close they were to me. When I could not afford to stay there longer, I slipped away as easily as I could and went west, though expecting to be fired on every minute. Hope had revived and I was doing all I could in every way to escape, with my life.

"When daylight came I had crossed the railroad where I thought the enemy would not be so thick, and cautiously moved from one point to another, after surveying the landscape as well as I could each time before starting; for I was certain that they were still looking out for the helpless men.

"I came upon a negro at work in a little garden, or field, and slyly approached him and asked him if there were any Union men close by. He said that I was almost in White's Station. It was in the possession of the Union soldiers; and I was in nine or ten miles of Memphis, our starting place. I went in and to the table, for the soldiers were eating their dinner when I arrived. I had not tasted food since Friday morning and it was then Tuesday noon. I had walked 115 miles, besides the many crooks and creeks I had made, and had slept but little and had virtually died once, all without even one morsel of food, and I went to eating without being invited. My clothes were mere strings, but I did not care for that. Soon I was the attraction of the station, and I had plenty of friends. I went in to Memphis that evening on the train that came that far east daily.

"I told the boys of the death of poor Frank Pankey of our own company and the other five men, including the captain and yourself. Not the remotest idea did I have that I would ever see one of you in this world again.

"News of the death of Captain Sommers having reached his home, on the following Friday, the seventeenth day of the month, I led the way to the place with a company of cavalry, at the request of a brother of the captain, who wished to bring in the bodies of the men. But there was nothing to move but the bones. An old negro said that he tried to cover the bodies with dirt, but he had nothing except a poor weeding hoe and he could do only a poor job with that. The bones were not all together. Two had gotten a short distance away."

Parks told the one-armed man that he was very glad to meet one who, like himself, had escaped from the murderers of their comrades, and that if Dick Davis was in prison he believed he could select the man, though he were with hundreds of others. He said he would be glad to do so.

The meeting and the statements just recorded occurred on a Sunday evening, and the very next morning Parks and the one-armed soldier were called for at the Irving Block prison. Only one of the men were admitted at a time. Many different persons were pointed out to them as probably the man they were seeking. Each time they said that he was not Davis. The real Davis was not noticed by the officer, but he was selected by the men.

Davis laughed at their mistake, but they assured him that they knew him to be the "Dick" that commanded them and their five comrades to be shot. They were absolutely certain of his identity. Each in his turn refused to select any other prisoner, and both unhesitatingly selected the same one, and both persistently contended that he was no other than the one who had commanded his men to shoot the helpless prisoners before named.

The court-martial called citizens, as well as soldiers, to testify in regard to "Dick's" cruel doings. For he had instigated or committed the murder of citizens and burned their houses and taken their money and property, as well as to wage relentless war against the Union forces. The court closed its sittings, but not one word could be heard of "Dick's" sentence. It was believed that he would be hanged, yet no one knew when, if at all. All waited with anxiety to know if indeed such a traitor would come to receive the reward of his own sins.

CHAPTER XIV.

THE twenty-third day of December, 1864, came, with its northwest clouds and its Arctic winds, more piercing than was common for that clime, and with them came the welcome news that Dick Davis was to be hanged in Fort Pickering that very afternoon. The reason the authorities had for keeping the sentence and its execution to themselves doubtless was to preclude the remote probability of an attempt to liberate him. For even Dick Davis was not without pals, called friends. And no one knows the other man's heart.

The city always had Southern sympathizers and even rebel soldiers dressed as citizens inside its lines, who might devise a scheme, unthought of before, to liberate Davis. Desperate men conceive desperate enterprises. Again, men sometimes enlisted in the Union army for the evident purpose of accomplishing some treacherous scheme, and many of them might be ready for such an hour and no earthly brain could detect their plan, if wisely laid. Caution is the better part of valor. But the six hours intervening between 8 a. m. and 2 p. m. afforded little opportunity for scheming in his behalf.

Captain William Roark, our commander, had the news early and hastened to camp, and selected Sergeant Jeff Slaten and myself to accompany him to the execution if by any means we could gain admittance. The fort was located on what was, before

the war, a farm, adjoining the city on the south, and had been extended in to the city as the war progressed. Many dwellings and other structures were torn away to make room for it.

The inclosure extended more than one mile southward down the river, and it was from 200 to 600 yards wide. Walls of earthwork, called breastworks, were erected, four to six feet high on the east, north and south, with portholes at intervals of 150 yards for the cannon to operate through, and openings of larger dimensions for the wagons and men to pass through at greater distances apart.

The west side was bounded by the Mississippi, whose banks were nearly perpendicular and more than fifty feet high, as I now remember them.

Two years previous to that day we had camped on those banks for two months as we were gradually descending the river to Vicksburg. There we were initiated into some new and unpleasant phases of service that pertains to camp life in times of war. We found that the tents we were to occupy had been vacated by only one class of their tenants.

The 13th Regulars had been sent away, but the parasites that seemed to be almost or quite as plentiful as house-flies in summer, were there for business. We had met in our boyhood days, flies, gnats, mosquitoes, bees, yellow jackets and hornets, besides other headfellows and bedfellows, and leeches and lizards; but these Canaanitish flesh-feeders and blood-suckers came nearer causing a stampede from our duties than all the other vermin together, and the tick and chinch tribes thrown in. Each individual seemed to have many feet and teeth in each foot. The alternatives were to die, to run them off, or clean them out.

A war of extermination was waged and kept up from day to day—scratching, scalding, scraping and burning till we were victorious, and we could sleep in peace.

We carried water up those high banks, and, as I went into the army to return again if possible, I was particular to bathe often. Though it was almost beyond my power to endure, I waded into the river there and bathed my body and neck and head and shoulders, while the wind was blowing down the river on my skin, from day to day; and I did not forget those events when we were to enter the fort again.

Here we were accustomed to be called out as we were sleeping soundly, to rush to the breastworks to meet Vandorn, Price or Forest, and stand shivering in the cold till the sun was high, just to please some fat general, as we thought, who went back to bed as soon as we were out. We learned to severely hate those false alarms.

During those two months we learned that an army camp was not the place for one to be afflicted with measles. In our company alone three men died in one night —the first men we lost. Bill Carter, Jack Davis and George Davis were the men. Wess Horn died later, and others barely recovered from the disease.

But during our two years' absence we heard of other tragedies beside the one now about to be enacted that lent an additional pathos to the plaintive memories of the experiences we had there when our men were fresh from their homes, entering on a service which had already cost so many of them their lives.

One of those sad events was the shooting of a citizen for being proved a spy. After due process of military trial he was condemned and shot to death. I was not very well informed of the circumstances of his crime and execution, else I forgot them, as we were hundreds of miles away at the time that the man was executed. But one of my company, Jo Harris, who

is yet living, told me of the deplorable case that follows:

Three men belonging to the Pennsylvania and New Jersey cavalry, while out on picket or scout duty, mistreated some helpless citizens, causing the death of one, a lady of respectability, and injuring one or more other persons. The regulations of the United States army require that each soldier shall act the gentleman toward civilians and non-combatants, and prescribes that condign punishment shall be meted out to those who dishonor the stars and stripes by wearing the uniform of a Union soldier while disgracing the name. Our army proposes to bless and not to curse our fellows. The soldier is sustained to serve, not to hinder nor to destroy.

Those men were of very different ages. One was about forty, one thirty, and one twenty years of age. After a fair trial and due conviction they were brought out to the fort to be shot, in the presence of all the convalescents and other soldiers at or about the city that could be spared from duty. Those 2,000 or 3,000 men were placed in two lines, facing each other, the lines being fifteen feet apart, extending more than half way around the fort.

The condemned men, following the band rendering the death march, in single file, and their coffins following in the same order carried by four men each, walked all the dreary way till the place of execution was reached. The coffins were placed fifteen feet apart, each man seated on the end of the one which was soon to contain his body.

Twenty-four soldiers were detailed to do the shooting. Eight were placed before each criminal. Four of the guns to be fired at each man were loaded with ball cartridges and four were loaded with powder and paper only. The men were not blindfolded nor bound, as it would seem humiliating for one wearing the uniform to meet death so.

At the command by the proper officer, rapidly given, "Ready, Fire!" the men fell backward on ther coffins—dead. They were calm, but pale almost to whiteness, and a sharp shriek escaped one of them at the word "Fire!"

It was a sad execution, an incident brought about, doubtless, by the evil leadership of the elderly man. But one sinner destroyeth much good. Proverbs 9:18. Those men had brought scandal and shame upon the Union army, which nothing but their life blood could expiate. "When lust hath conceived it bringeth forth sin; and sin when it is finished bringeth forth death." James 1:14. Heartrending as it was to the mother to know that her son died not in defense of his country, but for deliberate sin, it was done —and in his execution the honor of the army was vindicated and the ends of justice subserved.

The history of Davis, as we had it, was that in the early months of the great war he enlisted in the Union army and served in some regiment in the east. But he heard of the death of his brother, who fell in battle while fighting in the Confederate army. Immediately Dick deserted and went to the South, organized a band of guerrillas, and pillaged and plundered and robbed and killed all classes of people, especially Union prisoners, till he was captured. Hence he was an object of hatred and detestation to all Union people, as well as many of the Southern people also.

He was devoid of bravery and humanity and a devil incarnate in human form. He kept his own secrets to the last, except what he might have told the priest. Perhaps none but the God of heaven knows how many lives he caused to be destroyed, but I believe that one hundred would not include them all.

We started early that afternoon to the fort, that we might have time to wrestle with the difficulties as we met them. We came to many hitches, as the sentinels had extra orders that day; but our captain managed to overcome them all. How he did it we could not tell. However, we surmised that, as he was a member of the Masonic fraternity, he had an influence with some persons that we did not have. Be our guess correct or incorrect, we passed through every port and by every guard. Doubtless the relation of the fact that we were of the same company of some of the men that Davis had murdered, and that for that reason we were very anxious to see him hanged, helped us to get in.

After we had passed entirely through all obstructions, we went south to the center of the fort, where the gallows was erected. I took my stand on a parapet seven or eight feet high and about fifty feet west of the platform and gallows. From that point I could see well what was done, but I could not hear what was said in a low tone.

There were several thousand soldiers in the fort, and many of them under arms. As I now remember, there was quite a sprinkle of citizens admitted also. Of course, there were only those known to be loyal to the Union admitted.

At the appointed hour a wagon came through the gates to the gallows, on which sat the prisoner and the Catholic priest, behind the driver and between the guards. The march was a slow one on account of the solemnity of the occasion and the difficulty of getting through the crowd, which was solid for 200 feet or more every way from the place of execution.

Davis, the priest and two or three officers ascended the steps to the scaffold. Soon the condemned man kneeled before the priest, and while his body stood erect over his knees, he and the priest held a low conversation, which I understood to be questions by the priest and answers to them by Davis. The only words I heard perfectly were the words of the priest pronouncing absolution to the man. In other words, he said, in some way that I did not

he rose in a very sprightly manner, and when asked to say what he might want to say, he refused to say anything. The noose was then adjusted and the black cap drawn over his face.

The unbroken silence continued to reign

FRANKLIN W. PANKEY,

One of the victims of the Dick Davis massacre.

comprehend, that he extended mercy and the forgiveness of all the sins the man was guilty of. The stillness of death prevailed while the solemn service, or, as some thought, the solemn mockery, was taking place. When the penance was over

throughout that vast multitude. The executioner sprung the trigger and Dick Davis, the multi-murderer, swung between the heavens and the earth. He seemed still, except the little twirling of the rope by which he hung, for several minutes. Then writhings of the body, struggles, surges, kicks of the legs and contortions and twitchings of the arms and fingers continued for fifteen minutes or more, as I now remember. The last signs of life were the twitchings of his fingers, which moved so fast that no eye could follow them. His hands being bound behind his body, I could view them from my position well, and I knew that he had been strangled to death. I think he hanged there forty minutes or more. His neck had not been broken by the fall.

We all stood silently while his fingers were moving so rapidly for two or three minutes, waiting for him to die.

When the physicians pronounced him dead, the executioner reached up and cut the rope in twain while two men held the body and lowered it into the coffin at hand.

Dick Davis was one of the sandy variety of mortals, about five feet four inches high, and of 135 to 150 pounds weight. He was, therefore, easily handled by the two men.

I saw the man who cut the rope reach up again and cut a piece of it off and put it away, and the thought came to me that we should have part of that rope to send to the bereaved families of the men he had murdered, and I ran down the embankment and pushed my way to the gallows and cut off what I wanted and retired before anyone questioned my right to do so. I divided it, and its lasting qualities reminded me of the cruse of oil and the vessel of meal out of which the poor widow fed Elijah so long and it failed not. The more I untwisted it the more strands appeared. All who had special reasons for them received a strand, and especially the families bereaved most.

Frank Pankey's old blind mother could never hear the voice of her beloved boy again, but she could feel with her fingers the hemp that hanged the cowardly rascal that killed him. That did some good.

We returned to our camp, happy to be able to tell the friends of our murdered men that Dick Davis was dead in very truth.

One piece of that rope was kept by P. D. Dollins till he died about six years ago, and then by Captain Roark till he died three years ago, and is now in possession of his eldest son, Columbus Roark, of Kansas. All others, so far as I know, are lost, as having subserved their mission of the plaintive long ago. And the parties of that time and the things in existence then have largely passed away and have been superseded by other things, perhaps somewhat more modern and costly, but not more loyal and religious.

CHAPTER XV.

EXPEDITIONS were made to different places and for different purposes all through the winter, but our camp was not changed. Provost and picket service was the ordinary duty, unless detailed for tramps into the country or rushed to some place to aid some army or to cut off some expedition of the enemy. The variety of duties expected of us or the bright, diversified or gloomy prospects of our arms had no effect on me, so far as my desire for eternal life was concerned. Even the belief in the possibility of my coming into the possession of it made me a comparatively happy man. Yet I was as certain that if I should die as I then was, I would be lost as I was that any other one would be lost.

It was my daily desire and prayer to God to lead me some way to his salvation and to his service. I read books I secured at the Christian Commission rooms. One was "The Anxious Inquirer." It was a very good book, as I afterwards found, but I did not comprehend its teachings at the time. I attended the different churches every time I had a chance, and I went to one of the Catholic churches a few times.

At the first I thought it a cheap way of being entertained, for I went to the theaters once in awhile for recreation. I thought it a saving of the admittance fee. But a few times sufficed to disgust me with the tomfoolery of the institution, and I quit. I could not afford to patronize such mockery for recreation's sake, nor could I accept the empty whinings of the lusty priesthood for Christianity. My soul was too hungry to accept wind for bread.

No one in the world knew of my great quest, and I saw no change in my condition, unless it was that I was growing more anxious but less hopeful. I knew that I was seeking the way of life in the best way that I understood. But I knew that I had not met with any evidence of progress as I had expected. I knew that one traveling found signboards or other evidences of progress, and at the close of each day he was aware of his position and could calculate the length of time he would be engaged in his journey with reasonable certainty. I had thought that one seeking service in the army of the Lord would be similarly enlightened.

But all those months of seeking and thinking and reading and praying had brought me no light. It appeared more like I was going the wrong way, so far as any evidence of progress was visible to me. Yet I did not stop to consider whether I should go on. If my prospect had seemed ten thousand times more gloomy, I could not think of stopping; I knew that there was nothing else I could afford to accept instead of eternal life. I wanted the religion of the Bible. I knew there were people in the world who possessed that kind of religion, and I must have that kind or I would die seeking it.

The eighth day of February, 1865, came on in due time, and I was twenty-five years old that day. It was a beautiful Wednesday, for a winter one. I was busy discharging my duties as orderly sergeant and seeing after the sick at the general hospital, etc., that day.

Our men captured and brought in twenty prisoners that day, who were engineering some scheme to capture our men, or smuggle goods, or something to help the rebellion—I forget what it was now.

But all the business I did and all the things that happened did not remove for one minute from my mind and from my heart the one thing I craved and was starving for. I remembered that I ought to be a Christian then. I felt that I should have been many years ago. I tried at intervals to pray. After the day had passed, I think I made a more serious effort to come to the Lord that evening than I had ever made before. Nor did I cease my praying, as I now remember, till 10 o'clock that night. As I found no help, I was greatly troubled lest I should fail at last; for by that time I was conscious that if there was any way to find the joys of salvation, I knew not where to go nor what to do to find it. I had come to realize that there was no virtue in my prayers; and, as for tears, I could not cry. If I had shed one tear in four years, except those forced out by smoke, I had no recollection of the fact. My heart would cry, but my eyes would not. I had nothing to depend on nor to look to. I knew nothing to do but wait.

The evening of the next day my duties required me to visit my company, who were quartered in the second story of a vacated brick mill. I heard, while there, someone below suddenly begin to praise God. I hastened to an opening in the floor, through which bands had been run and through which I looked down to see the shouter.

To my surprise, I found that it was William Fitzgerald. I had no doubt of his honesty and of his true conversion. He walked back and forth across the floor of the large building and shouted; and the astonishment of sinners and the joy of the few Christians alike seemed to be almost unnoticed by him. I looked on and wondered why I could not find peace with God and be happy like that man. I regarded myself as wise as he. I never had sunk as low in society as he had, and was fifteen years younger than he was. He was a profane man, a dancer, a fiddler, a drunkard, a gambler and a fighter. He attended the frolics, or dances, and the shooting matches, and moved in the lower strata of society. He was very poor and his family lived in the crudest fashion of the backwoods, uneducated early settlers.

But Bill Fitzgerald, as he was called, was honest in his way then, and lived up to his profession afterwards. He had not forgotten the teachings he had received before. He believed in the old-fashioned religion of the fathers, and, having had enough of the folly of sin, was seeking the Savior during the last few months of the past, while his comrades were thinking him indisposed or homesick. But he was all right then.

I asked how it was that he was converted; for I had known him as a wicked, fearless man only, while I, who had not lived so profane a life, and had not condescended to keep so disreputable public company as he had kept, and had much better training than he had, and had—though seeking the Lord for nearly seven months, abstaining from all sin, as I understood it—been unable to make any progress at all.

, They told me that for five or six months past he had turned from all his obnoxious ways, had said but little to anyone, and wanted to be alone, and did only what he was detailed to do. They had no idea what was the matter with him, unless he had grown homesick or was losing his mind or he was going to die. Yet no one had bothered him, as he was known to be a man that it would not pay to bother, if he wanted to be left alone.

They said further, "That he had been attending a revival meeting in Chelsea, a suburb in the north part of the city, and had been at the altar of prayer a few of the last meetings." On hearing that Bill Fitzgerald had been going to the mourner's bench at the meetings in Chelsea, I was much more surprised than at witnessing his rejoicings at his conversion.

The mourner's bench had become a veritable bugbear to me. I classed it with the imbecile ceremonies of the heathen gods and the Catholic worship of Mary and adoration of St. Patrick and other superstitions which keep them in mental childhood and moral slavery all their lives.

But as the man was too brave and too independent to be hypocritical,: I had no doubt of his real conversion, regardless of the weakness manifested in going to the mourner's bench. I attributed that act to early associations which he had not learned to despise. But as for me, I'd not degrade myself by going to a meeting where such superstitious methods of worship were tolerated at all. Still I was glad for the saved man and for myself.

My prospect of being saved was better, in my own judgment, than it was before I saw the evidences of Fitzgerald's conversion. I knew all of the wickedness that he reveled in that I wanted to know, and a great deal more of better things than he did, yet he only was saved. The more I pondered the question, the less I understood the mystery. That matter, to the exclusion of all other subjects of meditation, occupied my every thought.

On the next evening I concluded, as I had nothing else to do, as a mere matter of pastime, that I would go to the meeting. Comrade D. L. Riley accompanied me, and, as we arrived late, the long room was full.

The house was one of the many two-story residences there, formerly occupied by factory hands. The partition was removed and it was used for religious purposes.

There was no organization called a church there. Christians of any faith preached and labored in the meetings. The citizens who took part were mostly refugees, far from their own churches, and were located there till they could go north or return to their homes after the war should close. The soldiers who attended the services were Christians or those desiring to become such, generally speaking.

However, we crowded inside the door and stood till the invitation was extended to those who wished the prayers and instructions of the Christians to come forward. As I had not once thought of receiving benefit from such a meeting, I looked only for foolish, shameful things to occur. There were twenty-five or thirty, I think, who went forward and bowed at the altar of prayer. More than half of them were soldiers; but I do not think I regarded any of them as men of judgment or ability.

I thought the Christians, in their anxiety and shallowness of soul, would soon get most of them to believe they were all right and they would claim to be converted. For I supposed that those seekers were merely affected in a sympathetic manner. I do not remember who preached nor what was said, nor anything else except what I saw. I went to see the meeting and expected nothing else. While I meant no harm, I expected no good.

When the song was closing I bade my companion to come away. On our way to camp I said, "Riley, I want religion; but I don't want that kind." He approved my idea. That was the first time I had ever hinted to anyone that I wanted to become a Christian. Perhaps he underestimated my statement. I had not told even my dear mother. I feared to do so, as I thought I might fail at last.

My curiosity was satisfied. I had no more idea of visiting that meeting place again than I had of buying a pair of wings to fly to heaven with. I remembered seeing many honest and intelligent persons bow at the mourner's bench in former years, and that I had known true conversions there. But I had learned of the ignorance or meanness of some workers who had told seekers to rise and tell the people they were saved and to give God praises, thus inducing false professions and deceiving the poor souls to their probable ruin. I had come to believe the anxious seat a mere machine by which the weak-minded and unfortunate were deceived by other silly or designing persons.

The awful opinion I held of the public altar had been growing on me for several years before I entered the army. I think the denunciation of it by the people called Campbellites and the Hardshell Baptists were responsible in some measure for the delusion that held me firmly in its embrace to that time.

I dismissed the meeting from my mind and went to sleep. During a lull in my business at 2 o'clock the next day, while wondering what would be the outcome of my cravings and searchings for Christ and his salvation, it came to my mind that from July 31, 1863, to May 31, 1864, I was so perfectly convinced that there was nothing in Christianity that I would not give one cent for all that ever was on the earth; and that till July 15, 1864, I did not confess God as the Creator of all things and the Author of the Bible. But that I saw plainly that I was in darkness then, and the reason for that darkness I saw also.

Might I not be mistaken again, I asked myself. I admitted the mere possibility, but not the remotest probability, that I was mistaken in my estimate of the merit of such protracted meetings or the altar of prayer or of the instructions that were given to the seekers by those who were in the habit of speaking and praying in public.

As I had nothing else to do (for I had quit praying, as I had found it useless in my case till something else was done), I decided to go to that meeting again that night, and to go early and alone. So I went.

The sun had just gone down when I arrived, and I found five person there already. They were earnestly consulting or advising concerning the meetings, I thought. I sat down as far away as I could get, lest someone should say something to me; so I did not understand much of their conversation. Neither did I want to, for I still had no confidence in the words or wisdom or prayers or sermons of any man or all men, as doing me any good whatever. I came alone, to observe the exercises in the altar—to learn if I had misjudged their nature and their merits or their demerits. I intended to get close when the people filled the space to a proper degree.

As the twilight passed into darkness the house filled to overflowing. The number of officers in attendance increased, since the evening previous, and I was in a dilemma. If I sat out there I would learn nothing of that for which I came. If I went where I could accomplish the object of my mission they would see me and perhaps conclude that I was one of the weak-minded class that was feeling an interest in the kind of religion that those people had or, perhaps, they pretended to have. Much as I disliked to go near, my desire was so great to learn anything pertaining to true religion, if there was any chance at all, that I took my seat next to the one placed for the anxious on that side of the altar.

I soon thought all eyes were fixed upon me, especially those of the officers. I cringed and crouched and twisted and looked down and up and away from them as well as I could. I don't know who preached nor what the preacher said. I did not come to listen to him. I wanted to see and hear workers do altar work.

It seemed long, but finally the altar was presented and calmly and deliberately quite a number bowed before me, all round the open space left for the workers. When the people rose I rose, and when they bowed in prayer I maintained a reclining position, as if I was not interested at all except to be polite. I wanted the people to think that I was there by accident, but was too gentlemanly to leave the place. It cost me dearly to act the hypocrite, but I stood it and accomplished my mission.

I listened to the instructions given to those who were seeking Jesus, but I listened in vain for the shoddy-like device that I was tuned for. The words that I knew were in the Book were meekly offered, such as: "Believe in the Lord Jesus Christ and thou shalt be saved" (Acts 16:30), and, "Come unto me all ye that labor and are heavy laden and I will give you rest" (Matt. 11:28), and other texts and other exhortations which I remembered to have heard the honest old servants of the Lord quote in their labors for sinners' instruction in the days of my childhood.

I listened to the prayers and observed the movements of the seekers closely, but found nothing objectionable in word or deed. However, they were so quiet and self-possessed that I could hear very few of their words. If the services rendered to God in the public worship of my mother and her fellow-members were right, those were correct also.

After fully satisfying myself that I had in some way or other been led to misjudge the meeting, I rose and pressed backwards two or three feet to escape the scrutiny of the eyes that I felt had been set on me all through the service; I surveyed the prostrate mourners, waiting at the feet of Christ, craving life, eternal life, as I had done for nearly seven months.

All at once the reasonableness of their actions appeared to me as if I had read it from a book. Christ had life to give. The mourner needed it and was begging to be admitted to the fellowship of the saints and to have his sins washed away. I thought I had not in my life seen a more proper thing done than those mourners were doing. I believed that every one of them would be saved before long, for I had a very big idea of God's truth and I knew that the words of Jesus in John 3:16 were very encouraging.

I was as happy as I was on July 15, 1864, when I first found that God's words as recorded in the Bible were true. I had made a great discovery. I decided to act the part of wisdom and honesty without delay. The meeting was closing. I considered the cost to my pride and the loss of standing I should sustain in humbly bowing in the congregation to one whom we could not see. But I had seen the beauty and propriety of the guilty party submitting to the terms of the offended one, especially if the offender was altogether wrong. I knew that the sinner was wrong; that I had not been ashamed to do wrong, and that for many years, and publicly as well as privately. But now that I had found all was vanity and vexation of spirit, and wanted to do the other way, I was actually ashamed to publicly declare my desire to lead a righteous life and to acknowledge my sins to God in the congregation. I had thought my carefulness to keep my intentions to myself was the outgrowth of my honesty alone; but when I analyzed it, I found much vanity and more

cowardice in it. I rejoiced to believe that at the next service I should be permitted to kneel at the altar of prayer with other lost but awakened sinners. I was convinced that I knew the reason of my inability to find the peace for which I had so long and earnestly sought.

I remembered that Jesus said that "Whosoever shall deny me before men, him will I also deny before my Father which is in heaven; but he that confesseth me before men, him will I confess before my Father which is in heaven." I relied implicitly on the Word of God as I understood it, and, therefore, when I should be able to do as it directed, I expected to be saved from all my sins and have eternal life.

I went home, not doubting that I was on the way to glory and to God. I craved the hour to arrive at which I could fulfill my vow. I went alone to the meeting that Sunday night. I sat in one end of the house, as far away from the altar of prayer as I could be. That circumstance, however, was accidental.

Lieutenant Bean, of my own regiment, preached. He was an influential man, and I was glad he was there. Still, I remember nothing about his text or sermon. A great conflict was going on in my mind. I was determined to go to the mourner's bench; yet it seemed almost impossible for me to do so in the presence of the officers.

CHAPTER XVI.

THE number of officers had increased each recurring evening, till at the meeting that I had determined to confess my desire to enlist in the Christian service, I think a dozen or more of them were present.

The preacher asked those who were willing to do so, to come to the altar. With much effort I rose and gradually advanced through the mass of people, till I reached the altar. The preacher extended his hand

and exclaimed (involuntarily, as it seemed to me) "Bless God!" Doubtless he was greatly surprised. I knelt there, placing my hands and my head on one of the seats. It was a real mourner's bench to me. I had gained the greatest victory I had ever gained. It required more effort and self-denial and courage for me to kneel at that altar of prayer than it had ever took for me to discharge any other duty or to meet any danger in my past life, even to fight a battle. All my shame seemed to be gone as I bowed down humbly there. I knew that I had done all that I could do. My will was broken.

My heart's desire was that the Lord in some way would bless me. Hedged in as I was, I could only wait on the Lord. I don't think I had moved my lips in prayer since late in the evening of my birthday. I did not move them at the altar. I had found that I received nothing for my words. I had no confidence in them. In my heart I said to the Lord that I had come to him for mercy and if he extened it I should be blessed; if not, I was helpless. My mind was fixed. I would seek him till death overtook me. I could only offer myself to him just as I was; sinful, ignorant, poor, starving for eternal life. Not even one tear could I shed. Not one thing could I do. I knew he had saved others, but I did not know how; else I'd see how to be saved myself. Just how God could save me from the penalty of my sins and be just in the act was an unsolved problem in my mind, and unsolvable so far as I could comprehend. However, I realized the fact that I had submitted my case to the proper court. I could only hope and wait. I had a degree of comfort in knowing all was known to God and that he had blessed others. I had distrusted self, as I thought, and venturing all on one I did not know, because there was no other chance. Eternal life

was in him or there was none. I had looked everywhere, tried everything. There was salvation in no other. I was submitting to the inevitable. I was almost reconciled to my doom.

Probably there were some persons there not fit to labor in the altar. Those or others may have instructed me. It made no difference whether they did or did not. I already knew all that they could tell me. Yet I did not object. Their words and sympathy and anxiety did me no harm; they did me no good. I had gone beyond human help or harm. I was perfectly indifferent to the opinion of others or their actions towards me. I had no idea that I should die soon, yet to live as I had lived all my life without life after this one was over and to continue to do so to the end was so unwelcome a prospect to me that I was indifferent on that point. I wanted the services to continue, but they closed early. I went to camp and to my bed somewhat in the attitude of one on trial after the case had been given to the jury, waiting in suspense.

I had fully believed heretofore that if I should be seen bowing in prayer to God I could not bear to look my comrades or anyone else in the face. But, to the contrary, I could then look at them with a more honest heart than I ever could before. If I could have proclaimed to the whole world the fact that I was in my right mind for the first time in my life in regard to my obligations to God and my own soul's interest, I would gladly have done so. I wanted them to know that I saw that I had been wrong; that I was seeking to turn to my Creator, to serve him as a righteous act; that I was acknowledging what I had been denying by action; that God had a right to demand my services and my affection; that I owed my creation and my preservation and all that I was then or ever hope to be to him;

that I had been an ungrateful sinner all my life; that I was now going to seek him and honor him till death, whether anyone else did or not, for I owed it to him and I craved to discharge my obligations so far as I could. I was so well accustomed to the realization of the fact I was in a lost condition that I was not alarmed. But when I went to bed that night I enjoyed a sense of pleasure in the confidence that I had found the road that would lead to the salvation of my soul. I rose the next morning in the same hopeful mood. At the meeting that night it was not a cross for me to kneel at the altar of prayer. It was just what I wished to do, and I had some expectation of receiving the desire of my heart, for I knew that I had done all that I could and I believed that the Lord was going to save me. He had saved others and he had said he would save those who looked to him. Yet it was incomprehensible, to me how he would or could do it. The meeting broke again and I had made no progress. I was hopeful however till afternoon the next day, the 14th.

Nothing else was on my mind but the pursuit of life eternal, except as my military duties claimed my attention, and that evening, returning from a business trip into the city, I considered the status of my case and found that the last duty that I could do had been done, and yet I was unsaved. To believe God's word would be to expect to be saved then, and yet it was not done. I was perfectly willing to continue to offer myself to the Lord at the altar of prayer and intended to do so as long as I should be permitted to.

But accepting the Lord as one of mercy and wisdom, I did not believe he would take pleasure in my starving for life if there was not something lacking. I could think of nothing unless it was that I might be one of the non-elect. If that was true, I was lost. I grew more and more

despondent. But while I was at the mourners' bench again on time that night, went there almost destitute of one ray of hope. Not believing that God would trifle with a needy sinner and that his Son had died to save such sinners and that I had come to his terms and was not yet saved, I was driven to the conclusion that I was not of the elect or that I had not been convicted and that I had been seeking the Lord from selfish motives and the Spirit of the Lord had not convicted me at all. How could I come to any other conclusion? But I determined to lay it all on the Lord. I saw that I had no more to lose; for I was already lost, and if I should be saved at all it would be a clear gain. I had needed salvation a long time and had looked for it with much pleasing anticipation, but at that time it seemed a real disappointment only was in store for me. And no more could I see any way for my escape from the doom of all unconverted men who die in their sinfulness than I could see how I could fly to the moon in an instant. Both seemed impossible to me. I was not noticing what went on around me, very much.

I think the meeting was encouraging, and I learned afterwards that John H. Parks, the soldier who escaped the Dick Davis massacre, professed faith that night. I could see that all was done that ever could be done for me, and that if I was not saved then I could never be saved.

As I could see no signs of mercy, whatever, in feeling, in hearing, in understanding, in shedding of tears, nor in hoping that at some future time my case would be better, I was driven to the only conclusion possible from the evidence before me: that there was no hope at all for me thenceforth and forever. I had no fear of physical death at that time, yet I felt my hope die within me as plainly as if my body was dying inch by inch. The last ray of hope at last departed. I am perfectly ignorant of the time that elapsed or of what transpired around me for a time. It might have been only one second. It may have been an hour. God knows.

The first real thing that I remember I was standing on my knees and the tears of real joy were roling down my cheeks and I was telling the Lord that he could save me. I was not speaking in a whisper either. At that moment I remember that Comrade Parks, who only a short time before had professed conversion, came to me and told me how to do; but I had already believed in Jesus. I also remember that Patent House, a very bad boy soldier who professed that night or previously, came to me and tried to help me, and at that moment I had but little confidence in him, yet I cared nothing about that. It seems curious that at that interesting moment I should consider one's honesty, but I did so, and left the matter to the Lord. He did me no good nor no harm. I was very happy. A man who had never seen any terrestial object before, to be permitted to behold with his eyes the physical objects we see, would be no more enlightened thereby than I was enlightened at seeing with my heart or with my soul how God could be just and still save me. I saw that it was simply because Jesus had died for my sins and had risen for my justification that God was willing to save me. He had said so. He was able to save me. He had saved others. I was needing to be saved and was willing to be saved. I was happy because I saw that I certainly would be saved. God was able and willing and I was willing and my salvation was a certainty, unless there was a stronger or wiser one than the God of heaven. Of course, I had not fear of that.

I was surprised that I had not understood the plain terms of salvation sooner. I had done many things that I ought to have done in my searchings for life, and many useless things. But the one thing and the only thing that I needed to do to be saved as a penitent sinner I had not done: that was to believe in the Lord Jesus Christ. I found that with the heart one believes unto righteousness: that the affections and the will acquiese with the understanding, or rather leads the understanding. Distrusting my own efforts of every kind, realizing that there was absolutely no hope at all in me or man, God led me to look to him to hope against hope; to try where I almost knew there was no use, for there was no other way.

I saw it plainly that night—just forty-one years ago. I have not forgotten it, nor have I been able to improve on the knowledge of the way of salvation one whit since.

I think now that I should have been saved at one o'clock, July 15, 1864, for I then believed in the word of God and true Christianity; but the mass of superstition or rerror that I had contracted kept me from the whole truth those seven months.

While I was very happy for the spiritual knowledge imparted to me by the Holy Spirit, showing me beyond the shadow of a doubt that God could and would save me, yet I did not think I was saved. If I had known that I was saved I do not think my ecstacy would have been greater; for I saw that it would certainly come to pass. While I was looking for the word to be spoken in my ears or my eyes to see Jesus or some other sign to be given me, assuring me that I possessed eternal life and had religion and was already a child of God, the meeting came to a close.

I saw two men near me of my own company, who I did not know were at the meeting, and both of them I took to be

Christians—Lewis Stricklin, a Baptist, and A. J. Sisk, a Methodist. I feared that they would say something to me, as they were my friends, and, of course, they wished me well; but I still preferred to deal directly with my Redeemer without any prompter or instructer, especially as I felt positive that it would not be long till the Lord would present me with such a revelation of his regenerating love and power and glory that I would never be like the Christians who can only say, "I hope I have been converted."

I really thought that when God converted a person, that person was given physical evidences of the fact through the organs of sense; that he saw Jesus Christ as Paul did, or that he heard the voice of Jesus saying, "Your sins are forgiven," or, "You are a child of God," or he would see a great light; or be made to shout loud and long in spite of himself, so that he would know that he was a Christian without having to merely hope that he was one.

I was looking steadfastly for something similar and no one in this world at that time could have made me believe that I should not receive such manifestations of my acceptance with God at my real conversion.

Crowding through the people I reached the door, and, instead of going to the road eastward that came into a street that went south and west to our barracks, I went down the bayou along a little path, alone, nearly south to my place of sleeping. I was so delighted with the Lord's way of saving sinners and the surety of my own salvation soon, that it was with much effort that I could restrain myself from shouting aloud every breath, "Reconciled to God! Reconciled to God." I would chide myself for my presumption in wanting to hollow for joy before I had anything to shout about. I actually had to

use my hands to keep the exclamations of delight from rolling off my tongue. It was my good fortune to meet no one as I went down that unused path, and when I came near my barracks all was in repose so I was not found out.

I was so sure that God was going to save me soon that I did not lie down till midnight or later, and, when I did at last, I merely dreamed or thought over the great things the Lord was doing for me, and the things that he WOULD do for me. I did not lie long. I rose and looked for the manifestation, whatever it would be, which accompanies conversion, and rejoiced at my good fortune; for there was not one doubt that I should soon be saved forever.

The day passed and the night found me at the meeting again. I had not said a word to anyone, neither had anyone spoken to me on the subject of the meeting or my interest in it. My exceeding joy was not known to any but myself. But when someone started a good spiritual song that night the people came near finding that I was happy, because I almost rose and shouted praises to God before I was aware of it.

Just then I discovered that I was about to do something that would be deceitful and sacreligious, as it was not reasonable nor rational for persons to give glory to God before they were converted. With much difficulty I kept my mouth closed and my body pressed to the seat; though my joy was so great that it seemed that I must praise God for what he was going to do for me.

The anxious seat was presented, I went and bowed there, the happiest man, in all probability, that ever knelt at a mourner's bench. I remained in exactly the same delightful mood all that night and next day. I saw that God would save me certainly, as viewed from the standpoint of logic, philosophy, scripture and experience. I never in all my life had any possession or privilege or prospect that could be compared in value or dearness by me to the blessings the Lord was bestowing on me. Yet I had not even once thought of having been saved already.

On returning from the city where my military duty called me, the next evening, in company with Comrade Stricklin, he, in a very cautious and kind way, ventured to suggest to me that in his opinion I had enjoyed the new birth already and that I would not enjoy any other than what I had experienced previously. I was astonished from the depths of my soul. I had known him, from the time I was ten years old, as an orderly church member and a friend of my family and a special friend of mine for nearly three years just past, and I could not believe him willing to deceive me; yet I turned to him and said, "You may deceive others but you cannot deceive me." He said no more, and I soon turned away.

I was at the meeting again that night and was still happy; but, during the services, while at the altar of prayer, I realized that my hope was declining. Despondency was creeping on me. I knew that all the joys I had felt were real and my views were correct concerning Christ and his salvation, but after being so near the Savior for nearly forty-eight hours, he seemed to be going away from me without giving me eternal life. I had not seen Jesus with my eyes, nor heard him with my ears speak to me. Nor had I seen a great light, nor had any other unmistakable token of his pardon appeared that I thought all Christians had and that I would certainly have if ever I was truly converted.

I considered the strange things that had come to me since my birthday the 8th inst, and even since I had been coming to the altar of prayer, and how very nearly Jesus came to me, yet I thought I had made a mistake somewhere and gone the wrong way.

I grew more and more sorry and mournful, till the next morning I wended my way to Chaplain's tent, one mile away, where I told him meekly of my desires and my efforts, and how I came so near being converted, and how much I wished I could have been; but that all my prospects had flown, and that I could not go on nor get back to the place where I was a month ago, so that I could start right, as I believed that I had gone wrong some way and I needed help awfully bad; and that I had come to him to help me if he could. I told him that I had never before conversed with anyone on my condition, as I wished to be very cautious in my future life, to make no mistakes, and that I saw it was much easier to go wrong or to be lead wrong than right. In a meek manner he advised me to go to the meetings as usual, and, instead of going to the altar of prayer, engage in singing and to speak to the seekers some word that I knew was in the Scriptures. He said that he believed I would get light as to my duties. I do not think that he hinted that I was a Christian; for I did not give him time to do so if he had intended such a thing. I was so surprised and hurt at what I thought to be so dangerous instruction from one whom we honored as a sincere, Godly man; one who seemed to think it the greatest misfortune that could befall a human being to miss heaven that I rose and hurried back to my barracks.

The chaplain was an humble but not an educated man. He enlisted as a private soldier and we elected him as chaplain rather than one who would not enlist unless he could be chaplain. He was sent home on furlough and was ordained as a minister by the authorities in the Cumberland Presbyterian church. We did not regret it ever afterwards. He did what he could to help us all during our three-years army service.

I was growing more disconsolate all the time. If I had known anything else to do I should not have gone to church that night. When the altar was presented I felt that I had gone wrong some way and that I could not go on till the wrong had been corrected. I sat away back, out of the way of others, for quite a number of persons—some of my own company—were professing conversion. It was my own condition that I wanted to improve. I was trying some way to get back where I was fifteen days ago so I could pray and seek the Lord; for I could not make any progress nor think of anything but my wrong move in some way just before I was about to be saved.

I sat there in silence and distress till the meeting had been dismissed and all were gone, save twenty or thirty in a circle around five or six seekers who wanted to remain longer. The lights were out except the light in the little circle. After a while I moved quietly up to the ring and peeped over to see who was there. Very near my feet I heard one prayer from the lips of one whose voice I recognized as W. R. Baker, of my own company. I wished I could aid him and the words of the chaplain, which I had spurned that morning, came to me—to speak to some inquirer some word of truth. Of course, I had no idea of committing such an error as that. However, I stood there in the rear of all those on that side of the circle. Perhaps no one had noticed me.

I did not know why the chaplain said that. I knew that I was doing no good. I thought it might be that he knew what was best. If I told the man the truth it surely would not hurt him. No one would know it but me and my Maker, and God understood my honesty of purpose. I quietly bent down and meekly told my comrade to trust in the Lord. I felt that it was presumption to do so and was suffering for it, when Baker rose and, with much delight, said he had trusted in Jesus and was saved by His blood. He went all round and talked so intelligently and looked so bright and happy that I could not stay there, but went back to the darkest corner and sat mourning over my pitiable condition, growing worse at each move I made. I thought Baker had recognized my voice and that he knew that I was not fit to tell him what to do and that I was a ruined man. I did not let anyone see me.

The next morning I went to the chaplain as soon as I could and told him that I had done what he said to do, and that I should not have done it; that no one not a Christian was fit to instruct seekers. It would soon be known to all my friends that I had acted hypocritical in so serious a matter. I knew that God understood my desire, but Baker would not know my heart. I asked him to help me some way to get out of my troubles which he led me into. I supposed he would be sorry that he had given me such instruction as he had, and would do all he could to correct matters. Instead of doing so, however, he seemed to me to be glad of his words to me and to enjoy my predicament. He actually bade me to do the same thing the next night, and he said that I would certainly get light from the Lord. Those words confirmed my late suspicion that our chaplain was either a very ignorant man, else his love for our immortal souls was very shallow. I determined to have no more conversations with him.

I had lost almost every particle of hope of finding Jesus, my Savior, and was trying to undo my mistakes and then get away back to the place where I had lost the true way and start after the life I so much needed where I left it. At the meeting the next night, the 18th, having grown more hopeless, I sat back—not because I objected to the mourner's bench, but because I thought I had scandalized every seeker there by my mistakes.

The meetings closed and about the same number of seekers and workers remained as the night before. I drew silently up to the circle and heard the voice of S. S. Hampton, another of my company, exactly where Baker was the night previous. The caplain's words came to me, and, in my despair, I stooped and said to him, "Believe in the Lord Jesus Christ and thou shalt be saved." Money could not have influenced me to do what I did. Desperation drove me to do what seemed to me to be wrong, because the preacher who ought to know had told me to do so and I knew nothing else to do.

Well, Hampton soon rose and in his simple but honest way rejoiced in the Savior's love. I had no doubt that he, too, as really converted. While I was glad for him or anyone else to be happy in the Savior's love, his profession served to render me miserable. The idea of my talking to two men, both of whom doubtless recognized my voice and who had later found the Savior and knew that I was what everyone would term a hypocrite, made me so ashamed of my conduct that I despaired of ever finding the way of salvation at all.

I decided to say no more about the matter to anyone, and let the Lord do just as he pleased with me; but that I would do right all my life and die craving eternal life and the fellowship of the Lord.

Then the question of Abraham came to my mind: "Shall not the Judge of all the earth do right?" I answered, "Yes; and

I'll trust him henceforward to lead and guide me, regardless of consequences, for I belong to him and he has the right to do as he pleases with me. I'll do what he says in the Bible to do, and risk it all in his hands, for I can do no better."

Immediately I began to feel relief, as having cast all my care on Jesus. 1 Pet. 3:7. I grew more and more satisfied to rest and wait, as it was all resting in the hands of Jesus. The conviction that the Lord would do right, and that he was merciful and could save me, and be just, as I had seen, suited my needy condition exactly, and I have loved that great truth to this day.

I gradually became willing to believe that I was a Christian. Only it seemed to me that all the Christians I ever heard of had seen Jesus or heard his voice or had seen angels or had seen lights, or had received indisputable evidence through one or more of the natural avenues of knowledge or organs of sense, that they might know beyond the possibility of a doubt that they were true Christians. Only for that one deficiency in my experience I would be very happy. I saw how God could save any penitent sinner and be just. I loved that way. It was exactly what all sinners needed. I never had known anything else worth living for but the religion of Jesus. I loved him and the race of mankind for whom he died. I loved his word and his service, and longed to love them more and more.

I knew that the great change from darkness to light came to me at the anxious seat, the third time I went there, on the 14th of the month. But it seemed that the one thing that I must have was a certain kind of Christian experience, such as I had not had to that time nor to the present day. My mistake grew out of my inability to understand persons relating the leadings of the Lord in their cases.

They were measuring heavenly things by earthly things and Christians could comprehend them, but I did not know that the "Natural man receiveth not the things of the Spirit of God: for they are foolishness unto him: neither can he know them, because they are spiritually discerned." 1 Cor. 2:14. And I had failed to comprehend the words of Jesus to Nicodemus, in John 3:3, "Except a man be born again he cannot see the kingdom of God." I really supposed that I knew about those things in my imagination as well as many Christians. In that, however, I was completely deceived. I had it all wrong. Every particle of all my spiritual experience, from the day I turned from sin to this day, were the exact opposites of what I had conceived as an unconverted man.

I gradually gained light for three months, when I was fully established. Yet it was not all peace along the way. But reading and praying and doubting and rejoicing, I grew in grace and in the knowledge of the Lord and Savior Jesus Christ. After I began to indulge a hope that what I had already received might prove to include regeneration, notwithstanding I had not experienced the evidences of it that I had expected to experience, I had three successive conflicts of unexpected natures and of awful severity.

The first was a return of my atheistic fears. There was no use to read; I had done that before. All the reasons and fair arguments were on the side of Revelation. My mind was convinced; but there was fear, it seemed, that all the things that the Christian possessed and all that he hoped for, in some way might be a myth. That nearly all the people on the earth we knew were wrong. Might we not be? Was positive knowledge possible?

Those soul-sickening suggestions had been away from my heart for more than eight months, and I never expected to entertain one of them again after I saw their lying nature at that time. I was helpless. I could not drive them away. It did not satisfy me that I could defeat the assertions of disbelievers in divine revelation. I realized that there was so much that I did not know and so little that I did know, that I wondered whether I knew anything.

But in due time the Lord came to me and lifted me out of my despondency and sorrow, and I was very thankful to him. I was happy awhile.

Then the query came into my mind, whether Jesus was the Immanuel. We had read of twenty-four false Christs. Could one come into the world without an earthly father? I read the book of Isaiah through without finding the prophecies relating to his coming, which had helped to enlighten me several months ago. I was so depressed that I overlooked them. I did not think of the mystery that pertains to all life, and that we could no more understand the mystery of natural conception than spiritual conception.

The Lord, by his Holy Spirit, enlightened my heart again, and I could see that there was one that could solve difficulties that man need not undertake. The last assault that was made on my delightful advancement in Christian growth and knowledge was that the doctrine of the resurrection of the body was an impossibility, and was, therefore, an absurdity of superstitious origin.

I had, at the first time of beholding the dead bodies of soldiers decaying before they were buried, declared that they could not be raised as Christians expected. And now the unreasonableness of that central and important tenet of the Christian system came forth, clothed in its seeming impervious panoply, fairly laughing at my weakness and terror, while I trembled, as it were, for the safety of the religion which was dearer to me than life itself, and all other things I had ever known.

But before despair had broken my heart, light came, and I could believe that one who could form the intricate material of the human body according to a law of his

have met and conquered those foes. I could not risk what was so dear to me on mere tradition or supposition. It was not enough for me to merely think I was right; I must know that I was right. I could afford to be mistaken about unim-

W. S. BLACKMAN,

As he appeared during time of Civil War.

own devising, could disintegrate that body by his own chemical agents and build it again at the time and in the way that he pleased to do so.

The Lord sent his Spirit and gave me the victory each time, else I could never

portant matters. If I paid all the property and money I had for a home, and, after it was too late, I found the property belonged to other parties, it would be unfortunate; or, if I find myself drowning, beyond any power to save myself, it would be more deplorable. But, if my religion be a fraud, then all is lost.

The Bible was the only book, comparatively speaking, in the world; and the Christian religion the only possession, comparatively speaking, known to men, in my estimation—hence my absorbing interest in them.

When joy sat enthroned in my heart as a permanent possession, after the victory over those great foes, I realized that I was truly converted to the true religion of Jesus Christ, and that it was just what I needed for this world and for the next.

I thought, at that morning when peace filled my heart, that if any other one had been so often led wrong and had been so ignorant and so severely attacked by the devil as I had been, he would never have escaped. I thought that my escape from those terrible influences were accidents that would not happen again in a century, perhaps never.

At that moment the thought came to me that it was the Lord who had been with me and permitted me to be tried as in the fire. And that he had said, "My grace is sufficient for you, and you shall not be tempted above that you are able to bear." I then understood that the Lord had been near me and was my friend. And I have found it so ever since that time, forty-one years ago.

During my investigations as to the possibility of conversion without external signs, I read to great profit several books, among which were "The Anxious Inquirer," Dodrige's "Rise and Progress of Religion in the Soul," "Theory of Conversion," all of which were very helpful to me, and I thank the Lord of glory for enabling the authors to publish them. They aided me to look at the Scriptures in a clear way, and I could see the reasonableness of the true way and rejoiced in it.

Later on I could enjoy the services of Christians everywhere I met them, whether I met them at the churches or at the Christian Commission.

Almost as soon as I was established I bought T. Scott's "Commentary on the Bible," T. Dick's complete works and Josephus's complete works, and various other books, as I craved to know how I might grow in knowledge, so as to be more useful to my fellow men, though I could not believe that I could ever preach.

CHAPTER XVII.

EARLY in April, with deep sorrow, our men heard of the loss of two hundred members of the Fifty-sixth regiment, Illinois infantry. The tragedy did not occur in a battle. This narrator does not intend to note battles, except as they affected The Boy of Battle Ford directly or remotely. But this sad event was so unlooked-for and so pathetic that I'll venture to record it.

On the 31st day of March, 1865, the steamship "General Lion," carrying twelve officers and 193 soldiers of said regiment, whose terms had expired several months previous, while the Fifty-sixth was with Sherman as he marched to the sea, were started home as soon as the coast was near, so they could ship to Washington city and take the cars for their homes.

The other members of the regiment reenlisted and did not come home at that time. There were hundreds of others on the ship at the same time.

When the ship reached Cape Hatteras a fearful storm was raging, the ship riding on the crest of a very tall wave one minute and sinking low between two waves the next minute. A large tank of oil on the top was loosened from its fastenings somewhat and leaked its contents on the deck until the oil found its way down to the furnace, when an explosion occurred.

Several of the soldiers nearest the deck succeeded in climbing out, but only five of the 205 of the Fifty-sixth survived the fire and the flood. Those who did not get to the deck were burned to death in the ship. Many of the lost had relatives in our regiment, which caused additional sorrow here.

The five who were saved were Martin H. Ozmeet, Williamson county; Isaac N. Willhite, Franklin county; Michael Brockett, of White county; George W. Williams of Gallatin county, and Jasper Gerald, of Saline county. The last two named are dead; The other three are yet living. The experiences of the five men were wonderful to relate. They were in the cold salt water from three to six hours. Passing vessels picked them up and resuscitated them.

Captain William E. Weber, of Galatia; Josiah Joiner, his first lieutenant, and thirty-nine men of his company, were destroyed on the ill-fated vessel. In battles, with a uniformed enemy, to lose one's life is not out of the ordinary; but to die, as did those brave men, without any chance for their lives, after defending the old flag for three years and more, is pathetic indeed. But they are not forgotten by a loyal people.

I shall digress now to give a short statement in regard to the life of William Fitzgerald, the member of Company G, who professed religion in the brick mill while I was in the story above him and whose profession started me in search again of life eternal. He had firmly believed in Christianity from his childhood. I heard that his parents were religious people, and he had no doubts of the reality of their regeneration. His great delight was in shooting at matches and fiddling for balls, called frolics then. In those exercises he earned money which he very much needed, for he was a very poor man, with a dependent family. He indulged a hope that some

time he would be saved, but, of course, he was by no means sure of it.

As noted in a previous page, he was seeking the Lord when his comrades had not the remotest idea of it. When he was converted he knew what he wanted to do. He wanted to be baptized, but not by someone who was not clothed with proper authority to baptize him. So he was content to wait until he came home. He read all he could while he stayed in the army, and attended the services in the city and elsewhere. He was a very happy Christian, not once wanting again the worldly pleasures he had tested so many years.

When he returned to his home, northwest of Stonefort, he offered himself to the Baptist church nearby as a candidate for baptism and church membership. He was baptized by the pastor and began to talk and lead in prayer in the meetings. He said he had served the devil all his life to that time; but he wanted to honor and serve the Lord, who had saved him, the rest of his life. His acquaintances had perfect confidence in his conversion, and he began to preach to them. His influence was so great and his zeal so intense that the church soon called him to ordination. Though he could barely read, he was sound in the gospel faith and safe in leadership, as far as he was willing to go. The presbytery, at the will of the church, laid hands on him and solemnly set him apart to the work of the ministry. He was so poor and was so unlearned that if he ever went to an association or other large religious gathering I never heard of it. But among the neglected and poor he was a useful power. He preferred to preach in the summer time in the woods, and many have been the conversions, true and lasting, at his meeting in some wood on the Big Saline.

He would serve as pastor for little, weak and backwoods churches when he could do so, and what the people contributed for his labors satisfied him. I have never been able to learn the actual number of professions under his ministry, but they must have been one hundred or two hundred.

Perhaps, since the apostolic times, no one ever did labor more unselfishly than he. He resorted to no clap-trap methods of securing professions, but preached that sinners should repent and believe the gospel. He did not try to generate the force to carry men to Christ, but prayed to God for grace and wisdom and power to lead sinners to him. He believed it to be his duty to preach and pray, and the Lord's pleasure to save believers. I suppose he baptized as many as he led to the Savior. He died in the early part of the year 1875, just about ten years after he made profession of the Christian religion.

He was converted, five days before I was, in the same city; both belonged to the same regiment; both lived in the same region, and both became 'Baptists. But he began his public ministrations, completed his work, and went home to glory before I had fairly started. I was as honest and steadfast as he, but I was fearful, doubtful and inquiring; while he was trustful, zealous and venturesome. He was a sinner saved by grace who will shine as the brightness of the firmament forever and ever.

"For ye see your calling, brethren, how that not many wise men after the flesh, not many mighty, not many noble, are called: But God hath chosen the foolish things of the world to confound the wise; and God hath chosen the weak things of the world to confound the things that are mighty; and base things of the world, and things which are despised, hath God chosen, yea, and things which are not, to bring to nought things that are: that no flesh should glory in his presence."

I am exceedingly happy to realize that God shall also call me from labor to rest with him and all the saved when life and its labors are over. There will be no more temporal nor spiritual soldiering there.

At 4 o'clock, a. m. April 27, 1865, I was awakened by the cries of soldiers who had been thrown out of the boat and were helplessly floating down the cold stream and in imment danger of drowning or chilling to death. The most pitiable cries that ever reached my ears came from those perishing men. They were returning to their homes from rebel prisons when the awful tragedy occurred.

About noon of the 25th the "Sultana," an antiquated steamboat of large size, landed at the wharf of the city of Memphis and remained there till 10 o'clock at night. At Vicksburg, Mississippi, the vessel had been condemned unseaworthy. Yet the precious lives of 2,150 were committed to its capability to transport them safely to the Northern states. Fully five-sixths of the number were persons who had just been released from Southern prisons and had been exchanged and brought to Vicksburg to be sent to their homes to be treated and fed, in order that at least some of them might be restored to health and many of them saved from death.

It was said that 350 citizens were on the boat coming north as refugees, of all ages. Through the heartlessness of transportation officers, the boat, though old and condemned, was crowded to its utmost capacity. There should have been not more than 1,000 well soldiers put on the boat at one time if it had been sound. But to put 350 citizens, mostly women and children, and 1,800 men, just out of nasty, wet and sickly prisons, aboard one boat, and it an old condemned one at that, was not only foolish and criminal, but was murder, demanding the penalty of death on the guilty officials. Yet we suppose no one was punished for the awful crime. There were so many great questions occupying the public mind at that time and soon afterwards, and it was so difficult to establish guilt under such circumstances, that if there was anyone punished for the awful calamity I never knew it.

I cannot account for the failure of the army officers at Memphis to at least clothe the poor men, for they were in tatters and strings; and were going in the direction of cooler atmosphere.

The boat left the wharf and plowed her way through the swift current of the overflowed Mississippi for twelve miles, till it struck an island submerged below the surface of the waters. The boiler exploded, blowing ofl the top part of the boat and the sides away, with most of the thousands of human beings that were on it. The hull then took fire and burned to the water's edge. Not one escaped except those who some way reached the banks or trees or were taken out next morning after floating twelve miles.

I rose and quickly aroused those near me and we hurried to the landing, nearly one-half mile below, and in all ways possible aided the poor men. All was confusion in the darkness. But we were soon in possession of the fact that a boat had burned, for when we arrived at the wharf we could plainly see an object burning, up the river, that seemed round, and about as large as a large hogshead. It was still fast on the island. We supposed it to be the "Sultana." It was yet dark, but began to dawn immediately. Water craft of every available character were busy doing what they could to save some, and in most instances were successful; but were, in a few instances that I witnessed, the immediate cause of the loss of the person they were trying to save.

One man, whom I could not see, just as I arrived called out to us to help hm, not more than fifteen feet from the bank; but at the next instant a wheel of a vessel was put in motion and the voice was heard no more. He could call but faintly. No one could see him and the boats were so thick that we dared not go out in search of him in perfect darkness at that moment.

I think one hundred or more floated the twelve miles. A few were overtaken one or two miles below, after it became light, and were saved. They could float, but could not reach land. One of those reached and saved was a woman with a child in her arms. When the boat was blown to pieces she was standing, with her babe in her arms, in some part of it. In some way the explosion did not kill her, but threw her far out into the river. As was the fashion then, everywhere, the woman wore hoopskirts. As she alighted in the water, feet foremost, enough air gathered under the skirts to hold her up while she floated fourteen miles. When her rescuers found her she was down in the water to her neck and clinging with a deadly grip to her lifeless child. The air was still confined there, forming an effectual buoy that held her from certain death.

Boats soon began to ascend each bank of the river, and men were gathered from the trees or high banks till all that ever was found were recovered, except those who were fortunate in finding a way out to a friendly house, which, in a few instances, was the case.

When the sun was two or three hours high, I remember seeing one man in a tree opposite the landing, over on the Arkansas side. He rested there contentedly till parties from the Tennessee side went over and brought him across.

Mrs. J. W. Mullinax, of Vienna, this state, is the only person I have ever met who told me of sustaining a family loss in that accident. Her brother, a soldier from Tennessee, was on the boat, and was anxiously looking to the arrival home to his family and friends, when he was blown to his death; as was reported by one who escaped from his side, where both were stationed on the top of the boat at the awful moment of the explosion.

Scott Prindle of Benton, Illinois, with whom I am personally acquainted, is the only one among those who escaped I have met, that I am aware of, since the day of the rescue. He says that in the efforts to save themselves the men hung to one another and that large numbers went down together. A stage was thrown into the water at the time of the explosion and a number was on it, but many more struggled to surmount it, and, despite the effort of those on it, the men at last turned it over and all went down. He says that he stayed on the burning boat till all but one had gone. Not having been thrown off, he waited till the water had swallowed up or carried away every one that had been thrown in or had plunged in. When he could remain there no longer, to escape the fire, he plunged in and swam to the Arkansas shore and hastened down the river, and climbed a tree opposite the city. Perhaps it was he whom I saw there.

The Christian Commission and soldiers and citizens did all in their power to revive the exhausted and chilled ones and save those in their reach. Yet a few died, after bravely fighting the chilly waves for four hours or more, in spite of all that could be done. For it was in addition to months of starvation and exposure to all sorts of weather in a sickly climate that those brave men were called upon suddenly to engage in a life and death conflict.

The prisoners were nearly all from Indiana, Ohio and Kentucky. My diary, written at that time, recorded 1,500 lost in all. Mr. Prindle, whom I visited lately in the interest of the truth, says of the catastrophe, that 1,550 were lost and that 600 were saved. I hope that the report that he and I remember—that 600 were saved—was correct; yet I never had evidence that the number of the saved was half so many.

If anyone should read these notes and want to inquire further of the terrible catastrophe that befell the "Sultana" and her precious load, he may address Mr. Scott Prindle at Benton, Illinois. He is in fair health and good mind, but is a worn-out man, having labored as a miller all his life, till too much worn out to work at all now. He has a splendid grown-up family, of which he is justly proud. Other incidents relative to the disaster could be related, interesting enough of the escape or the loss of individuals; but the tragedy was so fearful and irreparable that I'll drop the curtain here.

CHAPTER XVIII.

IT was early in May that I came to understand that I was already a true Christian. Four more months elapsed before my regiment was discharged and sent home. The great war was practically over. There was enough to do to keep all of us busy, in the service of the government, in and around the city. Those wishing to do so could have the benefits of the ministrations of various churches and other religious services. Also the library of the Christian Commission was for all of us. I had the best opportunity to grow in grace and the knowledge of the truth during that four months that I have had during any other four months since that time. I attended church every time I could and read and learned from day to day. It seemed as if I was in a new world. I had something to live for. I was full of peace and purpose. I did not have one-half day's gloom in the four months.

The captain and I had not been particular friends till I took the orderly sergeant's place after he was killed. Then we began to get acquainted. We grew in friendship ever afterwards. He was a surly looking man and was generally regarded as such a man. But if one found him out he found a man of good principle and of much general knowledge. During those months we were often mutually blessed by conversing together on religious subjects and other departments of knowledge pertaining to man—his origin, his environments, his opportunities, his obligations and his destiny.

The summer months were very wet and warm. Much chills and fever were engendered by them. I had several light attacks of them. James Dunning, an old man, educated as an old time cook and a practical nurse, took special care of me, and not even once did he fail to find what he thought I ought to have. He would set before me new Irish potatoes, so delicious and so nutricious that even my mother, my wife nor any other of God's creation during the forty years gone by since that time, has been able to equal them. Poor old Jim! He died nearly thirty years ago; yet I remember his kindness to me. The principle of love written on the tablet of my heart by his acts of consideration remain there to this very hour and shall remain there till I die. Only one of my company died that summer, however. That was George Clark, who had served his country well. Many of the convalescents were discharged and sent home through the summer as a matter of mercy to the men and economy to the government. Army after army of the enemy were captured or willingly surrendered, and the reconstruction period generated questions of immeasurable moment.

Lincoln, the great president, had been assassinated, and Andrew Johnson was at the head of the nation. I read only enough of secular news to keep along as a citizen and enjoy my new life and its privileges and its possibilities from day to day.

During the month of August the men became impatient at not being sent home, as the war was over and the heat was terrible. We were mustered out and took the steamboat "Superior" for Cairo at seven o'clock, September 4, 1865. Some of the men declared they would not risk boats nor cars again as they had escaped that far they would walk home to make sure of their safe arrival there. The last week was a very busy one for me, as the captain was sick and there were a great many rolls and reports to make out.

We were very glad to leave the "Sunny South," but our gladness was tempered with the pathetic reflection that we were leaving many that went there with us three years before. At Camp Butler, a few days later, our colonel had us in line, where we stood in dress parade three years previous, and raised his hand and uttered those words: "Men, go home and make as good citizens as you have soldiers. Farewell!"

On September 14, the train came for us at 4 p. m. All were hurrying to board it. James H. Dallas and Gilbert Clark were very low with fever. As we were all citizens then, without an officer, I said that I would never go home till the two sick men went, either dead or alive. The other men said we will all go. At that the beds of the sick men were carried to the train and the men on them. Tender care was bestowed on them night and day till they were with their friends at home. Dallas recovered after many weeks, but Clark died after being with his family several days. We were very sorry to hear of his death. He was a good boy and a splendid soldier.

We were met by friends at Carbondale, and arrived at our homes on the 16th, nearly three years and one month from our departure. It was noon and Lieutenant A. O. Hill, Comrade D. L. Riley and James Dunning took dinner with our family.

My dear mother was the happiest of all

friends, near and far. I was still suffering from chills which I contracted at Memphis and which continued their hold on me. My visitors, doubtless, expected me to tell war incidents, but it seemed to me that I could not be satisfied to dwell on any sub-

MRS. MARGARET HARRIS,

Mother of The Boy of Battle Ford, who died at the
age of 83 years and 7 months.

of us, I think, as she had witnessed the safe return of the last of the three who went from under her roof in the interest of the preservation of the union.

We were visited from day to day by

ject except the subject of the Christian religion. I visited my brother one night in each week and some one of the neighbors one night and remained with my mother the remainder of the time. My mother and I visited Stephen Pankey's family, our particular friends the 20th and spent the day.

On Saturday, the 23rd, the family, including Jo Harris (step-brother) and myself, attended the church service and we offered ourselves for membership. I had been so much engaged in the pursuit of religious knowledge, and the enjoyment of religious duties, that I had not paid much attention to the ceremonies required, as I knew that they were not vital to one's salvation and that I had been handicapped by being a soldier to some extent. However, I regarded the true and proper way to follow the Lord in the ordinances and in the particular church relationship that he approved, to be no light matter. And I thought I should never take one step in the direction of those ceremonials till I found a perfect Scriptural way.

I saw the consistency of immersion with the command to baptize, to my satisfaction. But I did not understand the communion question. However I could not see how I could arrive at any other conclusion than that what is commonly called open communion was the way to please Jesus, its author. At least, I wished it might turn out that way, for I wanted all the converted ones in the world to enjoy every privilege that could aid them in honoring the Lord of Glory.

Indeed I had taken the bread and wine very reverently at one of the meetings at Chelsea, when they called it the Lord's supper. I did not know how to refuse, being a pupil in the school of the Redeemer. But I had very serious doubts of the validity of baptism administered by Tom, Dick and Harry there. So I was not persuaded to be baptized till it could be done by one whose actions were recognized by the most active missionary churches holding the tenents of real conversion, and

one at least that was regarded as a branch of the Lord's own church.

I had no idea that I could learn what I must know as an honest follower of the Lord on those disputed points in many months, and, as it was plainly my duty to be baptized, I fell on the following plan: as all the missionary Christians called the Baptist churches branches of the church and as their baptisms were received as perfectly legal by them, if I was baptized in a Baptist church and changed my mind I could easily transfer my membership; while if I was to receive baptism at the hands of one who did not believe in immersion or had not been immersed himself, I could not be regarded as baptized by Baptists, neither could I be well satisfied with my own baptism, seeing that some of the churches were wrong and that wrong might invalidate the ordinance as respected my own baptism so far as I could know. Hence, the only safe way was to receive baptism by the authority of the Baptists, or delay the performance of the duty till I might be able to ascertain of a truth the exact way the Scriptures taught.

When the little body commenced to sing and I recalled their faithfulness and patience and their prayers, I decided to offer myself for membership that very day, as it was a perfectly safe step to take. After preaching and at the beginning of business I invited Joe to accompany me to the pastor and we presented ourselves as applicants for membership. Neither of us said much. But the answers to the questions asked us by those desiring to do so were considered satisfactory and we were unanimously elected to membership after baptism. It had never occurred to me that our acquaintances had confidence in us, as we were converted in the army. But when we were receiving the hand of Christian fellowship I was surprised to hear Mrs. Millie Barker, in shouts of praise to God, say that he had saved the lives of the boys through the war and had made them soldiers of the Lord.

It was a great cross to me to sit among the old church members, and I could not afford to sit back where I sat in the years gone by. I thought all eyes were on me. So I carefully secured a seat about the line between the two classes.

I opened my school at the New Salem school house on the 16th of October, just thirty days after my return home.

On the 5th day of November we were baptized. It was a cold day for the time of year. My blood was thin and I was yet in very poor health. After services at old Liberty church, the congregation rode four miles, facing the northwest wind, to the Bankston creek. I did not follow the example of those baptized in my presence previously. I would have nothing around my waist or on my head. I had never seen a time when I felt less like going into the water. But we were buried beneath the water and raised out of it again, as Christ commanded, for we could not afford to do less.

It had been eight months and twenty-two days, or, strictly speaking, 264 days since I had believed with the heart unto righteousness. I did not look for any miraculous display at my baptism and I realized none. I had by that time understood many things that were very dark to me as an alien from God and as a stranger to grace. I knew that pardon of sins had no more connection with baptism than burying the dead had to do with killing the body of the person to be buried. I had obeyed Christ, that's all.

The school was then on my heart. Many of the students were without religious examples, and, as I found to my sorrow before long, there were heads of families as much concerned to break up my school,

though in an undermining way, as I was to succeed. The great question with me was what to do in certain events. I was not afraid of every enemy of the school, if it were right for me to clean them out at any cost. I had started on the new and glorious way and wanted to be a blessing to old and young. But the opposing element did not want enlightenment. They wanted to have the name of tearing up the school. It had been so for four years past and continued so there for thirty years onward. The element causing the trouble was small but inverterate.

Eternity alone will tell the damage sustained by the meanness of one man and those under his influence. I believe that I had one thousand times more love for his own children really than he had. I thought till then that all people had a desire to see all others do well. I never forgot what I learned there of the depravity of the unregenerated heart.

While I worked very earnestly all that winter—the last two monts at the Bankston school—for the directors came for me the same day, I engaged for four months at the first school. I was trying to decide what to do in a secular way as a useful Christian, during my stewardship in this world. By spending what money and property I could command, and work at intervals, I could graduate in Shurtleff college and move in the higher walks of society. Otherwise I could content myself to teach in the country schools and improve from year to year and open my farm and put all my energies forth among my own people, where scarcely any of them could much appreciate my endeavors.

I loved to labor and improve my own farm and encourage the improvement of other's farms and stimulate the improvement of the methods of instruction in the schools and their general efficiency. I also saw room for improvement in the morals of the people throughout the rural districts, even if it could not be done in the towns. Places of public resort, for horse-racing, for gambling on shooting, whisky drinking, and dancing were tolerated in various places in the country but they were detested by the moral and progressive element of society.

It was a hard question to decide. If I chose to labor in the higher department of Christian activity, I might be of benefit to some, but not much to my own people. If I labored in the lower sphere of human opportunities I might in some degree compensate my own friends and relatives for kindnesses to me, and, as a responsible servant of God, "Replenish the earth and subdue it." Gen. 1:28.

I was conscious of my ignorance to a moderate degree. That tempered the manifestations of my zeal. Nearly all the education I had, I had acquired without a teacher, and, as I courted difficult undertakings if in my way, I finally decided to forego the remunerative and honorable positions beyond the years of pleasant toil in college, inviting me to occupy them ,so long as life lasted, together with the associations of the cultured, the wealthy and the popular men of the civilized world. I felt happy because I saw so much that I could undertake for my own county and people as I became more competent. I was especially happy that I could be near my mother and could help her to educate her little girls and lead them to Christ for salvation.

Then another question arose in my mind and demanded an answer almost as soon as the former had been disposed of. That was: Should I as a servant of God continue in the state I so far had maintained, or enter the marriage relation? The former question had been a subject of earnest prayer, but it had been disposed of and was out of the way. The latter one had

taken its place. I was almost submissive to the will of the Lord, yet my preference was to continue in the single state. I spurned all considerations from my mind, as far as it was possible for me to do, in constructing a verdict, except one. That was, As a married man, or as a single man, can I be of greater influence for good immediately and remotely, to my fellow men, to my country and to Christianity? That was THE QUESTION.

I was twenty-six years and two months old when I decided the first question and dismissed it from my mind. For six months I had been ardently following the path decided on. I had taught eight months, made a crop and had began another school. I had come to estimate women, since my conversion to Christianity, very highly; but did not know of one in all the world that wanted me as a husband. Neither did I know of any one that I could sincerely tell that I wished to become my wife. I knew that I could not with any degree of safety choose a wife under such circumstances, neither did I have an idea of doing so.

The kind of woman I intended to secure for my wife was not to be found near my home. I intended to possess an educated wife, as knowledge is power, and all the power I could bring to my aid in elevating my kind, and accomplishing the undertakings of my life, the better. I expected also to secure a wife that was endowed with a sufficiency of this world's goods to enable us to be a blessing wherever we lived or wherever we went. For I saw plainly that a proper use of the things of the world was pleasing to God and a blessing to men in many ways. I knew that money was a great power for good if used as not abusing it. I thought it my duty to utilize all advantages for God's glory and humanity's good.

And lastly, I preferred a beautiful wife,

as there was such to be found, and that beauty would be no drawback to my wife's successful endeavors along the line of my purposes in life. For my wife must be a real fellow-helper, fully committed to the uplifting and the enlightening and the blessing of our fellows.

I was so fully determined that those three qualifications should characterize my wife that I did not once think of looking for her where I was acquainted. Indeed, I did not want to find her. I expected the Lord to settle the question, and, if it was his will, that I should possess a wife, he would in his own way point her out. If not he would not. The only possible accomplishments in the reach of men that I was perfectly sure was impossible for me to do was to preach the gospel. When such an idea flashed through my mind I almost dodged. I would not consider the matter. I craved to serve the Lord all my life with all my power in the humblest sphere he would permit me, but I thought I would prefer to die in honor than to try to preach and disgrace him as I certainly would. I was happy on account of what I thought the Lord would let me do for his cause in my own private way, but I did not believe that I could ever lead a prayer in public.

Later, when I was told by my stepfather in a very diffident way that the church thought I ought to take some public part, seeing I was such a reader and so zealous in Christian activities, and loved to talk religion so well, that I would be called on to pray in the meetings, publicly. Well, I thought to pray publicly I cannot. But to refuse to try is to run before the enemy is in sight and a square going back on all my profuse engagements to follow the Lord wherever he might lead me. Although I resolved to try if it killed me to do so, I carried a dread in my heart henceforth.

I think it was one or two months before I was asked to lead the prayer. I regarded it as hypocrisy to repeat what some other person or I had made and therefore I had read none nor made any. I remember bowing quickly and closing my eyes and shaking as if I had the severest ague. The rest was a dream, till I pronounced the "Amen." I rose very quickly and my shaking ceased. I never could recollect one word that I uttered except the first two and the last two. Neither did anyone ever tell me anything about what I asked the Lord for. I would be afraid to let one tell me, if he had tried to.

They continued to call on me to lead the prayer, and, as I saw no way to escape from trying to pray and be guiltless, I tried every time, and for at least a dozen times shook as helplessly as at the first. I have never known anyone else to be so affected, nor do I know why I was.

Secular business about my little farm and my school teaching detracted somewhat from my religious fervor, but I have been told since, that I was thought to be the most happy man the people had ever known. I did not know I was attracting anybody's attention to me. I know I was happy and I could not avoid speaking of Jesus and his salvation. It was not myself that I was trying to exhibit to my people, but the Christ the Savior of sinners. I did not forget how the Lord had answered my mother's prayers and I loved her and I loved everyone else. I craved to do something for the Lord who had saved me.

I did not hint to anyone that I was praying for my brother and our dearest young friend, George W. Russell, but I wrestled with the Lord for their salvation. I do not think I said a word to them on the subject, except what I said of my experience or of the Lord Jesus Christ's preciousness in a general way. I always thought the people doubtful of me because I was converted while in the army. I knew Ben and George loved their wives and children and were honest men, and if they ever decided for the living way the victory was almost won.

About one year from the time of my return home I went to church, three miles from my mother's, where a series of religious meetings had just commenced. When the minister asked those who wanted to offer themselves to the Lord as needy sinners desiring salvation through the merits of Christ, to meet the Christians in the altar, my brother and our friend George, rose, and, coming to the altar of prayer, kneeled there for instruction and the prayers of the Christian people. I had not seen either of them, neither did I expect them to be there that night. But I was so glad that I did not know what to do. If I had been clear out of hearing of anybody I think I should have told the Lord how I loved him and his ways and how I thanked him for his mercy on my brother and my friend as loud as I could. I had no fear of a failure on their part. I knew them and I knew the Lord knew I was happy because they were going to be saved. I could hardly keep my mouth closed and my tongue almost praised God in spite of me some times.

It seemed that I would be compelled to tell of the love of God or I could not remain. But, I thought for a strong-minded, matured man to talk out like I was about to do might ruin the meeting and I would be thought a simpleton. I was afraid to walk to the men and even let them know I was there or was interested for them. I was afraid to look at any of the working saints. The very blessings I had been seeking had come and I knew they had, and all my endeavors were required to stop my mouth. I was filled with peace

and love and joy and hope. I wanted to praise the good Lord with all my voice and my heart and my strength. For my eyes to see that my brother was to be a Christian and serve God and go to heaven at last, my cup was full and was about to run over.

I went away happy and unhappy; happy because the Lord was saving my brother and my friend, and unhappy because I did not let my mouth and my tongue praise his holy name. My exertions to hold in and squelch the Spirit had cost me the suffering of headache nearly all night. But I returned the next night and took a little part and then waited for results.

In about seven weeks I saw old Pastor Hester lead those two manly men into the water and baptize them near the same place where our dear mother had been baptized more than twelve years before. Brother Russell died ten years after his conversion, but my brother is living yet. I had fullness of joy when I saw the seekers at the altar. I knew the Son of God came to save sinners and I knew those wanted to be saved. There being no power strong enough nor wise enough to interfere in the business, I knew in my heart the mourners would find the Lord in the pardon of their sins. I was very happy about it then, and I am happy about it now and of thousands of other blessings I have been receiving and am still receiving.

"Oh, how I love Jesus!
How can I forget him?
He is all to me.
I'd rather be the least of them
And be the Lord's alone,
Than wear the royal diadem,
And sit upon the throne.

Praise the Lord, Oh, my soul.
Let all that is within me praise His
 holy name.
Forget not all his benefits, Oh, my soul!"

CHAPTER XIX.

ABOUT November 1, 1866, I attended a series of meetings at the South America Baptist church of evenings, but taught school each day. I was very anxious to see sinners converted and often felt like I wanted to instruct inquirers, but could not afford to try lest I be in someone's way.

I had attended a few times with no other purpose than to receive spiritual strength and lend my influence to the well-being of the meetings, without any thought of noticing any of the young ladies, nor the old ladies more than the old men.

Standing on one side of the house of worship, facing the altar of prayer one evening I raised my eyes and saw on the other side of the house one standing, contentedly singing; her attention seemed to be fixed on those in the altar. I had seen her previously, but had not noticed her. I do not remember whether at that time I recognized her or inquired her name of someone. Her face was not fascinating, but honesty was stamped on it. Her dress was not gaudy, but neat and becoming. Her form was not robust but symmetrical and sprightly. She exhibited no signs of forwardness, nor did she cringe and crouch from the view of anyone. She presented to my mind the picture of childish innocence, simple virtue and noblest womanhood.

A kind of wireless telegraphy, it appeared, had communicated with me. I came to suspect treasures of untold worth where I had not even thought of looking. It was not a case of love at first sight; but a gentle hint that the Lord might be leading me.

I decided to speak to the lady after the close of the services. I did not lose sight of her, though I do not remember anyone else on that side of the house. The people in the rural districts are not used to much red-tape, and one does better to act with common sense and honesty than to put on airs among them. I knew that fact, and it suited me best, as I had not progressed much in style, anyway.

I sought an introduction and soon had the young lady's permission to walk along the way with her to her home a mile away. The foolish thoughts and words and actions of myself and the companions of my earlier years were so distasteful to me then that I did not want to act like them now. I intended to demean myself as if in the presence of Angels. I resolved to visit the young woman in the day time only, that our conversation should not be conducted in whispers, and that nothing should be said or done that I was not willing for God to inspect. I thought that, as I was asking God to lead me the way he chose to lead me, I must act honestly. He would not bless me while I was acting the fool and disgracing his name. Then I had no desire to act foolish, in the matter anyway.

As we walked along I told the young lady that I did not need to seek amusement in the company of young people. Hence had not sought her acquaintance as a matter of pastime. That I had been in this world nearly twenty-seven years, and much of that time had been wasted and that I was happily pursuing the Christian way then, as best I understood it, and that I had settled the matter of location and the sphere of activity for the future for me, but that I had not yet been lead to know whether to lead a single life or to seek a companion, as was the common way in the person of a woman as a wife.

I told her that for me the question that above all others needed to be answered next was, "Does God will that I shall remain single or enter the marriage relation?"

In other words, "Can I be of more benefit to my people as I am till life shall end, or if at the head of a family?" I told her that I was almost indifferent as to the answer except to do God's will. That I had not spoken to anyone on the subject or paid any attention to anyone till I spoke to her. I had expected the Lord whom I served to guide me in the matter and that I was asking him to impress me as to my duty. I told her honestly that I saw her that night and thought it might be wise to cultivate an acquaintance with her, with no other view in the world than to learn if the Lord had lead me to seek her as my wife. I told her that I was far from any decision on the subject as yet, but that if she felt willing to pray over the matter, as I was doing, we would be led correctly. I told her that if I continued to have any special interest in her I would learn of her merits and demerits as best I could, and asked her to do the same regarding myself. I was not willing to be deceived nor was I willing for her to make a bargain to her sorrow. As usual for me, I did most of the talking.

During the next twelve months I visited her father's home seven times and at very irregular periods. As we had slowly and cautiously and prayerfully decided to be united in the holy bonds of matrimony, I spoke to the old people of our decision, provided they raised no objection.

I do not think it necessary to state how I went at it, as all young men succeed in some way or other. I was asking them for their baby girl. They had raised five boys and five girls. All had been married but two. All had been baptized but two. Those two were afterwards baptized and, like them their sons and daughter, remained members of some Baptist church to the present or till their death. The youngest son also married soon after our wedding day.

The good old people gave their consent to our marriage as they kind o' liked me, and their daughter was in her nineteenth year.

At that time I did not think of the importance of giving a dear girl, and the baby girl at that, to another in marriage. The old man merely indicated that marriage was not child's play. But his words were clothed in such tenderness and solemnity that I did not feel all their force for many years.

The good old woman's pathos, when compelled to answer yes or no, generated in my heart the first hint that I had ever had of the solemn task of committing to the keeping of another a dear child of one's own bosom. She made one request: That I would never move her child so far away that she could not see her and know of her well-doing. I told her that I would never do so. I could not afford to break my promise to her, even if I had wanted to move away. Those dear people lived fifteen years and three months after that sacrifice on their part, and were buried together in the same grave, crowned with good works. Not once did an unkind word and, so far as I ever knew, or an unpleasant thought pass from either of them to me nor from me to them. Heaven seems to me more inviting because of their presence there.

When I left my intended bride I arranged to come and let her know if I saw that I could not afford to proceed with the marriage the next Sunday. It was with great diffidence I had advanced so far. And yet it was possible to remain unmarried still. But if the current of events continued as seemed likely it would soon be too late. On Wednesday morning I woke determined to break the engagement. I thought that day I might be mistaken. Nothing could induce me to go on. My mind was made up to go at as early an hour as possible and stop preparations for the wedding. Though I had not found a woman possessing the characteristics I had supposed she must have which I could spare, yet I had found one possessed of those cardinal traits absolutely necessary to the making up of a wife to suit me. It was not that I was not pleased with her, not that I had not been honestly engaged in the pursuit of the right one, but I thought it was possible that I had been deceiving myself in deciding to get married. I had business for all my waking hours, and, as time passed on, the awfulness of the enterprise assumed a more tolerable phase.

On Saturday I had to attend a teacher's institute at the county seat and my friend secured a marriage license for me. Then, for the first time, I felt that I must go forward at all hazards. When we reached my mother's home that evening I was told that I had been licensed to preach the gospel by my church that day. W. D. Russell had been licensed at the same time. I cannot picture my confusion and my sorrow. I said, "Oh, if I had been there they could not have done so." They said, "It would have done no good for you to be there." Brother Russell had remonstrated and plead that the matter be laid over. The church was of one mind and would not hear him. Neither of us had been given any intimation of the intention of the church to license us to preach the gospel, though it seemed that they were all aware of the fact themselves.

I could do nothing but wait—believing it impossible for me to preach. We were at our regular meeting the next day as usual but I did not feel like I was in a very happy way.

That evening a large congregation met us at the residence of the elder, James Miller, the bride's home, to witness the wedding and to congratulate us on our good fortune. As buggies were about as scarce as townships we went on horseback. I rode in a kind of stupor, as I now remember it, resigned but in the dark as to the future. The ceremony was pronounced by Elder B. H. Rice, a Baptist minister, and a former lieutenant in my company for a short time.

Everything pertaining to the wedding was simple, sincere and businesslike.

When we were pronounced husband and wife, my dallying was past. The mountain of fear and faltering and hesitancy and indecision was lifted from my heart in a moment. Though we have lived together for more than thirty-eight years since that time and have experienced the vicissitudes common to a life of service in the world and suffered many sorrows; but I have unceasingly believed that God led me in the finding of the woman I married, I have never been sorry that I found and chose and married the baby daughter of the good, old, humble, clean, industrious, Christian farmer family that I did. Long years afterwards my wife told me that she had chosen me already and had decided to remain single if I did not come for her.

We did not miss our monthly meetings or any other meetings where we were expected to go. On Sunday night, one week after the wedding day, we attended the protracted meetings at Bankston Fork church, where I was teaching, and the preacher decided that I should open the service.

It was the custom throughout the country to read a hymn and then re-read two lines at a time and lead the congregation in singing the lines just read. I was expected to discharge that duty and lead the opening prayer. The air being chilly that evening I feared that when I stood to read I should be unable to hold my nervous heels on the floor and that they would render an involuntary tattoo to the merriment of some of the congregation and the consternation of others. I was aware that such weakness in me would most certainly tend to the damage of the meeting. In that moment of deepest anxiety some good brother began to sing the old hymn, "How Tedious and Tastless the Hour when Jesus no Longer I See!"

I saw my opportunity in the twinkling of an eye, as it were, and quietly went out of the house and hurried away to a place where no one was apt to see me while I ran from one tree to another and back again, repeating the exercises till I heard the last four lines commence "O, drive these dark clouds from my sky," when I ran to the house and took my seat in exactly the right time to begin my part of the service-warm and composed. Fertility in expedients served me well that time and saved the day for me when it seemed that there was no way out of the difficulty.

Having selected my own county as the field of my immediate energies and having been married to the woman of my choice, the subjects of second and third importance that had ever come before me, like that of the first, the object of worship, had been happily settled and I was therefore relieved from further solicitude on their account. I was then ready from the basis of a Christian man, a married man and a country man to commence the labors of life in earnestness and happiness.

My large and excellent district school made pleasing progress and I gave it much of my time each day besides the eight hours required then, from the time of opening to the closing.

The school was classed well but sometimes I heard the best class I had while the rest of the school had the forenoon recess. I never failed to give each pupil his proper amount of attention.

Play? We all played, too! When very cold days made it unpleasant to be out of doors I challenged the whole school to catch me and started out. Of course all was soon running through the woods like wild horses. The larger boys understood my object and rather helped. I have not forgotten the loss of one half of my coat-tail on one occasion. After the chase in which I came out only second best generally, we had a good rest and commenced business again. Pleasant exercise was very helpful to the hard study required of each pupil in the school. I did not teach the sciences for I believed then and still believe that the seven primary branches are all that can be well taught by one teacher in one room. However I taught vocal music as a kind of dessert. Fifteen minutes at convening for the afternoon work was devoted to principles except the rendering of one or two short pieces. Those supplied the place of the rod or long lectures. We met and sang one night in each week. The parents and people were there also, as long as room could be had for them.

My wife and I agreed at the first that if one of us was not permitted to attend church the other would attend unless required to discharge duties as citizens or as neighbors of more immediate importance. We attended each our own individual churches at New Salem and South America monthly and the Bankston church near us and other churches on odd Saturdays and Sundays. I was confident that there was no half-hearted way of being a Christian, that could be profitable to anyone. If the word of God was to be my guide I must understand its teachings and obey its instructions before I could expect the Lord to bless and protect me and my interests; without which I would have no assurance and influence. In view of the fact that there were so few things that I did know and so many that I did not know

I endeavored to be economical with my time and put to the best use possible so far as I knew how all the spare moments I had to the investigating of the scriptures.

The pursuit of knowledge was ever pleasant to me but after I became a Christian it was much more so. I was happy in tne determination to live and labor for the benefit of my fellows. I knew in that business I could not fail. I realized that the worldly man would soon pass from his possessions but the honest, watchful Christian had happiness here and in the future world, life everlasting.

Mr. F. M. Ozment, a former teacher of mine for a very short time and a member of the same church as myself taught in the same township and like myself had a large school. We were like brothers working together for the mutual betterment of the school interests of the county. Each year we visited each other's school. Each of them excelled the other in that particular that the teacher of it excelled the other. It seemed that a rapidly increasing and lasting impetus came to the schools of the county as our two schools drew wide attention to them. The schools, like their teachers, were real friends.

On the twenty-sixth day of March, 1868, the patrons of my school made a splendid dinner for the pupils of the school and other schools and parents in adjoining districts. It was to be the last day of the session. All the classes passed examinations before the people and each class and pupil showed great progress. The regular recesses were enjoyed that day as on the other days and every hour was needed to finish the examinations in. The dinner was a great success and all present were delighted. I was offered my price to teach the next school there that day. One of the most admirable accomplishments that the pupils had acquired, in the judgments of the patrons, was that of reading

music in the round note system and rendering the different parts of the tunes. The pupils who were too small to read the notes stood on the floor and kept the kind of time with their hands that we were singing to, and named the beat as they made it. They were too busy to grow idle or tired. During the examination day at intervals between recitals or examinations vocal music was rendered out of a large glee book called the "Jubilee." From six o'clock p. m., to ten o'clock p. m., the school gave an exhibition in the large church house at hand before a large and interested audience. It was perhaps the first school exhibition ever held in the county and it was a real good one. The young ladies and young men as well as the smaller pupils worked hard and deserved the praise they received. I announced at the close of the entertainment that we could not afford to have another under four years. And we had one four years later as good as the first one.

I am glad to have known most of my pupils in later years as acceptable teachers or lawyers or physicians, county officers, successful business men, citizens or ministers of the gospel. I think that four at least out of every five of them professed faith in Christ in early life. Fully one-half of them have before this time gone to people the pale nations of the dead. My timidy kept me from urging them to seek the kingdom of God first, and assuring them that all necessary things would be added unto them. O, how I wish I had been more bold in praying for them before them each morning in school as well as in private. But it is too late to improve the opportunity now, afforded me then.

I had determined to make the best out of my life for every one that I could so I began to farm in an improved way as I became able. I would have no thickets in my field, no crooked roads through or by my farm nor dead trees in it. I hired hands and at a good price and began in earnest to bring things to pass. I undertook too much but made very good progress. Though a weak man I did not expect a hired hand to do more than I did and always dismissed him from service an hour before I finished the chores. About the middle of May I was so much impressed with the duty of family prayer that I summoned courage to tell the two young men that we were going to hold prayer each evening and if they preferred to do so they could retire. But they never did, not even once that summer retire till after the services. I very much feared I would fail to let my light shine before them as I ought, but I am not conscious of any ugly behavior on my part though it rained more than I had expected it would, the breachy cattle belonging to my neighbors damaged my produce and other unpleasant circumstances tried me sorely. On one occasion, however, I had a painful experience in the absence of my hired men that I was glad they did not witness. For more than two weeks I had suffered with an abcess on the front of my right leg two inches above the knee. Part of the time I limped into the field leaning on the hoe handle and cut weeds and briars where work was needed worst. On the day referred to my boys were both compelled to be away. I thought rain would fall by night. A few rows of corn near the house in a piece of new ground had not been plowed. I concluded to try to plow them as I had improved some. The stumps and roots were thick and I felt before I finished the first row that I was in great danger of being struck on the boil by a wicked root.

The plow would run under them and they would run up on the handle and fly back very hard and make me cringe fearfully. I tried then to watch and walk more carefully and have the horse walk more slowly. But when the work lacked only three rows of being finished, having crossed a little ravine thirty-five feet from the fence the horse went up the little hill very fast and as he went the plow passed under a strong white oak root which slid up the handle as the others had done. I believed the root would strike my boil and I hollowed to the horse to stop just as the root hit me an awful stroke exactly on the boil. Somehow I remained conscious though I was nearly killed. I found myself on my back rocking like a cradle, groaning in language more eloquent than beautiful. The dirt had no terrors for my clothing nor the sun my naked countenance. By blood rushed through my veins so fast they strutted into the likeness of so many blue sticks. I was so hot that my skin seemed almost ready to blaze. Sweat exuded from every pore, and tears of anguish from my eyes. I suddenly found that my stomach was too sick to admit of further rocking. I may have fainted. If I did I do not remember it.

After suffering inexpressible anguish for some time I discovered a change in my feelings which I judged was for the better. I reached my foot and rubbed it a little. Then I rubbed my hip a little. I continued to put my hand nearer the wound as I improved. Inch by inch I exposed the flesh to the light. Tenderly I uncovered the spot where my affliction had persistenly resided. There was no boil in sight. The spot it had occupied was covered with flesh of a sickly blue that looked to have been exposed to a wintry wind all day. When I fully came to myself I thought of my horse, and looked around for him. He had heard my order to stop and had stood at the end of the row where he happened to be as he heard me, against the fence.

When I saw that I was out of danger I thought of a man who lived for no good but harm, and imagined him present ing me in my sufferings and I discovered in me a desire to shoot him. I had been praying for my enemies as well as my friends as a Christian duty, and had no idea that anything could arouse a feeling of revenge toward my enemies that my imagination aroused in that evil hour.

In a short time my sore was healed. The root cured it but the remedy was worse than the disease. From my earliest memory extreme sensitiveness possessed me, rendering my suffering from an injury to my body many fold more painful than that endured in an ordinary nature.

I did not forget the strange and wicked thoughts I had about wanting to shoot my enemy as I was recovering from my accident. I had not had anything like them since I had been a Christian, and did not know such feelings could be realized by a Christian. But I found that Paul meant something when he said, "For I know that in me (that is in my flesh) dwelleth no good thing." I learned that I still needed the Lord to keep me and watch over me all the time else I should bring disgrace on my profession and failure to my hopes.

Thirty-eight years of experience since that time has taught me the need of watching and praying lest I fall into temptation. If anyone has come into sinless perfection it is some other person than me.

After commencing to keep house for ourselves I decided to begin the study of communion at the table of the Lord as the Baptist church practiced. I had not investigated the subject to that time though intending to do so at my earliest convenience. I owed that duty to myself and to my fellow men and to God. I could not afford to be in error in any point of doctrine or practice through laziness, neglect or indifference of mine.

I knew that my judgment should not be formed from sentiment, policies nor majorities. That truth alone should influence my opinion, in that matter as well as all others. I determined to rely primarily and chiefly on the teaching of Jesus and the apostles. I well knew that I could never have a good conscience toward God if I did not respect his wish and word. It is recorded in John 15:14, "Ye are my friends if ye do whatsoever I command you." And in John 14:23, "If a man love me he will keep my words, and my father will love him, and we will come unto him and take up our abode with him." And in Luke 6:46, "And why call me ye Lord, and do the things I say?" And in Luke 14:27, "Whosoever doth not bear his cross and come after me cannot be my disciple." There was no alternative left to me but to faithfully learn Christ's will and obey it or cease to profess to be a disciple of his at all. I understood that if I pretended to honor Christ, yet did not obey him, he would know of it and distrust me; and that my fellows would be shocked at my ignorance or stubbornness or hypocrisy. During the ensuing nine months I made a pretty thorough examination of the subject pro and con in addition to performing the school work and farm work required of me.

Though my sympathies were entirely with the open communionists to that time I was compelled to give up that view and accept the practice of the restricted communion Baptists. I have reviewed the subject time and again since and have steadily become more pronounced in my opinion that the doctrine and practice of open communion ignores the teaching of Jesus and the apostles and fosters disloyalty to the Lord of Lords and betrays a sacred trust committed to his own institution to be kept sacred till he returns to earth again. Here follow the reasons for my decision. Each of Christ's churches is an independent democratic body responsible only to him for its religious actions. All free institutions being responsible for their own conduct and progress have laws for their guidance, government and protection. The republic of the United States of America has such laws framed by our past and present wise men that have been found adequate to our needs and on the point of fellowship or communion in the administration it is restricted in its franchise while unlimited in its friendship to all within its territory.

The voter must be a male twenty-one years of age who has not forfeited his citizenship in the United States nor his voting right in his precinct. If a foreigner he must live in the country two years and take the oath of allegiance before he can have fellowship in elections of any kind. Neither wealth, wisdom, fame nor beauty entitles its possessor to the right to vote in elections or to hold office. The youth may love his country, serve in its army, and die in its defense but he has no fellowship in administering its laws. The foreigner may give his life in freedom's cause as did the Baron DeKalb or lead an army against our country's foes, as did the Marquis LaFayette but neither act entitled the actor to citizenship in the republic. Those welcome services elicited warm friendship from every patriot but no fellowship can be had but by the lawful method. The fathers decreed it so, and no harm can come of their wise and cautious foresight. All deserving men and women, foreigners and minors enjoy our human fellowship as well as our friendship but national fellowship is restricted to persons possessing the prescribed qualifications. No one of intelligent mind and loyal heart would permit all persons everywhere to vote in our elections. We wisely govern ourselves. Others would not if they could and could not if they would. We only of all the world know the responsibilities and the privileges of freedom. Neither do we apologize to other nations for our restricted

fellowship. It suits us because it is safe, while it injuries no other person in the world. And our practice really benefits others, as what benefits our people indirectly blesses other people also. We can do our voing better than others can do it and we are better prepared to fill our offices than they are. Yet we invite them to come in at the national door of citizenship and snare equally with us in the blessings and burdens of our free institutions. They are not expected to bear witness (false witness however) against us for faithfulness to our convictions of duty. Other nations are restricted in their fellowship like ourselves. It is the only safe way. Fraternal institutions are close communionists in principle and practice as well as nations.

I was truly a Mason in principle in 1865 before I had been elected and initiated, passed and raised to the Master's degree as I was after I had become a Mason. But I had no fellowship in the lodge whatever. I had not come in as all my fellows had before at the only door into the ancient order, and could not expect to obtain fellowship there without knowledge or obligation. I would have been unfit for the place and the place unfit for me. The Masonic fraternity restricts its fellowship to its own membership and it must continue to do so as long as it shall continue in business; yet no patriot blames it for its prudence and consistency. All its members should be friends to all humanity and its true ones are. But their friendship to their fellowmen does not confer fraternal fellowship.

All other secret orders occupy the same ground. They are, every one, what would be termed close or restricted communionists. They have friendship with their fellow men whether they belong to one lodge, a dozen lodges, or to no lodge at all. Their friendship is the same, but their fraternal fellowship is restricted to those under the same obligation and the same discipline. They are wisely constituted. No fair-minded man will find fault with a nation or lodge or corporation for refusing him fellowship unless he is able and willing to fill the place he seeks.

The fitness of the applicant must be approved by the membership and the ceremonies must be observed and the rights secured by each candidate alike. The rule is universal. Open fellowship or open communion in secret societies, in business, corporations or in nations has never been nor can be.

Different denominations of churches, i. e., different kinds or classes of churches, were constituted by their founders for particular purposes. So far as other persons were concerned they had a lawful right to organize with any kind of material, with any number of persons, into any form of government, with any number of ordinances for any particular purpose on any set of principles, provided disloyalty to the United States government, or immorality among the people, or other undesirable teachings or practices degrading and injurious to the commonwealth were not to be inculcated nor fostered by it.

Every church to be found is the product of the brain of the founder or founders, with revisions as later decades seem to necessitate changes. But the imprint of the head or founder remains. Each church has its own terms of admittance to fellowship and its rules for dismissal from fellowship. Whether it teaches much of the gospel or denies it in toto; whether it is materialist or spiritualist, whether its adherents be many or few, none dare to molest or make afraid. Each one must answer to God for himself. Perfect freedom to organize for any purpose not inimical to the rights of others or for no purpose at all belongs to every person. If the church he belongs to does not suit him

he does not have to remain in it. There are other churches willing to receive him.

If one should fail to secure membership in a church to his own notion he has the right to institute a campaign of instruction and proselyting and to organize one of a kind that does suit him, as others have done. Teaching and suasion is a right that everyone possesses, but persecution and misrepresentation is cowardly, mean and belittling in an American citizen, or in any other, as for that.

Baptists had nothing whatever to do in prescribing the terms of admission into the Baptist church, nor in fixing the terms of admittance to the Lord's table in those churches, the nature of church, the duties of the church, the doctrines of the church, the officers of the church, the ordinances of the church, nor the government of the church. Jesus Christ and his apostles, by precept and example, endowed the first churches with all those and the name was furnished by their enemies, from age to age, as appellations of reproach in the different countries of the world; as Novations, Petrobrusions, Paulicians, Waldenses, Albigenses, Mennonites, Anabaptists, Baptists, and so forth.

The New Testament is their discipline and Jesus Christ is accepted as their founder and head. The teachings of that Book is their guide in all matters of ethics, morals and religion.

The New Testament teaches very positively and plainly that two qualifications are necessary in a participant at the Lord's supper: Regeneration, a spiritual one; and baptism, a ceremonial one. Regeneration confers spiritual or Christian fellowship and scriptural baptism, i. e., baptism administered by the authority of the Scriptures, confers church fellowship.

Hence all true Christians have fellowship in singing, in prayer, in reading the word of God, in opposing sinfulness, in hearing the gospel preached and in working for the salvation of sinners according to the light they have regarding their duties. Each regenerated person belongs to the family of God, but not to the visible church of God.

The church of God as an institution was founded by the Savior for certain purposes. The two ordinances belong to it and that of baptism is to be administered first, and the Lord's supper second. Never in any other order, in the Testament.

In the Acts of the Apostles, 2:38-41, the order of duty from the convicted sinner to the acting church member is written there. "And they that gladly receive His word (were regenerated) were baptized (were scripturally dipped) and the same day there were added unto them (received into the church) about three thousand souls. And they continued steadfastly in the apostles doctrine and fellowship (walked as becomes a child of God and did not follow off some crank or heretic) and the breaking of bread and prayers. (partook of the Lord's supper." Baptists believe now and have believed from their earliest history that the above is the proper order of the ordinances, and they have observed that order invariably to the present time, except in isolated instances, for lack of understanding or pressure from without, loyalty to the Lord's teachings has yielded to sentimentalism and that, to the injury of all concerned.

Baptists believe unrestricted or open communion to be not only unscriptural, but antiscriptural, sinful and disloyal to the Great Head of the church. In Paul's letter to the Thessalonians, 2, Thess. 3: 6, "Now we command you brethren, in the name of our Lord Jesus Christ, that ye withdraw yourselves from every brother that walketh disorderly and not after the tradition which he received of us." Again,

1 Cor. 5:11, "But now I have written unto you, not to keep company, if any man that is called a brother be a fornicator, or covetous, or an idolater or a railer, or a drunkard, or an extortioner; with such an one no not to eat."

The unscriptural practice of open communion did not obtain in, nor was it heard of among Catholics, Protestants or Baptists, till the celebrated Robert Hall in the beginning of the nineteenth century, for some supposed reason, permitted it, or rather, upheld the soundness of the practice. His idiosyncrasies of that character abridged his usefulness. His severe bodily suffering evidently injured his mind and cut his life short. Otherwise his usefulness would have been exceedingly great As an orator he had few equals.

But though the churches known as Baptist churches are perhaps the only ones known as pure democracies, yet nearly all others, in doctrine whether in practice or not agree with them in their principles of close communion. Hence the cry of close communion hurled at the Baptists of late years, to turn unsuspecting Christians from their churches, springs either from malice or ignorance, and should be exposed.

Dr. Wall, the historian and champion of Pedobaptism, says, "No church ever gave the communion to any persons before they were baptized." Among all the absurdities that ever were held, none ever maintained that any persons should partake of the communion before they were baptized. Chancellor King and Dr. Dodridge and other eminent scholars and historians agree with Wall.

The Friends, or Quaker church, and the General Baptist or small Robert Hall, church, both of which understood the family of God to be identical with the church of God, do not restrict the Euchrist at all. The first do not believe in nor practice either baptism or the Lord's supper, and the latter disclaim any right to restrict the supper. There are no other churches in the world, with the possible exception of one or two very small bodies, who are really open communionists.

The Methodist Discipline, on page 37, says, "No person shall be admitted to the Lord's table among us who is guilty of any practice for which we would exclude a member." If that church believes and practices that rule they could no more admit a Baptist, especially a Baptist minister, to their communion than a Baptist can admit an infidel. But Baptists find no fault with the Methodist people for their belief. They regard the rule as wise and necessary. But Baptists think it fair and honest in these teachers to present the facts truly to their people, as some have done who regard their standing in the world of letters and others whose sense of honor compels them to estimate truth above the interest of sect. The Methodists are close communionists in principle and they must be also in practice, or ignore their Book of Discipline.

Baptists believe that Methodists, Presbyterians and others are consistent in their strict communion, but they think it un-Christian policy to turn converts away from Baptist churches by urging that Baptists are close communionists when they are no more so than themselves.

F. G. Hibbard, one of the ablest of the Methodist divines and the author of a book on infant baptism used in the Methodist colleges, said, "It is but just to remark that in one principle the Baptists and Pedobaptists agree. They both agree in rejecting from communion at the table of the Lord and in denying the rights of church fellowship to all who have not been baptized. Valid baptism they consider as essential to constitute visible church membership. This also we (Methodists) hold.

The only question, then, that here divides us is: What is essential to valid baptism?"

A Presbyterian divine said: "Open communion is an absurdity, when it means communion with the unbaptized. I would not for a moment consider a proposal to admit an unbaptized person to the communion, and can I ask a Baptist to so stultify himself and ignore his own doctrines as to invite me to commune with him while he believes I am unbaptized? I want no sham union and no sham unity, and if I held the Baptist notion about immersion I would no more receive a Presbyterian to communion than I would now receive a Quaker. Let us have unity, indeed, but not at the expense of principle; and let us not ask the Baptists to ignore or be inconsistent with his own doctrine. Let us not, either, make an outcry at his close communion, which is but faithfulness to principle, until we are prepared to be open communionists ourselves; from which stupidity may we be forever preserved."

Another Pedobaptist, and a D. D., has said: "You regular Baptists are fighting the battle for us all. Open communionism rests only on a sickly sentimentalism, and if that sentimentalism carries the day in your churches it will soon be making trouble in other churches. May God help you Baptist stand firm."

I could copy many other friendly concessions from Pedobaptists and others, some of whom think more of their scholarship and their consistency than they think of their creed and some of whom concede the truth for conscience sake, though they do not feel willing to overcome the difficulties in the way to uniting with consistent restricted communion churches.

The Jewish theocracy was restricted to perfection, yet it was instituted by the God of heaven. Every male that was not circumcized was killed. Every male proselyte was circumcised before he became a citizen in the commonwealth. No nation had any right to cry out, "close communion" to the Jews. And every worthy man of other nations could become a Jew if he really desired to do so.

Every man and every woman can become a Baptist if he can bring fruits meet for repentance and receive baptism according to the scriptural order and so Christ obeying, become a member of the institution tracked by the blood of its members from the apostolic period. How strange it is for persons to cry out close communion, the second ordinance, while they pass silently over baptism, the first ordinance.

The Jews were restricted communionists; all nations are restricted communionists, all business corporations, all lodges, and all churches, including the Baptist churches, are close communionists. But if no others were so the true Baptists would be, because they can not afford to change any of the doctrines and ordinances of their New Testament discipline.

Jesus said to the body instituted to execute the commission, "Go teach all nations, baptizing them in the name of the Father and the Son and the Holy Spirit; teaching them to observe all things whatsoever I have commanded you; and lo, I am with you all way, even unto the end of the world. Amen."

Baptists deeply regret the divisions among professed followers of Jesus Christ and are willing to do all that can be done, and are doing and have been doing since divisions came, all they could to unite all Christians in one and the same order by remaining in the middle of the road, the one made plain by Christ and the apostles, the only ground that is now, ever has been, or that ever will be possible to unite in church fellowship on.

In thus believing, Baptists disclaim any

righteousness of their own, or that they are superior morally or mentally to others of God's regenerated millions, but they believe the devil sows the seeds of division, confusion and error in the minds of Christians to impede their work and hinder the enterprise Christ is engaged in all that he can. Many times he causes Christians to oppose other servants of God by deceiving them and having them do what they would not do at all if they understood themselves. All true Christians have spiritual or Christian fellowship with one another so far as they have it with Christ. They ought to have church fellowship with one another throughout the world also, but it is impossible to do so till each accepts the Bible teachings altogether instead of accepting some of the teachings of the Scriptures and some of the teachings of men in its stead.

In opposing the restricted communion of the Baptist churches some have quoted with assurance the language of Paul in the letter to the Corinthian church, 11:-28, "Let a man examine himself and so let him eat of that bread and drink of that cup." Everyone to whom Paul wrote of those Corinthians were members of the church at that place and the letter certainly did not contain an invitation to outsiders. He istructed those members to receive the emblems as memorials of Christ's broken body and spilt blood, but not to do as some of them had been doing —eat the bread because they were hungry and others drink because they loved its flavor till they were drunk. It's as plain as day to one who will read through no other person's glasses.

Others ask, with triumphant pride, "If we can not eat together here how can we eat together in heaven?" We answer all that eat together spiritually here will eat together spiritually there. We will have the bread and wine here, thus showing his death till he comes only. There will be none in heaven. If there had never been a devil open communion would not have been thought of.

Early in the month of August, 1868, when little John Franklin, our first born, was very young, after the summer work was finished and the hired men had gone, one forenoon I attended a series of meetings just beginning at the Bankston Fork Baptist church, less than two miles away. Elders Bickers and Manier were the ministers in charge of the services, which were expected to result in a revival of religious interest in the community and the salvation of lost men and women. To my surprise, both ministers asked me to preach. I had never tried to preach, though licensed to do so by my church more than eight months previous. I had thought my church inexcusably mistaken concerning my call to the ministry, as I could fly in the air as easily as I could read a text and preach a sermon from it, and I had left the matter with the Lord to manage. I told the ministers, therefore, that I could not preach and that I had not even thought of trying.

I had no hesitancy in tackling any necessary secular enterprise and was almost devoid of doubt of my successful accomplishment of life's duties, as God was my leader and strength. But I thought that God knew I could never preach the gospel. I thought if I had wanted to try and if I should succeed, no one would want to hear me and that I should soon become a hiss and a by-word. I believed I could do service in other ways and I craved to be led by the Lord to do them.

One of the ministers sat on my right side and the other one sat on my left. They persisted in their request to have me preach, ignoring everyone of my many reasonable excuses and utterly refused to be put off at all. In my confusion and perplexity I chose a text to read, judging that if I could say nothing it would perhaps do but little harm.

The scripture had come to my mind just before rising from my bed a few mornings previous, "I that speak unto thee am he."—John 4:24. I did not remember where the text was to be found but I knew it was in the 'Bible and I soon found it. A halo of light seemed to surround the words of Jesus to the Samaritan woman, and I enjoyed them as never before. I saw that Christ was often speaking to men by his Spirit and through his providences when they do not suspect his presence. If I had not at that time remembered considering the pleasing services to be rendered to God by obeying such calls instead of neglecting them as untaught novices, I could not have tried at all. But the thought that I might persuade others to observe the will of our great High Priest as spoken to us by his Spirit and providences; though I had no idea how to do it, I undertook the momentous task. I could talk about the Christian religion for hours without tiring, but as to the contents of a sermon I thought that a turnip had as much blood in it as I had a sermon in me, if not more.

Just then W. D. and R. H. Dallas entered the house and took seats facing me on the opposite side of the building. They were older than I was, but had grown up with me. Both of them were industrious farmers and business men of good standing in the country and friends to morality and Christianity, but neither of them was a Christian. That is, they were without spiritual light and life and hope. However, they were close observers of persons and things with which they came in contact, and especially of the conduct of professors of Christianity. I really believed they wished every convert to prove a real one, but they had no respect for a hypocrite or a deceived professor. I am confident they wanted to understand how to secure eternal life and wished some time to enjoy the hope other Christians enjoy. But not possessing the light of regeneration, they could not understand the weakness of the flesh as Christians do. I was very sorry they had come to the meeting that day.

I was satisfied that they knew I could not preach as well as I did. I feared that my effort would tend to darken the way to Christ to them and do them a real injury instead of a benefit. It was an awful moment for me. I had already taken the Bible and consented to try. After my poor little prayer I read my text, and without one word of apology began. I thought of many apologies that fairly wrestled for the privilege of being first presented; but they were each ignored as being entirely inadequate to meet the emergency. I determined to say what I could and let the matter rest there.

I could see the Dallases cringeing for me from the time I took the Bible in my hand, as I thought then and as I think now. I do not know one word uttered. But as I stammered along, trying to mend what I was certain was poorly said, I thought I could see everyone who cared for the meeting and the cause of religion blush and turn away his head in sorrow. It seemed to me that I could say nothing as I wanted to say it and that in trying to correct the bad deliverance I made it worse and worse every time. I think I lost interest in everything for the time being but myself, for I saw that I was growing more and more confused.

Somehow I discovered I had a chill on me after I had floundered around for something to say for ten or fifteen minutes. That is the only time in my life that I was glad I had a chill. It gave good and reasonable excuse for quitting and I quit. I asked the pastor to excuse me, told him the cause, delivered the meeting into his hands and took a seat outside of the house in the sunshine.

After the meeting closed and during the social hand-shaking and conversation usually enjoyed in that day, by the congregations, the Dallases modestly but honestly advised the ministers that it would be a waste of time and a neglect of opportunity to do good to dally away any more time in experimenting on my preaching powers, for it would always be impossible for me to preach. However, they mercifully acknowledged that I knew much more than I could tell. Though I was still outside stretching and shivering with my chill and knew nothing of their conversation inside of the house, it was not many days till some one told me what the Dallases said about my sermon to the ministers that day. The cold-matter-of-fact words were exactly what I expected, yet they made me feel meaner and more ashamed of the effort to preach and of myself for making it than before I heard them. It was their privilege to listen to me and form an impartial judgment and to give the ministers their candid opinion, all of which they were not slow to do. Honesty required me to acknowledge that their opinion was similar to my own.

To this day I believe my first sermon was a very poor one. The source of my embarrassment was mainly my view of the exalted character of God and the unworthiness of mortals to approach him at all, and particularly to stand between the living and the dead to teach men about God and heaven and their duties in this life and the judgment. Secondly, fear of trying to labor in a sphere which none but God's called could ever expect to rise above a mere machine preacher, and, as I had no ability to preach nor a token of a call to the ministry, I should certainly prove to be one of that unnecessary kind of men in the pulpits of the country,whether educated or uneducated, whether saved or unsaved, who do not and cannot comprehend the work before them, or realize the responsibility resting on them nor the golden opportunities passing before them.

I believe I then would have preferred death rather than to assume the ministry unless called of God to the work. But if called I would prefer the ministry of the gospel, regardless of all conditions, to any other thing or place under the heavens. I believed then, and I believe it more surely now, that of all the foolish men who ever tried to serve the Lord the man who crowds himself into the pulpit uncalled is the most foolish fool. When God calls a man into the ministry he tells someone else of the fact in due time. On all very important occasions since that time I have been reasonably courageous, but on less important occasions I still hesitate and stammer.

I had another chill two days afterward and another one two days later. I then stopped them with quinine, the specific for chills then. I felt no signs of a chill till I had been trying to preach ten or fifteen minutes that day, and it might have been induced by my nervousness, so far as I know. I did not again visit that meeting nor do I suppose anyone grieved over my discontinuance.

In the interest and well-being of short-lived humanity everywhere, and the excellence of the only religion that saves in present and future world I have detailed a fair sample of the influences that contributed to the transformation of the Boy of the Battle Ford into the man of twenty-eight and one-half years, full of hope, and zeal and energy, happy in the fellowship of the Holy Spirit, happy in having something to live for worthy the attention and affections and unceasing service of all intelligencies on earth and in heaven.

CHAPTER XX.

THE task I had long expected to perform is done. I should here lay my pen down and rely on God to make this true and uncouth story a blessing to many whose souls weigh heavily on the author's heart but for the fact that the readers will generally wish to know if the Battle Ford MAN is still pursuing the straight and narrow path with the same zeal and energy and happiness after the passing of more than thirty-eight years of his pilgrimage in the world of sin and sorrow and toil and death. Hoping that a very brief summary of events along a very narrow line of action may be both interesting and profitable to those who have followed the boy of the Battle Ford to manhood, with humility and with joy, with tears and with ecstacy I here append the following pages:

The preachers who constrained me to first try to preach nearly thirty-eight years ago have long ago laid their Bibles down, closed their lips in death and surrendered their bodies to the earth. Their souls have returned to God who gave them. The plain old worshipers of that generation have largely disappeared and their places are occupied by a later and more up to date people. The old songs of the fathers with their charges of guilt and grace have been largely discarded and their places in worship are filled with modern productions, some of which entrance us with the beauties of heaven, but too much ignore the horrors of the pit. The hearty offhand singing of that time has been supplanted by the choir and the organ, which sometimes act as an octopus on the suffering worshipers.

The common seats of that period on which our parents sat for an hour or more at once listening with willing ears and throbbing hearts and tearful eyes while the red hot sermon or exhortation greeted their anxious ears, have passed away years ago, together with the house of worship built by those plain but earnest worshipers, and seats took their places so convenient and tidy that most church members and some worldly persons can without injury to their physical nature and with only partial interruption to their mental enjoyment sit for twenty or thirty minutes and listen to the minister of the gospel. The splendid new house with its belfry and bell and other modern conveniences built with funds left for that purpose by A. B. Bickers, a faithful deacon of the church, adorns the old school and church yard, and behind it rests the bodies of nearly all the old members of the church, their families and their neighbors. A new school house built and worn out since that day has been replaced by another of improved architecture. There was not a frame dwelling in the district then; all were made of logs. Now all are frames.

The beautiful forests have given place to fertile fields. Poor roads and poor tools to labor with have long ago been discarded and good roads, good bridges, good vehicles and good implements of labor are enjoyed by everyone alike. Two young men and their wives, only, of the adults, live there still. They are great grandparents now. All the others are dead except ourselves. More than half of the families there thirty eight years ago have no posterity there now. New comers occupy their places. Perhaps the great changes seen in my own school district since the bloody war which closed almost forty-one years ago is a fair sample of the change in persons, places and pursuits in general in most of our country. Greater changes still during the last sixty-three years, the period of my recollection, is recorded in my memory.

Only five people now living I knew then

besides my brother and myself. The four are cousins, who were little children then, and Mr. Pankey, referred to elsewhere. John Allen, Steve Reynolds, and Mack Boatright remain of the Brushy Fork people where I enjoyed my first school, except four others younger than myself. Of my companions in youthful fashion, fun and folly nearly everyone has paid the debt that each must pay sometime and perhaps knows more of the life beyond the grave than we know.

More than seventy-five per cent of those who campaigned with me to save the Union from forty-one to forty-five years ago are in their silent graves, and the remainder with unsteady step are bravely tramping to the same goal. Only two persons in my church were members there when I was received less than forty-one years ago. Only one Baptist minister in Gallatin, Saline, Hardin, Williamson, Johnson, Massac, Pope, Pulaski and Franklin counties, Elder G. S. Lewis of Golconda, and one Methodist minister, Eld. W. C. Roper of Carrier Mills, are living now, both of them tottering on the verge of the tomb.

The saints of God with whom I worshiped then and to whom I looked for advice and consolation often, are too few now to exert much influence in this busy world of ours, except as faithful guide-boards with trembling hand and quivering voice to point onward and upward to the place prepared for them of which Jesus told his disciples, happy in view of their approaching discharge from service here that they may enter into the rest that remains for the people of God.

The Dallases who heard me try to preach that August day have long since been numbered with the dead and their families, if living would be strangers where they lived, and their farms belong to other people.

Little John Franklin, our dear babe, and his brother Willie, and his little sister, Carrie, two others of our own dear children slept the sleep of death more than twenty-seven years ago, and three little mounds in the Russell cemetery still remind us that we buried our darlings there.

At the birth of each one I sought the secret grove where vegetable life which could come only from God, surrounded me and, on bended knees, gave it to God, waiving any and all right to it, with one petition only, that He would use the child for His own glory and the benefit of the world or take it to himself. I did not ask that it might become famous among men, or wealthy or have long life unless that life should be devoted to the advancement of the Redeemer's kingdom and the glory of His name.

At each recurring bereavement during the ten and one-third years from the first to the third death after we had done all we could to keep it and it lay cold in death before us, though with hearts all broken and prospects all blasted we could and we did say with Job "The Lord gave, and the Lord hath taken away; blessed be the name of the Lord." What else could we say if we would? To whom else should we go, if we could? The Lord only has eternal life. The Lord had accepted my offer. He had taken my dear children to a better sphere of action and I knew he could not make any mistake. We estimated heaven more highly than before and we tried more earnestly to please the Lord by rendering more faithful services from day to day in every way that we thought it our duty to do.

We bore our full share of burdens of every kind, legal and social, educational and financial, civil and religious. We kept in mind the fact that our opportunities to do good would soon cease. I deemed it erroneous to suppose anyone, after we should leave the world, would be able to use our property or money that he did not earn, more to God's pleasure than we could who had earned it. My wife fully acquiesced in my efforts to obey God as we learned his will.

I never did dread work or other hardships and had no fear that I should suffer poverty in the world. I knew that all we had or ever would have was the Lord's, merely loaned to us to use as stewards and servants; and the thought enabled me to be happy when engaged in prosperous enterprises, and to humbly submit to unexpected and heavy losses when they came.

But I sometimes thought myself a very miser and shamefacedly and mournfully went to the Lord in prayer for wisdom and grace and guardianship that I might be wise and liberal with his bounties in my possession. Before my God I do believe I lost much enjoyment and money and influence with men and power with God and the opportunity to lead persons to Christ for salvation and the privilege to lay up treasures in heaven because I lacked wisdom to resist selfishness and to give, give, give. "He that giveth to the poor lendeth to the Lord, and the liberal soul shall be made fat." No one knows a thing till he learns it. I did not nearly understand my duty then as well as I do now.

I could not afford to be unhappy long. Life is too short. I had to do the best I knew or be unhappy. Therefore I was compelled to learn my duty, if possible, and then discharge that duty.

I was a happy man and we were a happy family.

Lizzie, our only remaining child—intelligent, filial, musical, lovely and happy—was permitted to make our home a veritable paradise for nearly eight years after our latest bereavement. For the last three and one-half years of her life she was a happy Christian and an earnest seeker for recruits to augment the Christian army.

While I was away seeking souls for

heaven from week to week, from month to month, and from year to year, she and her mother supervised my farming and extended live stock interest, done with hired for me from day to day and rejoiced with me in the success of my labors. We were united in the belief that whatever reward might be given me, they would share

LIZZIE BLACKMAN,

Who died at the age of seventeen years less twelve days.

labor, and drove to their Sunday school and church, four miles away, when the weather permitted, regularly counting it a happy privilege and a duty. They prayed equally, as we were engaged together in carrying out the commission to "Teach all nations, etc."

Lizzie suffered many severe attacks of

fever, rheumatism, asthma, and other afflictions, perhaps two attacks in each of her earliest years. But she kept abreast of the best pupils of her age at school, though doing nearly all her studying at home.

The last winter of her life and part of the summer preceding it, she was permitted to enjoy the studies and the sports of her friends in the district school. Her mother, from early childhood, infused into her mind and heart the necessity of clean body, clean thoughts and clean tongue, the excellence of honesty, truth and courage, and the danger of bad books, bad company and bad habits. We were gratified to believe the child accepted joyfully the reasonable and affectionate teachings of her mother.

In order that she might develop into a strong-bodied, broad-minded, great-souled woman, we encouraged physical, mental and religious exercises along the line of propriety. We realized a deep measure of responsibility resting on us as to her future influence.

Solomon said, "Train up a child in the way he should go and when he is old he will not depart from it." We believed the wise man and we could not afford to be guilty, willingly, of contributing even one useless being to burden the needy millions of pitiable humanity. Those parents who raise a bad family are a nuisance and a curse to the country in which they live, but those parents who train their family to honor and usefulness are an odor of sweet incense and a veritable blessing to any country in any age.

We counseled together, and with our daughter, often and earnestly. We could not afford to run any risk of failure. If others had children they could let the devil have, we did not. I knew that nearly all the poverty and laziness and drunkenness and lying and theft and swindling and lewdness and domestic infelicity and murder and insanity and suicide which curses

the world would be eradicated from it if every parent of the present was then and would be in the future what he ought to be.

Lizzie was very sociable and kind to all and was loved by her acquaintances. I requested that she continue her simple sociability, but not to permit any affection for young men to get a lodgment in her heart at the peril of her whole future prospect. I told her that love, so-called, was blind and foolish; that a moral leper who understood the art of making love could captivate and secure most young, inexperienced girls, despite of parents and home and all else; that an artful woman could capture most young men, lead him to marry her, in spite of the tears of a loving mother and the threats of the outraged father; that thousands and hundreds of thousands of ruined wives and ruined husbands were in slavery worse than that the negroes were lately under, yet they could not break its shackles till death released them. I told her to treat young gentlemen politely, but never to keep company with them except as children. That she could excuse herself as being too young and that she relished the company of girls rather better. I requested that she discreetly avoid anything that savored of courtship till she should arrive at the age of twenty-two years. I gave her my reasons as follows:—1. She had a good home and loving parents and need not expect to better her condition by marrying any man, even the choice one among men. Second, she was naturaly weakly and had improved only two years and her body would not become strong and her health established earlier than that time. Third, That she was inexperienced in the world and unacquainted with men and their ways, and therefore entirely incompetent to select a husband with any degree of assurance. Fourth, That we would visit people and places as emergences required in the future as the years went by when we could mix pleasure with duty, and that if after such experience she felt it her duty to enter the marriage relation she would be known further and would know more worthy men than while young and the probability of marrying happily would be largely increased. Fifth, That as she had already chosen Christ as her Savior and leader she must depend on him to enlighten her very best judgment in determining the most important step yet before her. For a Christian to marry is a more important and dangerous move than to die, and she must not take the step rashly.

Sixth, That as she then was she could win souls for heaven, lend her influence to make the homes of others happy and lay up treasures in heaven for herself. Seventh, That as she was our only living child we needed her presence, her help and her songs. Eighth, The matter of her marriage if it should ever come to pass was of as much importance to us if not more than to herself. That we would much rather commit her body to the grave with her friends where we could shed the tear of love on the grass above her than to have her married to an unworthy or even a second-class husband, when the shedding of tears of anguish could do no good. That any man who is not a first-class man is not fit to be a husband at all. The girl who marries any other kind hoping to reform or improve him generally sells herself into slavery and misery and throws her life away.

Our dear child cheerfully and heartily acquiesced in all I said. As the months passed away the harvest of souls called more and more loudly for laborers. Few of us only, saw the golden grain ready to be reaped. My soul fairly flamed within me. I shifted part of my pastoral work and all my secular business to others or left it to take care of itself. Mostly in destitute places I labored day and night

for twenty-four months without intermission except as sickness or death interrupted me. God gave me souls for my hire in very great numbers. At the end of eight and one-half months our association convened. About three hundred had professed regeneration in my meetings, I had baptized two hundred and seven, and many more of the converts were baptized later.

Elders Blanchard, Estes, Trovillion, Baker and others went into the harvest and God poured out His spirit on their labors and the revival extended to many places in the counties of Saline, Pope, and Hardin.

The baptisms reported to the association that year were four hundred and forty-eight as against one hundred and twelve the previous association. Daughter had helped me a few days in each of two meetings and I was tempted to have her take up the work as singer and organist in my meetings, but decided for her and her mother to spend nine months at Ewing college before entering in the revival work. At her earnest pleadings to attend the district school after our visit to Springfield on account of the Baptist General association to convene there soon, till the Ewing college entered its second quarter, I consented. Five days after our return from the association she became sick and on the fifth day of her affliction she died of spinal meningitis. She had repeatedly said she would die soon and that belief may have dictated her anxiety to postpone her departure for college. She seemed as cheerful in calculating her early death as she did in anticipating meeting her friends in the church. Three other young girls, her particular friends and associates and church members, died in less than one year after she died. The people near and far deeply sympathized with us. Lizzie was loved for her Christian devotion and friendship and intelligence. A large concourse of people came to her funeral and Elder Caldwell delivered an able and sympathizing and hopeful sermon, and we buried her fair and pleasing countenance and beautiful form out of our sight. We were then as childless as when we were married twenty years before.

Our anguish was inexpressible; our loss irreparable and our loneliness immeasurable. We missed daughter every hour and everywhere. Our plans were destroyed and our greatest earthly joy was removed and every earthly prospect for us seemed as black as the darkest night. I knew the bereavement was more sorely felt by my wife than by myself. We had one resting place left. That was the Lord. We still believed beyond the shadow of a doubt the Lord makes no mistakes. We had no idea why he permitted death to mow her down when we were doing all we could to build up His kingdom. We had hoped she might be a great power for good, but that hope was seemingly blighted. Then we would deduce some comfort because we had so precious a child for the Lord to take. We could and we did say again from deeply chastised hearts, "The Lord gave and the Lord hath taken away; blessed be the name of the Lord." At the lonely home we could remain but a short time at once. Her vacant chair at the table was more than I could endure. I was compelled to occupy it myself leaving my own place vacant before I could eat at all. Though I knew God had done right and I did not feel dissatisfied with his providential dealings with us, yet my soul cried and my eyes wept, and my heart yearned for Lizzie. All the people and all the pleasures in the world could not fill the vacancy in our hearts caused by the absence of our own dear Lizzie. We went from home and returned again at short intervals between meetings for six weeks, for we could not remain away nor stay there.

However, God was blessing my labors and scores and scores of souls were being saved. At the end of that period relatives came to live with us and I left my wife at home and continued in the ministry. My business interests suffered for lack of my own better personal supervision. But I could not cease to seek for souls and at the end of the twenty-four months I had baptized four hundred and sixty persons whom we judged to have been regenerated. More than two hundred others professed regeneration at the meetings. My labors of that time were bestowed mostly in destitute places and broken down churches. We lived on the farm where we had our beautiful orchards and meadows and woods and squirrels and fish-ponds and home for three years. But it could never be the same home to us again. Strangers own it now. Too plaintive were the remembrances to remain there though thousands of pleasant ones are written on our hearts of the sweet days of the past at our old home. Nearly twenty years our hearts have hungered for the resurrection of the dead. For until then we can not meet Lizzie and other dear ones and Jesus the Redeemer. Our four dear children lie side by side in our church yard. There is room beside them for two more graves and there are two of us to occupy them there.

On the eighteenth day of the present century our dearest mother died. At the good old age of eighty-three years and seven months all bent with labors and trembling with age, filled with confidence and crowned with victorious Christian service, she bravely and cheerfully approached the door of death, guided by God's word and supported by his presence and entered into the realm incomprehensible to us in our mortal bodies. She had been a Christian fifty-one years and Christ was her stay in time of trouble and her joy every day.

We often conversed on her early depart-ur*3 from the scene of her long and laborious life, and the wonderful things to be enjoyed in the life just beyond death. Her mind was bright and her faith was strong in the Lord. She had lived to see all her children saved and many others near her heart and she believed to the last that God would mercifully hear her prayers for others still. On the next day friendly hands conveyed her to the cemetery adjoining her church and loving hearts committed her to the grave, between her late husband and her daughter Mary Russell, and near others dear to her, and ten yards from our own dear children. I estimate being near our dear ones at the coming of Jesus as worth something. When we arise in his likeness I want to see our dearest ones on earth next after Jesus, if it shall please him.

Our mother was ripe for the other world yet to give up mother is to give up a never failing friend. I rejoice that I had a faithful mother to surrender to the Lord of our salvation, however.

"Dearest mother, thou hast left us
   Here thy loss we deeply feel.
But, 'tis God that has bereft us,
   He can all our sorrows heal."

A faith well founded on Christ's word is the substance of things hoped for; the evidence of things not seen. I have never 3ed to be open for instruction. Truth is what I have craved most of my life. A mistake in the sphere of religion is a fatal one. Seeing that most of mankind are little interested in their eternal future I have been more and more critically careful to examine and re-examine the grounds of my hope and I do declare so far as I have experienced and understood and believed and enjoyed there can be no mistake in the old religion of our fathers. It endows its possessors with joy unspeakable and full of glory. He has a title to an in-

heritance incorruptible and that fadeth not away reserved in heaven for those who are kept by the power of God through faith unto salvation ready to be REVEALED at the LAST time. The assurance of immortality beyond the grave is of incomparably greater worth than all else that we can think or wish or know. My tongue can not tell, my pen can not write nor can my actions portray the joy I possess in Christ Jesus the Lord. I have lived a busy life for forty years, spending more than sixteen hours each day on an average as I sincerely believe in labor, business or study. Life to me has been worth living since I was saved from the love and the practice and the penalty of sin.

The fellowship of Christ was what I was perishing for when I was wandering in the world, trying anything and everything that held out hopes of satisfaction in my early manhood. It has made me what I am. It is more than all else to me. All is failure without it. All is success with it. I know in whom I have believed. "He that believeth on the Son of God hath the witness in himself." After my experience in sin and sadness till I was twenty-five years of age and forty-one years of light and love, hope and happiness in the Christian service I sincerely declare that if I had a thousand lives to live I would want every part of every life to be that of a Christian. My open, energetic life has encountered many obstacles. Discouragement, disappointments and opposition have often beset me, but I have never once faltered in the way. The fogs and icebergs and the storms confront those who go down to the seas in ships sometimes but they disturb not the depths of the deep below. Neither do the Christian soldier's adversaries of any and of all kinds injure his interests in heaven. I am exceedingly happy that through his grace I have been blessed of the Lord to finish. this work. Though I had been impressed to tell my story of Christ's power and willingness to give life and peace and joy to sinful men in print I had almost concluded I should never find time to do so. However, causes over which I had no control abridged my active ministry to such an extent that I have accomplished this, my ardent wish. I did not intend to chronicle any event since 1868, but in few instances it seemed proper as being so closely connected with others herein given. I hope and pray the Lord who saved me to make this production a great blessing to hundreds and thousands of my fellow-men. So mote it be. Amen! and Amen. And here I lay down my pen.

THE AUTHOR.

SOURCES INDEX

SOURCES FOR THE INTRODUCTION

W. S. Blackman, *The Boy of Battle Ford and the Man* (Marion, Illinois: Egyptian Press Printing Co., 1906).

Bruce Catton, *The American Heritage Picture History of the Civil War* (American Heritage Publishing Co., 1960), pp. 516, 520–21.

"Dreadful Fire at Sea; Five Hundred Lives Lost, the U.S. Transport Steamer *General Lyon* Burned Off Cape Hatteras," *New York Times*, April 3, 1865. This early account shows five survivors from the 56th Illinois Regiment, as does the *Adjutant General's Report*.

Frederick H. Dyer, *A Compendium of the War of the Rebellion*, vol. 3 (New York: Thomas Yoseloff, 1959), p. 1097.

History of Gallatin, Saline, Hamilton, Franklin and Williamson Counties, Illinois (Chicago: Goodspeed Publishing, 1887; rpt. Utica, Kentucky: McDowell Publications, 1973), pp. 176, 227, 237–38, 596–99, family history of Blackman and wife Allie (Miller) Blackman and full names of their four children.

Edmund Newsome, *Experience in the War of the Great Rebellion by a Soldier of the Eighty-First Regiment Illinois Volunteer Infantry* (Carbondale, Illinois: Edmund Newsome Publisher, 1880; rpt. 2nd ed., rev., Murphysboro, Illinois: Jackson County Historical Society, 1984).

Report of the Adjutant General of the State of Illinois, vol. 6, rev. (Springfield: Journal Company Printers and Binders, 1900), pp. 367–69, history of the 120th Illinois Infantry Regiment; 344–66, muster rolls; 356, Blackman a sergeant at war's end.

William B. Tubbs, "A Bibliography of Illinois Civil War Regimental Sources in the Collections of the Abraham Lincoln Presidential Library," Part 1, Published and Printed Sources, *Journal of Illinois History* 8 (summer 2005), p. 152.

Bluford Wilson, "Southern Illinois in the Civil War," *Transactions of the Illinois State Historical Society* 16 (1911), pp. 98–99.

INDEX

Shawnee Classics

A Series of Classic Regional Reprints for the Midwest

A History of the Ninth Regiment Illinois
Volunteer Infantry, with the Regimental Roster
Marion Morrison
New Foreword by John Y. Simon

Tales and Songs of Southern Illinois
Collected by Charles Neely
*Edited with a Foreword by John Webster
Spargo*

Eight Months in Illinois:
With Information to Immigrants
William Oliver
New Foreword by James E. Davis

The Outlaws of Cave-in-Rock
Otto A. Rothert
New Foreword by Robert A. Clark

Afloat on the Ohio: An Historical Pilgrimage
of a Thousand Miles in a Skiff,
from Redstone to Cairo
Reuben Gold Thwaites

A Woman's Story of Pioneer Illinois
Christiana Holmes Tillson
Edited by Milo Milton Quaife
New Introduction by Kay J. Carr

Autobiography of Silas Thompson
Trowbridge, M.D.
*New Introduction by John S. Haller Jr. and
Barbara Mason*

Life and Letters of General W. H. L. Wallace
Isabel Wallace
New Foreword by John Y. Simon

Army Life of an Illinois Soldier: Including a
Day-by-Day Record of Sherman's March to
the Sea
Charles W. Wills
Compiled by Mary E. Kellogg
New Foreword by John Y. Simon